THIS IS YOUR **PASSBOOK**® FOR ...

FOOD SERVICE MANAGER

NATIONAL LEARNING CORPORATION®
passbooks.com

PASSBOOK® SERIES

THE *PASSBOOK® SERIES* has been created to prepare applicants and candidates for the ultimate academic battlefield – the examination room.

At some time in our lives, each and every one of us may be required to take an examination – for validation, matriculation, admission, qualification, registration, certification, or licensure.

Based on the assumption that every applicant or candidate has met the basic formal educational standards, has taken the required number of courses, and read the necessary texts, the *PASSBOOK® SERIES* furnishes the one special preparation which may assure passing with confidence, instead of failing with insecurity. Examination questions – together with answers – are furnished as the basic vehicle for study so that the mysteries of the examination and its compounding difficulties may be eliminated or diminished by a sure method.

This book is meant to help you pass your examination provided that you qualify and are serious in your objective.

The entire field is reviewed through the huge store of content information which is succinctly presented through a provocative and challenging approach – the question-and-answer method.

A climate of success is established by furnishing the correct answers at the end of each test.

You soon learn to recognize types of questions, forms of questions, and patterns of questioning. You may even begin to anticipate expected outcomes.

You perceive that many questions are repeated or adapted so that you can gain acute insights, which may enable you to score many sure points.

You learn how to confront new questions, or types of questions, and to attack them confidently and work out the correct answers.

You note objectives and emphases, and recognize pitfalls and dangers, so that you may make positive educational adjustments.

Moreover, you are kept fully informed in relation to new concepts, methods, practices, and directions in the field.

You discover that you arre actually taking the examination all the time: you are preparing for the examination by "taking" an examination, not by reading extraneous and/or supererogatory textbooks.

In short, this PASSBOOK®, used directedly, should be an important factor in helping you to pass your test.

FOOD SERVICE MANAGER

DUTIES

Supervises the preparation and serving of meals; directs purchase of all food as well as necessary equipment used in food preparation and service; keeps records and prepares reports regarding the number and cost of meals served, inventory control, time and payroll records, etc.; attends and participates in meeting with other facility department heads and supervisors required; oversees the care and maintenance of food service equipment; consults with a dietitian regarding nutritional care of and special diets; inspects food preparation and serving areas to insure acceptable sanitary standards are being met; manages and coordinates the resources of the dietary department to achieve adequate and efficient food service at maximum cost effectiveness; directs in-service training programs for food service personnel and familiarizes new employees with duties and responsibilities; assists the facility administrator in preparation of the dietary departmental budget; and orients, evaluates and assigns employees as required for efficient and safe operation of the food service program in the facility.

SCOPE OF THE EXAMINATION

Written test will cover knowledge's, skills, and/or abilities in such areas as:

1. Food service management principles and practices;
2. Basic nutrition and dietetics;
3. Proper food preparation and serving techniques;
4. Sanitary food handling and storage practices;
5. Purchasing; and
6. Supervision and training.

HOW TO TAKE A TEST

I. YOU MUST PASS AN EXAMINATION

A. WHAT EVERY CANDIDATE SHOULD KNOW

Examination applicants often ask us for help in preparing for the written test. What can I study in advance? What kinds of questions will be asked? How will the test be given? How will the papers be graded?

As an applicant for a civil service examination, you may be wondering about some of these things. Our purpose here is to suggest effective methods of advance study and to describe civil service examinations.

Your chances for success on this examination can be increased if you know how to prepare. Those "pre-examination jitters" can be reduced if you know what to expect. You can even experience an adventure in good citizenship if you know why civil service exams are given.

B. WHY ARE CIVIL SERVICE EXAMINATIONS GIVEN?

Civil service examinations are important to you in two ways. As a citizen, you want public jobs filled by employees who know how to do their work. As a job seeker, you want a fair chance to compete for that job on an equal footing with other candidates. The best-known means of accomplishing this two-fold goal is the competitive examination.

Exams are widely publicized throughout the nation. They may be administered for jobs in federal, state, city, municipal, town or village governments or agencies.

Any citizen may apply, with some limitations, such as the age or residence of applicants. Your experience and education may be reviewed to see whether you meet the requirements for the particular examination. When these requirements exist, they are reasonable and applied consistently to all applicants. Thus, a competitive examination may cause you some uneasiness now, but it is your privilege and safeguard.

C. HOW ARE CIVIL SERVICE EXAMS DEVELOPED?

Examinations are carefully written by trained technicians who are specialists in the field known as "psychological measurement," in consultation with recognized authorities in the field of work that the test will cover. These experts recommend the subject matter areas or skills to be tested; only those knowledges or skills important to your success on the job are included. The most reliable books and source materials available are used as references. Together, the experts and technicians judge the difficulty level of the questions.

Test technicians know how to phrase questions so that the problem is clearly stated. Their ethics do not permit "trick" or "catch" questions. Questions may have been tried out on sample groups, or subjected to statistical analysis, to determine their usefulness.

Written tests are often used in combination with performance tests, ratings of training and experience, and oral interviews. All of these measures combine to form the best-known means of finding the right person for the right job.

II. HOW TO PASS THE WRITTEN TEST

A. *NATURE OF THE EXAMINATION*

To prepare intelligently for civil service examinations, you should know how they differ from school examinations you have taken. In school you were assigned certain definite pages to read or subjects to cover. The examination questions were quite detailed and usually emphasized memory. Civil service exams, on the other hand, try to discover your present ability to perform the duties of a position, plus your potentiality to learn these duties. In other words, a civil service exam attempts to predict how successful you will be. Questions cover such a broad area that they cannot be as minute and detailed as school exam questions.

In the public service similar kinds of work, or positions, are grouped together in one "class." This process is known as *position-classification*. All the positions in a class are paid according to the salary range for that class. One class title covers all of these positions, and they are all tested by the same examination.

B. *FOUR BASIC STEPS*

1) **Study the announcement**

How, then, can you know what subjects to study? Our best answer is: "Learn as much as possible about the class of positions for which you've applied." The exam will test the knowledge, skills and abilities needed to do the work.

Your most valuable source of information about the position you want is the official exam announcement. This announcement lists the training and experience qualifications. Check these standards and apply only if you come reasonably close to meeting them.

The brief description of the position in the examination announcement offers some clues to the subjects which will be tested. Think about the job itself. Review the duties in your mind. Can you perform them, or are there some in which you are rusty? Fill in the blank spots in your preparation.

Many jurisdictions preview the written test in the exam announcement by including a section called "Knowledge and Abilities Required," "Scope of the Examination," or some similar heading. Here you will find out specifically what fields will be tested.

2) **Review your own background**

Once you learn in general what the position is all about, and what you need to know to do the work, ask yourself which subjects you already know fairly well and which need improvement. You may wonder whether to concentrate on improving your strong areas or on building some background in your fields of weakness. When the announcement has specified "some knowledge" or "considerable knowledge," or has used adjectives like "beginning principles of..." or "advanced ... methods," you can get a clue as to the number and difficulty of questions to be asked in any given field. More questions, and hence broader coverage, would be included for those subjects which are more important in the work. Now weigh your strengths and weaknesses against the job requirements and prepare accordingly.

3) Determine the level of the position

Another way to tell how intensively you should prepare is to understand the level of the job for which you are applying. Is it the entering level? In other words, is this the position in which beginners in a field of work are hired? Or is it an intermediate or advanced level? Sometimes this is indicated by such words as "Junior" or "Senior" in the class title. Other jurisdictions use Roman numerals to designate the level – Clerk I, Clerk II, for example. The word "Supervisor" sometimes appears in the title. If the level is not indicated by the title, check the description of duties. Will you be working under very close supervision, or will you have responsibility for independent decisions in this work?

4) Choose appropriate study materials

Now that you know the subjects to be examined and the relative amount of each subject to be covered, you can choose suitable study materials. For beginning level jobs, or even advanced ones, if you have a pronounced weakness in some aspect of your training, read a modern, standard textbook in that field. Be sure it is up to date and has general coverage. Such books are normally available at your library, and the librarian will be glad to help you locate one. For entry-level positions, questions of appropriate difficulty are chosen – neither highly advanced questions, nor those too simple. Such questions require careful thought but not advanced training.

If the position for which you are applying is technical or advanced, you will read more advanced, specialized material. If you are already familiar with the basic principles of your field, elementary textbooks would waste your time. Concentrate on advanced textbooks and technical periodicals. Think through the concepts and review difficult problems in your field.

These are all general sources. You can get more ideas on your own initiative, following these leads. For example, training manuals and publications of the government agency which employs workers in your field can be useful, particularly for technical and professional positions. A letter or visit to the government department involved may result in more specific study suggestions, and certainly will provide you with a more definite idea of the exact nature of the position you are seeking.

III. KINDS OF TESTS

Tests are used for purposes other than measuring knowledge and ability to perform specified duties. For some positions, it is equally important to test ability to make adjustments to new situations or to profit from training. In others, basic mental abilities not dependent on information are essential. Questions which test these things may not appear as pertinent to the duties of the position as those which test for knowledge and information. Yet they are often highly important parts of a fair examination. For very general questions, it is almost impossible to help you direct your study efforts. What we can do is to point out some of the more common of these general abilities needed in public service positions and describe some typical questions.

1) General information

Broad, general information has been found useful for predicting job success in some kinds of work. This is tested in a variety of ways, from vocabulary lists to questions about current events. Basic background in some field of work, such as sociology or economics, may be sampled in a group of questions. Often these are principles which have become familiar to most persons through exposure rather than through formal training. It is difficult to advise you how to study for these questions; being alert to the world around you is our best suggestion.

2) Verbal ability

An example of an ability needed in many positions is verbal or language ability. Verbal ability is, in brief, the ability to use and understand words. Vocabulary and grammar tests are typical measures of this ability. Reading comprehension or paragraph interpretation questions are common in many kinds of civil service tests. You are given a paragraph of written material and asked to find its central meaning.

3) Numerical ability

Number skills can be tested by the familiar arithmetic problem, by checking paired lists of numbers to see which are alike and which are different, or by interpreting charts and graphs. In the latter test, a graph may be printed in the test booklet which you are asked to use as the basis for answering questions.

4) Observation

A popular test for law-enforcement positions is the observation test. A picture is shown to you for several minutes, then taken away. Questions about the picture test your ability to observe both details and larger elements.

5) Following directions

In many positions in the public service, the employee must be able to carry out written instructions dependably and accurately. You may be given a chart with several columns, each column listing a variety of information. The questions require you to carry out directions involving the information given in the chart.

6) Skills and aptitudes

Performance tests effectively measure some manual skills and aptitudes. When the skill is one in which you are trained, such as typing or shorthand, you can practice. These tests are often very much like those given in business school or high school courses. For many of the other skills and aptitudes, however, no short-time preparation can be made. Skills and abilities natural to you or that you have developed throughout your lifetime are being tested.

Many of the general questions just described provide all the data needed to answer the questions and ask you to use your reasoning ability to find the answers. Your best preparation for these tests, as well as for tests of facts and ideas, is to be at your physical and mental best. You, no doubt, have your own methods of getting into an exam-taking mood and keeping "in shape." The next section lists some ideas on this subject.

IV. KINDS OF QUESTIONS

Only rarely is the "essay" question, which you answer in narrative form, used in civil service tests. Civil service tests are usually of the short-answer type. Full instructions for answering these questions will be given to you at the examination. But in case this is your first experience with short-answer questions and separate answer sheets, here is what you need to know:

1) Multiple-choice Questions

Most popular of the short-answer questions is the "multiple choice" or "best answer" question. It can be used, for example, to test for factual knowledge, ability to solve problems or judgment in meeting situations found at work.

A multiple-choice question is normally one of three types—

- It can begin with an incomplete statement followed by several possible endings. You are to find the one ending which *best* completes the statement, although some of the others may not be entirely wrong.
- It can also be a complete statement in the form of a question which is answered by choosing one of the statements listed.
- It can be in the form of a problem – again you select the best answer.

Here is an example of a multiple-choice question with a discussion which should give you some clues as to the method for choosing the right answer:

When an employee has a complaint about his assignment, the action which will *best* help him overcome his difficulty is to
  A. discuss his difficulty with his coworkers
  B. take the problem to the head of the organization
  C. take the problem to the person who gave him the assignment
  D. say nothing to anyone about his complaint

In answering this question, you should study each of the choices to find which is best. Consider choice "A" – Certainly an employee may discuss his complaint with fellow employees, but no change or improvement can result, and the complaint remains unresolved. Choice "B" is a poor choice since the head of the organization probably does not know what assignment you have been given, and taking your problem to him is known as "going over the head" of the supervisor. The supervisor, or person who made the assignment, is the person who can clarify it or correct any injustice. Choice "C" is, therefore, correct. To say nothing, as in choice "D," is unwise. Supervisors have and interest in knowing the problems employees are facing, and the employee is seeking a solution to his problem.

2) True/False Questions

The "true/false" or "right/wrong" form of question is sometimes used. Here a complete statement is given. Your job is to decide whether the statement is right or wrong.

SAMPLE: A roaming cell-phone call to a nearby city costs less than a non-roaming call to a distant city.

This statement is wrong, or false, since roaming calls are more expensive.
This is not a complete list of all possible question forms, although most of the others are variations of these common types. You will always get complete directions for

answering questions. Be sure you understand *how* to mark your answers – ask questions until you do.

V. RECORDING YOUR ANSWERS

Computer terminals are used more and more today for many different kinds of exams.

For an examination with very few applicants, you may be told to record your answers in the test booklet itself. Separate answer sheets are much more common. If this separate answer sheet is to be scored by machine – and this is often the case – it is highly important that you mark your answers correctly in order to get credit.

An electronic scoring machine is often used in civil service offices because of the speed with which papers can be scored. Machine-scored answer sheets must be marked with a pencil, which will be given to you. This pencil has a high graphite content which responds to the electronic scoring machine. As a matter of fact, stray dots may register as answers, so do not let your pencil rest on the answer sheet while you are pondering the correct answer. Also, if your pencil lead breaks or is otherwise defective, ask for another.

Since the answer sheet will be dropped in a slot in the scoring machine, be careful not to bend the corners or get the paper crumpled.

The answer sheet normally has five vertical columns of numbers, with 30 numbers to a column. These numbers correspond to the question numbers in your test booklet. After each number, going across the page are four or five pairs of dotted lines. These short dotted lines have small letters or numbers above them. The first two pairs may also have a "T" or "F" above the letters. This indicates that the first two pairs only are to be used if the questions are of the true-false type. If the questions are multiple choice, disregard the "T" and "F" and pay attention only to the small letters or numbers.

Answer your questions in the manner of the sample that follows:

32. The largest city in the United States is
    A. Washington, D.C.
    B. New York City
    C. Chicago
    D. Detroit
    E. San Francisco

1) Choose the answer you think is best. (New York City is the largest, so "B" is correct.)
2) Find the row of dotted lines numbered the same as the question you are answering. (Find row number 32)
3) Find the pair of dotted lines corresponding to the answer. (Find the pair of lines under the mark "B.")
4) Make a solid black mark between the dotted lines.

VI. BEFORE THE TEST

Common sense will help you find procedures to follow to get ready for an examination. Too many of us, however, overlook these sensible measures. Indeed, nervousness and fatigue have been found to be the most serious reasons why applicants fail to do their best on civil service tests. Here is a list of reminders:

- Begin your preparation early – Don't wait until the last minute to go scurrying around for books and materials or to find out what the position is all about.
- Prepare continuously – An hour a night for a week is better than an all-night cram session. This has been definitely established. What is more, a night a week for a month will return better dividends than crowding your study into a shorter period of time.
- Locate the place of the exam – You have been sent a notice telling you when and where to report for the examination. If the location is in a different town or otherwise unfamiliar to you, it would be well to inquire the best route and learn something about the building.
- Relax the night before the test – Allow your mind to rest. Do not study at all that night. Plan some mild recreation or diversion; then go to bed early and get a good night's sleep.
- Get up early enough to make a leisurely trip to the place for the test – This way unforeseen events, traffic snarls, unfamiliar buildings, etc. will not upset you.
- Dress comfortably – A written test is not a fashion show. You will be known by number and not by name, so wear something comfortable.
- Leave excess paraphernalia at home – Shopping bags and odd bundles will get in your way. You need bring only the items mentioned in the official notice you received; usually everything you need is provided. Do not bring reference books to the exam. They will only confuse those last minutes and be taken away from you when in the test room.
- Arrive somewhat ahead of time – If because of transportation schedules you must get there very early, bring a newspaper or magazine to take your mind off yourself while waiting.
- Locate the examination room – When you have found the proper room, you will be directed to the seat or part of the room where you will sit. Sometimes you are given a sheet of instructions to read while you are waiting. Do not fill out any forms until you are told to do so; just read them and be prepared.
- Relax and prepare to listen to the instructions
- If you have any physical problem that may keep you from doing your best, be sure to tell the test administrator. If you are sick or in poor health, you really cannot do your best on the exam. You can come back and take the test some other time.

VII. AT THE TEST

The day of the test is here and you have the test booklet in your hand. The temptation to get going is very strong. Caution! There is more to success than knowing the right answers. You must know how to identify your papers and understand variations in the type of short-answer question used in this particular examination. Follow these suggestions for maximum results from your efforts:

1) Cooperate with the monitor

The test administrator has a duty to create a situation in which you can be as much at ease as possible. He will give instructions, tell you when to begin, check to see that you are marking your answer sheet correctly, and so on. He is not there to guard you, although he will see that your competitors do not take unfair advantage. He wants to help you do your best.

2) Listen to all instructions

Don't jump the gun! Wait until you understand all directions. In most civil service tests you get more time than you need to answer the questions. So don't be in a hurry. Read each word of instructions until you clearly understand the meaning. Study the examples, listen to all announcements and follow directions. Ask questions if you do not understand what to do.

3) Identify your papers

Civil service exams are usually identified by number only. You will be assigned a number; you must not put your name on your test papers. Be sure to copy your number correctly. Since more than one exam may be given, copy your exact examination title.

4) Plan your time

Unless you are told that a test is a "speed" or "rate of work" test, speed itself is usually not important. Time enough to answer all the questions will be provided, but this does not mean that you have all day. An overall time limit has been set. Divide the total time (in minutes) by the number of questions to determine the approximate time you have for each question.

5) Do not linger over difficult questions

If you come across a difficult question, mark it with a paper clip (useful to have along) and come back to it when you have been through the booklet. One caution if you do this – be sure to skip a number on your answer sheet as well. Check often to be sure that you have not lost your place and that you are marking in the row numbered the same as the question you are answering.

6) Read the questions

Be sure you know what the question asks! Many capable people are unsuccessful because they failed to *read* the questions correctly.

7) Answer all questions

Unless you have been instructed that a penalty will be deducted for incorrect answers, it is better to guess than to omit a question.

8) Speed tests

It is often better NOT to guess on speed tests. It has been found that on timed tests people are tempted to spend the last few seconds before time is called in marking answers at random – without even reading them – in the hope of picking up a few extra points. To discourage this practice, the instructions may warn you that your score will be "corrected" for guessing. That is, a penalty will be applied. The incorrect answers will be deducted from the correct ones, or some other penalty formula will be used.

9) Review your answers

If you finish before time is called, go back to the questions you guessed or omitted to give them further thought. Review other answers if you have time.

10) Return your test materials

If you are ready to leave before others have finished or time is called, take ALL your materials to the monitor and leave quietly. Never take any test material with you. The monitor can discover whose papers are not complete, and taking a test booklet may be grounds for disqualification.

VIII. EXAMINATION TECHNIQUES

1) Read the general instructions carefully. These are usually printed on the first page of the exam booklet. As a rule, these instructions refer to the timing of the examination; the fact that you should not start work until the signal and must stop work at a signal, etc. If there are any *special* instructions, such as a choice of questions to be answered, make sure that you note this instruction carefully.

2) When you are ready to start work on the examination, that is as soon as the signal has been given, read the instructions to each question booklet, underline any key words or phrases, such as *least, best, outline, describe* and the like. In this way you will tend to answer as requested rather than discover on reviewing your paper that you *listed without describing*, that you selected the *worst* choice rather than the *best* choice, etc.

3) If the examination is of the objective or multiple-choice type – that is, each question will also give a series of possible answers: A, B, C or D, and you are called upon to select the best answer and write the letter next to that answer on your answer paper – it is advisable to start answering each question in turn. There may be anywhere from 50 to 100 such questions in the three or four hours allotted and you can see how much time would be taken if you read through all the questions before beginning to answer any. Furthermore, if you come across a question or group of questions which you know would be difficult to answer, it would undoubtedly affect your handling of all the other questions.

4) If the examination is of the essay type and contains but a few questions, it is a moot point as to whether you should read all the questions before starting to answer any one. Of course, if you are given a choice – say five out of seven and the like – then it is essential to read all the questions so you can eliminate the two that are most difficult. If, however, you are asked to answer all the questions, there may be danger in trying to answer the easiest one first because you may find that you will spend too much time on it. The best technique is to answer the first question, then proceed to the second, etc.

5) Time your answers. Before the exam begins, write down the time it started, then add the time allowed for the examination and write down the time it must be completed, then divide the time available somewhat as follows:

- If 3-1/2 hours are allowed, that would be 210 minutes. If you have 80 objective-type questions, that would be an average of 2-1/2 minutes per question. Allow yourself no more than 2 minutes per question, or a total of 160 minutes, which will permit about 50 minutes to review.
- If for the time allotment of 210 minutes there are 7 essay questions to answer, that would average about 30 minutes a question. Give yourself only 25 minutes per question so that you have about 35 minutes to review.

6) The most important instruction is to *read each question* and make sure you know what is wanted. The second most important instruction is to *time yourself properly* so that you answer every question. The third most important instruction is to *answer every question.* Guess if you have to but include something for each question. Remember that you will receive no credit for a blank and will probably receive some credit if you write something in answer to an essay question. If you guess a letter – say "B" for a multiple-choice question – you may have guessed right. If you leave a blank as an answer to a multiple-choice question, the examiners may respect your feelings but it will not add a point to your score. Some exams may penalize you for wrong answers, so in such cases *only*, you may not want to guess unless you have some basis for your answer.

7) Suggestions
   a. Objective-type questions
      1. Examine the question booklet for proper sequence of pages and questions
      2. Read all instructions carefully
      3. Skip any question which seems too difficult; return to it after all other questions have been answered
      4. Apportion your time properly; do not spend too much time on any single question or group of questions
      5. Note and underline key words – *all, most, fewest, least, best, worst, same, opposite,* etc.
      6. Pay particular attention to negatives
      7. Note unusual option, e.g., unduly long, short, complex, different or similar in content to the body of the question
      8. Observe the use of "hedging" words – *probably, may, most likely,* etc.
      9. Make sure that your answer is put next to the same number as the question
      10. Do not second-guess unless you have good reason to believe the second answer is definitely more correct
      11. Cross out original answer if you decide another answer is more accurate; do not erase until you are ready to hand your paper in
      12. Answer all questions; guess unless instructed otherwise
      13. Leave time for review

   b. Essay questions
      1. Read each question carefully
      2. Determine exactly what is wanted. Underline key words or phrases.
      3. Decide on outline or paragraph answer

4. Include many different points and elements unless asked to develop any one or two points or elements
5. Show impartiality by giving pros and cons unless directed to select one side only
6. Make and write down any assumptions you find necessary to answer the questions
7. Watch your English, grammar, punctuation and choice of words
8. Time your answers; don't crowd material

8) Answering the essay question

Most essay questions can be answered by framing the specific response around several key words or ideas. Here are a few such key words or ideas:

M's: manpower, materials, methods, money, management
P's: purpose, program, policy, plan, procedure, practice, problems, pitfalls, personnel, public relations
   a. Six basic steps in handling problems:
      1. Preliminary plan and background development
      2. Collect information, data and facts
      3. Analyze and interpret information, data and facts
      4. Analyze and develop solutions as well as make recommendations
      5. Prepare report and sell recommendations
      6. Install recommendations and follow up effectiveness

   b. Pitfalls to avoid
      1. *Taking things for granted* – A statement of the situation does not necessarily imply that each of the elements is necessarily true; for example, a complaint may be invalid and biased so that all that can be taken for granted is that a complaint has been registered
      2. *Considering only one side of a situation* – Wherever possible, indicate several alternatives and then point out the reasons you selected the best one
      3. *Failing to indicate follow up* – Whenever your answer indicates action on your part, make certain that you will take proper follow-up action to see how successful your recommendations, procedures or actions turn out to be
      4. *Taking too long in answering any single question* – Remember to time your answers properly

IX. AFTER THE TEST

Scoring procedures differ in detail among civil service jurisdictions although the general principles are the same. Whether the papers are hand-scored or graded by machine we have described, they are nearly always graded by number. That is, the person who marks the paper knows only the number – never the name – of the applicant. Not until all the papers have been graded will they be matched with names. If other tests, such as training and experience or oral interview ratings have been given, scores will be combined. Different parts of the examination usually have different weights. For example, the written test might count 60 percent of the final grade, and a rating of training and experience 40 percent. In many jurisdictions, veterans will have a certain number of points added to their grades.

After the final grade has been determined, the names are placed in grade order and an eligible list is established. There are various methods for resolving ties between those who get the same final grade – probably the most common is to place first the name of the person whose application was received first. Job offers are made from the eligible list in the order the names appear on it. You will be notified of your grade and your rank as soon as all these computations have been made. This will be done as rapidly as possible.

People who are found to meet the requirements in the announcement are called "eligibles." Their names are put on a list of eligible candidates. An eligible's chances of getting a job depend on how high he stands on this list and how fast agencies are filling jobs from the list.

When a job is to be filled from a list of eligibles, the agency asks for the names of people on the list of eligibles for that job. When the civil service commission receives this request, it sends to the agency the names of the three people highest on this list. Or, if the job to be filled has specialized requirements, the office sends the agency the names of the top three persons who meet these requirements from the general list.

The appointing officer makes a choice from among the three people whose names were sent to him. If the selected person accepts the appointment, the names of the others are put back on the list to be considered for future openings.

That is the rule in hiring from all kinds of eligible lists, whether they are for typist, carpenter, chemist, or something else. For every vacancy, the appointing officer has his choice of any one of the top three eligibles on the list. This explains why the person whose name is on top of the list sometimes does not get an appointment when some of the persons lower on the list do. If the appointing officer chooses the second or third eligible, the No. 1 eligible does not get a job at once, but stays on the list until he is appointed or the list is terminated.

X. HOW TO PASS THE INTERVIEW TEST

The examination for which you applied requires an oral interview test. You have already taken the written test and you are now being called for the interview test – the final part of the formal examination.

You may think that it is not possible to prepare for an interview test and that there are no procedures to follow during an interview. Our purpose is to point out some things you can do in advance that will help you and some good rules to follow and pitfalls to avoid while you are being interviewed.

What is an interview supposed to test?
The written examination is designed to test the technical knowledge and competence of the candidate; the oral is designed to evaluate intangible qualities, not readily measured otherwise, and to establish a list showing the relative fitness of each candidate – as measured against his competitors – for the position sought. Scoring is not on the basis of "right" and "wrong," but on a sliding scale of values ranging from "not passable" to "outstanding." As a matter of fact, it is possible to achieve a relatively low score without a single "incorrect" answer because of evident weakness in the qualities being measured.

Occasionally, an examination may consist entirely of an oral test – either an individual or a group oral. In such cases, information is sought concerning the technical knowledges and abilities of the candidate, since there has been no written examination for this purpose. More commonly, however, an oral test is used to supplement a written examination.

Who conducts interviews?

The composition of oral boards varies among different jurisdictions. In nearly all, a representative of the personnel department serves as chairman. One of the members of the board may be a representative of the department in which the candidate would work. In some cases, "outside experts" are used, and, frequently, a businessman or some other representative of the general public is asked to serve. Labor and management or other special groups may be represented. The aim is to secure the services of experts in the appropriate field.

However the board is composed, it is a good idea (and not at all improper or unethical) to ascertain in advance of the interview who the members are and what groups they represent. When you are introduced to them, you will have some idea of their backgrounds and interests, and at least you will not stutter and stammer over their names.

What should be done before the interview?

While knowledge about the board members is useful and takes some of the surprise element out of the interview, there is other preparation which is more substantive. It *is* possible to prepare for an oral interview – in several ways:

1) Keep a copy of your application and review it carefully before the interview

This may be the only document before the oral board, and the starting point of the interview. Know what education and experience you have listed there, and the sequence and dates of all of it. Sometimes the board will ask you to review the highlights of your experience for them; you should not have to hem and haw doing it.

2) Study the class specification and the examination announcement

Usually, the oral board has one or both of these to guide them. The qualities, characteristics or knowledges required by the position sought are stated in these documents. They offer valuable clues as to the nature of the oral interview. For example, if the job involves supervisory responsibilities, the announcement will usually indicate that knowledge of modern supervisory methods and the qualifications of the candidate as a supervisor will be tested. If so, you can expect such questions, frequently in the form of a hypothetical situation which you are expected to solve. NEVER go into an oral without knowledge of the duties and responsibilities of the job you seek.

3) Think through each qualification required

Try to visualize the kind of questions you would ask if you were a board member. How well could you answer them? Try especially to appraise your own knowledge and background in each area, *measured against the job sought*, and identify any areas in which you are weak. Be critical and realistic – do not flatter yourself.

4) Do some general reading in areas in which you feel you may be weak

For example, if the job involves supervision and your past experience has NOT, some general reading in supervisory methods and practices, particularly in the field of human relations, might be useful. Do NOT study agency procedures or detailed manuals. The oral board will be testing your understanding and capacity, not your memory.

5) Get a good night's sleep and watch your general health and mental attitude

You will want a clear head at the interview. Take care of a cold or any other minor ailment, and of course, no hangovers.

What should be done on the day of the interview?

Now comes the day of the interview itself. Give yourself plenty of time to get there. Plan to arrive somewhat ahead of the scheduled time, particularly if your appointment is in the fore part of the day. If a previous candidate fails to appear, the board might be ready for you a bit early. By early afternoon an oral board is almost invariably behind schedule if there are many candidates, and you may have to wait. Take along a book or magazine to read, or your application to review, but leave any extraneous material in the waiting room when you go in for your interview. In any event, relax and compose yourself.

The matter of dress is important. The board is forming impressions about you – from your experience, your manners, your attitude, and your appearance. Give your personal appearance careful attention. Dress your best, but not your flashiest. Choose conservative, appropriate clothing, and be sure it is immaculate. This is a business interview, and your appearance should indicate that you regard it as such. Besides, being well groomed and properly dressed will help boost your confidence.

Sooner or later, someone will call your name and escort you into the interview room. *This is it.* From here on you are on your own. It is too late for any more preparation. But remember, you asked for this opportunity to prove your fitness, and you are here because your request was granted.

What happens when you go in?

The usual sequence of events will be as follows: The clerk (who is often the board stenographer) will introduce you to the chairman of the oral board, who will introduce you to the other members of the board. Acknowledge the introductions before you sit down. Do not be surprised if you find a microphone facing you or a stenotypist sitting by. Oral interviews are usually recorded in the event of an appeal or other review.

Usually the chairman of the board will open the interview by reviewing the highlights of your education and work experience from your application – primarily for the benefit of the other members of the board, as well as to get the material into the record. Do not interrupt or comment unless there is an error or significant misinterpretation; if that is the case, do not hesitate. But do not quibble about insignificant matters. Also, he will usually ask you some question about your education, experience or your present job – partly to get you to start talking and to establish the interviewing "rapport." He may start the actual questioning, or turn it over to one of the other members. Frequently, each member undertakes the questioning on a particular area, one in which he is perhaps most competent, so you can expect each member to participate in the examination. Because time is limited, you may also expect some rather abrupt switches in the direction the questioning takes, so do not be upset by it. Normally, a board member will not pursue a single line of questioning unless he discovers a particular strength or weakness.

After each member has participated, the chairman will usually ask whether any member has any further questions, then will ask you if you have anything you wish to add. Unless you are expecting this question, it may floor you. Worse, it may start you off on an extended, extemporaneous speech. The board is not usually seeking more information. The question is principally to offer you a last opportunity to present further qualifications or to indicate that you have nothing to add. So, if you feel that a significant qualification or characteristic has been overlooked, it is proper to point it out in a sentence or so. Do not compliment the board on the thoroughness of their examination – they have been sketchy, and you know it. If you wish, merely say, "No thank you, I have nothing further to add." This is a point where you can "talk yourself out" of a good impression or fail to present an important bit of information. Remember, *you close the interview yourself.*

The chairman will then say, "That is all, Mr. _____, thank you." Do not be startled; the interview is over, and quicker than you think. Thank him, gather your belongings and take your leave. Save your sigh of relief for the other side of the door.

How to put your best foot forward

Throughout this entire process, you may feel that the board individually and collectively is trying to pierce your defenses, seek out your hidden weaknesses and embarrass and confuse you. Actually, this is not true. They are obliged to make an appraisal of your qualifications for the job you are seeking, and they want to see you in your best light. Remember, they must interview all candidates and a non-cooperative candidate may become a failure in spite of their best efforts to bring out his qualifications. Here are 15 suggestions that will help you:

1) Be natural – Keep your attitude confident, not cocky

If you are not confident that you can do the job, do not expect the board to be. Do not apologize for your weaknesses, try to bring out your strong points. The board is interested in a positive, not negative, presentation. Cockiness will antagonize any board member and make him wonder if you are covering up a weakness by a false show of strength.

2) Get comfortable, but don't lounge or sprawl

Sit erectly but not stiffly. A careless posture may lead the board to conclude that you are careless in other things, or at least that you are not impressed by the importance of the occasion. Either conclusion is natural, even if incorrect. Do not fuss with your clothing, a pencil or an ashtray. Your hands may occasionally be useful to emphasize a point; do not let them become a point of distraction.

3) Do not wisecrack or make small talk

This is a serious situation, and your attitude should show that you consider it as such. Further, the time of the board is limited – they do not want to waste it, and neither should you.

4) Do not exaggerate your experience or abilities

In the first place, from information in the application or other interviews and sources, the board may know more about you than you think. Secondly, you probably will not get away with it. An experienced board is rather adept at spotting such a situation, so do not take the chance.

5) If you know a board member, do not make a point of it, yet do not hide it

Certainly you are not fooling him, and probably not the other members of the board. Do not try to take advantage of your acquaintanceship – it will probably do you little good.

6) Do not dominate the interview

Let the board do that. They will give you the clues – do not assume that you have to do all the talking. Realize that the board has a number of questions to ask you, and do not try to take up all the interview time by showing off your extensive knowledge of the answer to the first one.

7) Be attentive

You only have 20 minutes or so, and you should keep your attention at its sharpest throughout. When a member is addressing a problem or question to you, give him your undivided attention. Address your reply principally to him, but do not exclude the other board members.

8) Do not interrupt

A board member may be stating a problem for you to analyze. He will ask you a question when the time comes. Let him state the problem, and wait for the question.

9) Make sure you understand the question

Do not try to answer until you are sure what the question is. If it is not clear, restate it in your own words or ask the board member to clarify it for you. However, do not haggle about minor elements.

10) Reply promptly but not hastily

A common entry on oral board rating sheets is "candidate responded readily," or "candidate hesitated in replies." Respond as promptly and quickly as you can, but do not jump to a hasty, ill-considered answer.

11) Do not be peremptory in your answers

A brief answer is proper – but do not fire your answer back. That is a losing game from your point of view. The board member can probably ask questions much faster than you can answer them.

12) Do not try to create the answer you think the board member wants

He is interested in what kind of mind you have and how it works – not in playing games. Furthermore, he can usually spot this practice and will actually grade you down on it.

13) Do not switch sides in your reply merely to agree with a board member

Frequently, a member will take a contrary position merely to draw you out and to see if you are willing and able to defend your point of view. Do not start a debate, yet do not surrender a good position. If a position is worth taking, it is worth defending.

14) Do not be afraid to admit an error in judgment if you are shown to be wrong

The board knows that you are forced to reply without any opportunity for careful consideration. Your answer may be demonstrably wrong. If so, admit it and get on with the interview.

15) Do not dwell at length on your present job

The opening question may relate to your present assignment. Answer the question but do not go into an extended discussion. You are being examined for a *new* job, not your present one. As a matter of fact, try to phrase ALL your answers in terms of the job for which you are being examined.

Basis of Rating

Probably you will forget most of these "do's" and "don'ts" when you walk into the oral interview room. Even remembering them all will not ensure you a passing grade. Perhaps you did not have the qualifications in the first place. But remembering them will help you to put your best foot forward, without treading on the toes of the board members.

Rumor and popular opinion to the contrary notwithstanding, an oral board wants you to make the best appearance possible. They know you are under pressure – but they also want to see how you respond to it as a guide to what your reaction would be under the pressures of the job you seek. They will be influenced by the degree of poise you display, the personal traits you show and the manner in which you respond.

ABOUT THIS BOOK

This book contains tests divided into Examination Sections. Go through each test, answering every question in the margin. At the end of each test look at the answer key and check your answers. On the ones you got wrong, look at the right answer choice and learn. Do not fill in the answers first. Do not memorize the questions and answers, but understand the answer and principles involved. On your test, the questions will likely be different from the samples. Questions are changed and new ones added. If you understand these past questions you should have success with any changes that arise. Tests may consist of several types of questions. We have additional books on each subject should more study be advisable or necessary for you. Finally, the more you study, the better prepared you will be. This book is intended to be the last thing you study before you walk into the examination room. Prior study of relevant texts is also recommended. NLC publishes some of these in our Fundamental Series. Knowledge and good sense are important factors in passing your exam. Good luck also helps. So now study this Passbook, absorb the material contained within and take that knowledge into the examination. Then do your best to pass that exam.

———

EXAMINATION SECTION

EXAMINATION SECTION
TEST 1

DIRECTIONS: Each question or incomplete statement is followed by several suggested answers or completions. Select the one that BEST answers the question or completes the statement. *PRINT THE LETTER OF THE CORRECT ANSWER IN THE SPACE AT THE RIGHT.*

1. The one of the following entrees which offers the LEAST variation in texture is   1._____

    A. turkey, cranberry sauce, fried golden brown potatoes, peas
    B. chopped sirloin, mushroom gravy, French fried potatoes broccoli spears
    C. oven-fried chicken, baked potato, peas and carrots, salad
    D. meat loaf, mashed potatoes, creamed spinach, white bread

2. In planning a menu, the FIRST item which should be chosen is the   2._____

    A. vegetable   B. salad   C. entree   D. dessert

3. Of the following, the BEST method of tenderizing cuts of meat which are less tender is by   3._____

    A. broiling   B. stewing   C. baking   D. deep-frying

4. Which one of the following statements regarding proteins is CORRECT?   4._____

    A. The amount of protein in the body is a constant.
    B. The presence of nitrogen distinguishes protein from carbohydrates and fat.
    C. Protein provides more calories per gram than carbohydrates or fat.
    D. Protein provides the principal source of glucose to brain tissue.

5. The one of the following foods that provides MORE vitamin C per serving than the others is   5._____

    A. brussels sprouts   B. cabbage
    C. tomatoes   D. turnips

6. Liver is a PRIMARY source of which one of the following vitamins?   6._____

    A. A   B. B_6 C. C   D. D

7. Vitamin A is a fat soluble vitamin essential in an adequate diet for children and adults. Which one of the following statements concerning vitamin A is TRUE?   7._____

    A. The Recommended Daily Allowance for vitamin A for the adult male and female 10 years of age and older is the same.
    B. The Recommended Daily Allowance for vitamin A is expressed in terms of U.S.P. units.
    C. Vegetables have vitamin A activity equal to vitamin A in animal foods.
    D. Excessive amounts of vitamin A are well tolerated by adults.

8. Iron is a mineral required for growth and to keep the body functioning properly. Of the following, the combination of foods that will provide the BEST intake of iron is   8._____

    A. green peas, liver, enriched bread, dried potatoes
    B. cheese, oranges, liver, butter

C. peanut butter, milk, carrots, liver
D. liver, ice cream, chicken, peaches

9. Calcium and phosphorous account for approximately three-fourths of the mineral ele-   9.____
   ments in the body. Their intake is important for adequate nutrition.
   Which one of the following statements is CORRECT about both minerals?

   A. For children and young adults, the Recommended Daily Allowance for calcium is
      twice that for phosphorous.
   B. Their absorption and utilization are enhanced by the presence of vitamin E.
   C. They are not found in soft tissues.
   D. They constitute an important buffer system in the regulation of body neutrality.

10. When a menu is being planned for a specific holiday, the one of the following which is   10.____
    LEAST appropriate is to

    A. ask for suitable menu possibilities from the staff
    B. choose only foods which are familiar to those who will be served
    C. test acceptability of possible holiday items by serving one or two items at earlier
       meals
    D. include traditional foods associated with the holiday, if available

11. When a No. 8 scoop is used to serve mashed potatoes, the portion served should be   11.____
    _____ cup.

    A. 2/5   B. 1/3   C. 1/2   D. 2/3

12. A six-ounce ladle is equal to APPROXIMATELY _____ cup(s).   12.____

    A. 1/2   B. 1   C. 3/4   D. 1 1/4

13. The MOST accurate measurement of food is by   13.____

    A. volume
    B. weight
    C. can size
    D. number of pieces per container

14. Deep fat frying is BEST accomplished at which one of the following temperatures?   14.____

    A. 300° F   B. 350° F   C. 400° F   D. 450° F

15. When you are roasting beef, the indication that a well-done and palatable product has   15.____
    been achieved is an interior temperature in the range of

    A. 110° to 130° F   B. 131° to 150° F
    C. 151° to 170° F   D. 171° to 190° F

16. Of the following methods of roasting beef, the one that causes the LEAST amount of   16.____
    shrinkage is cooking at

    A. high temperature during the first half of the cooking time and at low temperature
       during the other half
    B. high temperature during the entire cooking time

C. moderate temperature during the first half of the cooking time and at high tempera-ture during the other half
D. low temperature during the entire cooking time

17. The method of meat preparation that calls for cutting the meat into small pieces, covering with hot liquid, and cooking at about 185° F is known as   17.____

    A. boiling   B. stewing   C. roasting   D. broiling

18. Of the following pressure ranges, the one in which three compartment steamers operate is the _____ lb. range.   18.____

    A. 1-5   B. 5-15   C. 15-30   D. 30-50

19. When vegetables are cooked for large numbers of people, the BEST results are obtained by *batch cooking.*   19.____
This kind of cooking is done in order to

    A. have high-quality vegetables available during the entire serving period
    B. prepare more vegetables using less staff
    C. use less equipment
    D. prepare several batches of vegetables at the same time

20. The one of the following procedures that could cause food poisoning is   20.____

    A. allowing cooked poultry to stand for an hour, slicing it, and covering it with broth, and holding it at room temperature for several hours
    B. keeping food mixtures on cafeteria counters for one hour
    C. cooking left-over food mixtures quickly by frequent stirring and then refrigerating in shallow pans
    D. chilling all ingredients for salads for at least one hour before preparation

21. When large numbers of people are to be served in a cafeteria setting, an estimate should be made each day of the quantity of food to be prepared and cooked.   21.____
This is BEST done by which one of the following ways?

    A. Having the cook make a list of the previous day's leftovers.
    B. Considering previous sales of the same menu combinations, as well as the weather and any special events.
    C. Cooking as much food as the staff and equipment allow so as not to be caught short.
    D. Using the capacity of the seating area as a base.

22. Which one of the following statements concerning frozen pre-cooked foods is NOT cor-rect?   22.____

    A. Certain pre-cooked foods are excellent when freshly prepared, but deteriorate rap-idly in an ordinary freezer.
    B. Some pre-cooked foods are so greatly changed by freezing and subsequent reheating that they become unpalatable.
    C. All food items which are carefully cooked, rapidly frozen, and then held at low tem-perature until used, are satisfactory products when served.
    D. Many foods may be frozen, stored in an appropriate type of freezer, and thawed without marked change in nutritional and esthetic value.

23. Of the following, the one which is NOT a method of controlling food costs in an institutional food service is

    A. avoiding the use of *leftover* foods since they are usually unpopular items
    B. maintaining an accurate food inventory
    C. knowing what yield can be obtained from various sizes, counts, and amounts of food
    D. ensuring the food-service employees use standardized recipes and portions

23.____

24. The direct labor cost involved in the preparation of meals includes wages paid to cooks, bakers, salad makers, counter workers, etc. and is MOST accurately determined by which one of the following methods?

    A. Making studies of the amount of time spent by employees in actual meal preparation tasks.
    B. Checking employees' time cards to determine total absence time.
    C. Dividing the number of meals served each week by the number of employees.
    D. Determining how much time is lost because of equipment breakdown and adding the value of this time to the cost of employees' wages.

24.____

25. Which one of the following would MOST likely enable the supervisor of a food service to attain better cost control over operations?

    A. *Increasing* the output of individual staff members.
    B. *Increasing* the size of the staff.
    C. *Reducing* the amount of time scheduled for food preparation tasks.
    D. *Reducing* the amount of time spent on training staff members.

25.____

KEY (CORRECT ANSWERS)

1.	D	11.	C
2.	C	12.	C
3.	B	13.	B
4.	B	14.	B
5.	A	15.	D
6.	A	16.	D
7.	A	17.	B
8.	A	18.	B
9.	D	19.	A
10.	B	20.	A

21.	B
22.	C
23.	A
24.	A
25.	A

TEST 2

DIRECTIONS: Each question or incomplete statement is followed by several suggested answers or completions. Select the one that BEST answers the question or completes the statement. *PRINT THE LETTER OF THE CORRECT ANSWER IN THE SPACE AT THE RIGHT.*

1. Of the following, the FIRST step in the control of food costs in an institution should be to   1.____

    A. make sure the delivery of foods is in accordance with the order
    B. store foods under tight security as soon as they are received
    C. follow purchase specifications in obtaining food products
    D. get the correct amount of raw food to the cook

2. Of the following, the area in which recipe costing aids are of MOST value is   2.____

    A. making yield studies
    B. planning menus
    C. taking inventories
    D. determining the cost of wasted foods

3. Control records of both the physical and cost aspects of food storage are MOST useful   3.____
as a basic guide in which one of the following areas?

    A. Receiving food deliveries   B. Issuing food to the kitchen
    C. Ordering food   D. Controlling food theft

4. The one of the following which indicates actual control over food costs in a food ser-   4.____
vice is that

    A. recipe costing is done
    B. waste is eliminated
    C. yield studies are made
    D. food cost data are regularly analyzed

5. The one of the following which is the MAJOR purpose of a perpetual inventory in the food   5.____
storage area of a kitchen or other dietary unit is to

    A. facilitate removal of shelf items that are needed for quick use
    B. reduce breakage and spoilage of liquified foods
    C. act as a control in the area of food purchasing
    D. facilitate the planning of balanced diets and menus

6. Walk-in storage refrigerators can be a very important aspect of a well-equipped kitchen   6.____
in a food service.
Of the following, the MOST desirable location for a walk-in refrigerator is near the

    A. receiving and preparation areas
    B. tray delivery area
    C. cafeteria
    D. dishwashing area

7. Food specifications are precise statements of quality and other commodity requirements. All food should be purchased according to specifications.
Of the following, the LEAST important aspect of a food specification is the

    A. quantity required in a case, pound, carton, etc.
    B. federal grade desired
    C. size of the container
    D. picture of the item

7.____

8. The aim in buying food is to obtain the best value for the money spent.
Of the following, the practice which is LEAST likely to accomplish that aim is

    A. buying the cheapest item
    B. purchasing by specification
    C. purchasing only the quantities required for the menus planned
    D. checking all purchases on delivery

8.____

9. When deciding whether to select a particular piece of equipment for a kitchen or other dietary area, the one of the following which would be LEAST important for you to take into consideration is

    A. whether there is space for it
    B. whether it is easily cleaned and maintained
    C. whether there is an employee currently on staff who knows how to operate it
    D. how well it has worked in other institutions

9.____

10. Of the following foods, the type that is MOST likely to cause staph food poisoning if improperly prepared or handled is _____ food.

    A. sugar-coated   B. dried
    C. pickled   D. cream-filled

10.____

11. Harmful bacteria are MOST often introduced into foods prepared in a food service operation by

    A. insects   B. rodents   C. employees   D. utensils

11.____

12. When planning menus for secondary school students, it is desirable for the manager to do all of the following EXCEPT to

    A. stay within the school's food budget
    B. include familiar ethnic foods
    C. include many food choices
    D. consider the size of the food service staff

12.____

13. Of the following, the manager's BEST evidence for a shortage claim on surplus food delivered to a school is

    A. her written report of the shortage claim
    B. the delivery receipt from the truck driver
    C. the container the food was delivered in
    D. an old container of the same item

13.____

14. The manager should prepare school lunch menus for a MINIMUM of _____ week(s) at a time.   14.____

    A. one   B. two   C. three   D. four

15. The manager must keep monthly inventories of all of the following EXCEPT   15.____

    A. paper goods   B. food items
    C. serving utensils   D. cleaning supplies

16. In the Type A lunch pattern for 10- to 12-year-old children, all of the following fulfill   16.____
the *meat or meat alternate* requirement EXCEPT

    A. two ounces of cheese
    B. one-half cup of fresh carrots
    C. four tablespoons of peanut butter
    D. one-half cup of cooked dry peas

17. A manager is planning to use tuna fish salad to comply with the guideline for the *meat or*   17.____
meat alternate requirement of the Type A lunch for secondary school students.
How much tuna fish will she need in order to serve 400 secondary school students?
_____ pounds.

    A. $37\frac{1}{2}$ B. 50   C. 75   D. 100

Questions 18-25.

DIRECTIONS: Answer Questions 18 through 25 SOLELY on the basis of information presented in the charts below.

STUDENT SALES COUNTER SHEET
March 4, 2005

Item	Price per Item	No. Items Offered for Sale	No. Items Unsold	Total Cash Received for Items Sold
Hot lunch	$2.25	250	75	
Milk	$0.60	525		$285.00
Soda	$0.75	300	163	$102.75
Ice Cream Bars	$0.45	181	59	$54.90
Buttered Roll	$0.15	200	150	
Cooked Vegetable	$0.90	325	40	$256.50
Pudding	$0.45	565	30	$240.75
Potato Chips	$0.30	610	50	$168.00

STUDENT SALES COUNTER SHEET
March 5, 2005

Item	Price per Item	No. Items Offered for Sale	No. Items Unsold	Total Cash Received for Items Sold
Hot lunch	$2.25	300		$585.00
Milk	$0.60	450		$255.00
Soda	$0.75	275	207	
Ice Cream Bars	$0.45	250	100	
Buttered Roll	$0.15	175	25	
Cooked Vegetable	$0.90	300	62	$214.20
Pudding	$0.45	490	47	
Potato Chips	$0.30	595	45	

18. Hot lunches accounted for APPROXIMATELY what percentage of all cash received for March 4, 2005?

   18.____

   A. 10%   B. 15%   C. 20%   D. 25%

19. Which one of the following items was sold LEAST on March 4, 2005 and March 5, 2005, combined?

   19.____

   A. Soda   B. Ice cream bars
   C. Buttered roll   D. Cooked vegetable

20. The number of milk containers which were unsold on March 4, 2005 is

   20.____

   A. 30   B. 50   C. 75   D. 95

21. How many fewer containers of pudding and soda were sold on March 5, 2005 than were sold on March 4, 2005?

   21.____

   A. 19   B. 81   C. 105   D. 161

22. Which single item, besides hot lunches, accounted for the GREATEST number of items sold on March 4, 2005?

   22.____

   A. Cooked vegetable   B. Pudding
   C. Ice cream bars   D. Soda

23. How many hot lunches were sold on March 4, 2005 and March 5, 2005, combined?

   23.____

   A. 435   B. 550   C. 625   D. 665

24. Of the following, the item that was bought MOST by the students on both March 4, 2005 and March 5, 2005 is

   24.____

   A. soda   B. buttered roll
   C. pudding   D. potato chips

25. The cumulative total of money received for all the soda, ice cream bars, buttered rolls, and pudding sold on March 4, 2005 is

   25.____

   A. $165.15   B. $405.90   C. $858.90   D. $1252.65

8

KEY (CORRECT ANSWERS)

1.	C		11.	C
2.	B		12.	C
3.	C		13.	C
4.	B		14.	D
5.	C		15.	C
6.	A		16.	B
7.	D		17.	C
8.	A		18.	D
9.	C		19.	C
10.	D		20.	B

21.	D
22.	B
23.	A
24.	D
25.	B

EXAMINATION SECTION
TEST 1

DIRECTIONS: Each question or incomplete statement is followed by several suggested answers or completions. Select the one that BEST answers the question or completes the statement. *PRINT THE LETTER OF THE CORRECT ANSWER IN THE SPACE AT THE RIGHT.*

1. In food service operations, the supervisor usually can arrive at a decision concerning an operations problem by considering the following steps to a solution:
    I. Analysis of available information
    II. Definition of problem
    III. Development of alternate solutions
    IV. Selection of decision
   In which of the following options are the steps given in PROPER sequence?

   A. II, I, III, IV
   B. I, III, II, IV
   C. I, II, III, IV
   D. III, I, II, IV

   1.____

2. The one of the following which is MOST important for improvement of the productivity of food-service employees is the

   A. use of convenience foods
   B. posting of food preparation schedules for employees
   C. adoption and implementation of a program of task analysis and work measurement
   D. advance preparation of as much food as possible

   2.____

3. Assume that all of the following problems are occurring in a kitchen under your supervision: production is slow in terms of food preparation; housekeeping is lax; the quality of the food prepared is very poor; morale is low.
   Of these four problems, the one that is *most likely* the cause of all the others and should probably be attended to FIRST is

   A. slow production
   B. lax housekeeping
   C. poorly prepared food
   D. low morale

   3.____

4. A common problem in food-service supervision is that improper supervisory practices can lead to situations in which subordinates disobey direct orders given to them by their superior.
   Which of the following supervisors would be *most likely* to promote such a situation? A supervisor who

   A. does not delegate authority
   B. does not make a decision without consulting his or her entire staff
   C. is unwilling to punish any employee for an infraction of the rules
   D. rarely holds meetings with his or her staff

   4.____

5. While reviewing kitchen operations, you notice that a recently-hired employee is using too large a scoop for serving mashed potatoes. Since you personally instructed this individual in the proper utilization of serving utensils, you believe that this employee should be reprimanded.
   In this situation, the *most appropriate* of the following actions would be to

   5.____

A. call the employee aside, inform him of his mistake, and plan for additional instruction
B. inform the employee of his mistake in the presence of the other employees
C. remove the employee from his work station and assign him to some less desirable tasks
D. assign another employee to serve the mashed potatoes with the appropriate size scoop and have the recently-hired employee observe

6. Assume that you are approached individually by two employees who work together in food preparation. Each employee registers her complaint against working with the other. Which one of the following would be the MOST effective action to take in order to handle this problem?

    6.____

A. At the next regularly scheduled staff meeting, mention the importance of good working relationships.
B. Ask your superior to make a judgment in this case, instead of deciding what to do yourself.
C. Reassign one employee to a suitable job where she will not have to work with the other employee.
D. Write a report to your superior detailing the problem and requesting transfers for both of the employees.

7. Suppose that, as a supervisor, you have an idea for changing the way a certain task is performed by your staff so that it will be less tedious and get done faster.
Of the following, the MOST advisable action for you to take regarding this idea is to

    7.____

A. issue a written memorandum, explaining the new method and giving reasons why it is to replace the old one
B. discuss it with your staff to get their reactions and suggestions
C. set up a training class in the new method for your staff
D. try it out on an experimental basis on half the staff

8. In preparing work schedules for food-service employees, the one of the following considerations to which the supervisor should give LEAST priority is the

    8.____

A. work skills of the employees
B. jobs to be done
C. physical set-up of the work area and equipment available
D. preferences of the employees

9. A new employee complains to you that she thinks the current method of serving meals is very ineffective. This employee strongly insists that another method is much better. However, the suggested method had been tried in the past with very unsatisfactory results. Of the following, the BEST way for you to handle the situation would be to

    9.____

A. assign the employee to a different work area to avoid conflict
B. try out the suggested method for one or two days to demonstrate why it doesn't work
C. briefly tell the employee that her suggested method will not work
D. discuss with the employee the reasons why the present method has proven to be more successful than her suggested method

10. Assume that you find it necessary to discipline two subordinates, Mr. Tate and Mr. Saw-   10._____
yer, for coming to work late on several occasions. Their latenesses have had disruptive
effects on the work schedule, and you have given both of them several verbal warnings.
Mr. Tate has been in your work unit for many years, and his work has always been satis-
factory. Mr. Sawyer is a probationary employee who has had some problems in learning
your procedures. You decide to give Mr. Tate one more warning, in private, for his latenesses.
According to good supervisory practice, which one of the following disciplinary actions
should you take with regard to Mr. Sawyer?

   A. Give him a reprimand in front of his co-workers to make a lasting impression.
   B. Recommend dismissal since he has not yet completed his probationary period.
   C. Give him one more warning, in private, for his latenesses.
   D. Recommend a short suspension or payroll deduction to impress on him the impor-
      tance of coming to work on time.

11. Assume that you have delegated a very important work assignment to Johnson, one of   11._____
your most experienced subordinates. Prior to completion of the assignment, your superior accidentally discovers that the assignment is being carried out incorrectly and tells
you about it.
Which one of the following responses is *most appropriate* for you to give to your superior?

   A. "I take full responsibility, and I will see to it that the assignment is carried out cor-
      rectly."
   B. "Johnson has been with us for many years now and should know better."
   C. "It really isn't Johnson's fault, rather it is the fault of the ancient equipment we have
      to do the job."
   D. "I think you should inform Johnson since he is the one at fault, not I."

12. Assume that you observe that one of your employees is talking excessively with other   12._____
employees, quitting early and taking unusually long rest periods. Despite these abuses,
she is one of your most productive employees, and her work is usually of the highest
quality.
Of the following, the *most appropriate* action to take with regard to this employee is to

   A. ignore these infractions since she is one of your best workers
   B. ask your superior to reprimand her so that you can remain on the employee's good
      side
   C. reprimand her since not doing so would lower the morale of the other employees
   D. ask another of your subordinates to mention these infractions to the offending
      employee and suggest that she stop breaking rules

13. Assume that you have noticed that an employee whose attendance had been quite satis-   13._____
factory is now showing marked evidence of a consistent pattern of absences.
Of the following, the BEST way to cope with this problem is to

   A. wait several weeks to see whether this pattern continues
   B. meet with the employee to try to find out the reasons for this change
   C. call a staff meeting and discuss the need for good attendance
   D. write a carefully worded warning to the employee

14. It is generally agreed that the successful supervisor must know how to wisely delegate   14.____
work to her subordinates since she cannot do everything herself.
Which one of the following practices is *most likely* to result in INEFFECTIVE delegation by a supervisor?

    A. Establishment of broad controls to assure feedback about any deviations from plans
    B. Willingness to let subordinates use their own ideas about how to get the job done, where appropriate
    C. Constant observance of employees to see if they are making any mistakes
    D. Granting of enough authority to make possible the accomplishment of the delegated work

15. Suppose that, in accordance with grievance procedures, an employee brings a complaint   15.____
to you, his immediate supervisor.
In dealing with his complaint, the one of the following which is MOST important for you to do is to

    A. talk to the employee's co-workers to learn whether the complaint is justified
    B. calm the employee by assuring him that you will look into the matter as soon as possible
    C. tell your immediate superior about the employee's complaint
    D. give the employee an opportunity to tell the full story

16. The successful application by a supervisor of work simplification techniques to food prep-   16.____
aration and service work is *most likely* to result in which one of the following?

    A. Employees working harder than before
    B. Food products of higher nutritional value
    C. Better employee attendance
    D. Elimination of unnecessary parts of jobs

17. Holding staff meetings at regular Intervals is generally considered to be a good supervi-   17.____
sory practice.
Which one of the following subjects is LEAST desirable for discussion at such a meeting?

    A. Revisions in agency personnel policies
    B. Violation of an agency rule by one of the employees present
    C. Problems of waste and breakage in the work area
    D. Complaints of employees about working conditions

18. Suppose that you are informed that your staff is soon to be reduced by one-third due to   18.____
budget problems.
Which one of the following steps would be LEAST advisable in your effort to maintain a quality service with the smaller number of employees?

    A. Directing employees to speed up operations
    B. Giving employees training or retraining
    C. Rearranging the work area
    D. Revising work methods

19. Of the following, which action on the part of the supervisor is LEAST likely to contribute to upgrading the skills of her subordinates?

    A. Providing appropriate training to subordinates
    B. Making periodic evaluations of subordinates and discussing the evaluations with the subordinates
    C. Consistently assigning subordinates to those tasks with which they are familiar
    D. Giving increased responsibility to appropriate subordinates

19.____

20. Suppose that a new employee on your staff has difficulty in performing his assigned tasks, after having been given training.
Of the following courses of action, the one which would be BEST for you, his supervisor, to take FIRST is to

    A. change his work assignment
    B. give him a poor evaluation since he is obviously unable to do the work
    C. give him the training again
    D. have him work with an employee who is more experienced in the tasks for a short while

20.____

21. To insure the safety of employees who must retrieve items from a food storeroom, the supervisor should direct that

    A. bulky items be put on the floor near the storeroom door
    B. newly-received items be put on the shelves in front of previously-received items
    C. ladders or step-stools be used to reach upper shelves
    D. frequently-requisitioned items be piled up just outside the entrance to the storeroom

21.____

22. Suppose that a cook receives a minor burn, which causes a blister on his hand, while handling a hot pan of food. After seeing that the employee gets proper treatment for the burn, the MOST advisable of the following actions for the supervisor to take is to

    A. send the employee home
    B. tell the employee to return to his work station
    C. help the employee to finish the day's food preparation
    D. temporarily assign the employee to a task other than handling food

22.____

23. Of the following, the FIRST step which should be taken by you, the supervisor, in the orientation of a new food-service employee is to

    A. include the new employee in the next regularly-scheduled staff conference
    B. discuss with the new employee the many problems which the kitchen staff faces daily
    C. give the new employee a task to see how well he can perform
    D. have a conference with the new employee and discuss what his duties will be

23.____

24. Assume that, as part of a step-by-step training process, the supervisor explained and demonstrated a food preparation task to a new employee. As a last step, the supervisor told the employee to perform the task himself.
The training given by this supervisor was

24.____

A. *good;* by putting the employee on his own, the supervisor indicated confidence in the employee
B. *poor;* he didn't ask whether the employee understood how to perform the task
C. *good;* he employed the technique of demonstration
D. *poor;* more than one instructor is required to make this method of training effective

25. Of the following, the BEST way to follow-up immediately after giving a new employee training in food preparation tasks is to

    A. have the new employee observe more experienced employees performing their tasks
    B. give the new employee an overall view of all the food service operations
    C. allow the new employee to perform the tasks herself under careful supervision
    D. have the new employee write a report on what she has learned

25.____

26. If one of your kitchen staff performs a particularly important task incorrectly, the one of the following times which is BEST for teaching her the proper procedure so that she will remember it is

    A. later on in the day after she has had time to think about the task
    B. immediately so that she can correct her error
    C. after the workday ends so you may speak to her with less distraction
    D. during the next regularly-scheduled staff training session

26.____

27. Assume that you are approached by a cook who is upset and who wants to give you her explanation as to why the day's food preparation went wrong.
In order to be an understanding listener, you should do ALL of the following EXCEPT

    A. carefully question the worker
    B. make a value judgment so you can take a definite position on the matter
    C. try to find out the meaning of the emotions behind the cook's statements
    D. restate the cook's position to assure that you comprehend what she is telling you

27.____

28. A troubled subordinate privately approaches his supervisor in order to talk about a problem on the job.
In this situation, the one of the following actions that is NOT desirable on the part of the supervisor is to

    A. ask the subordinate pertinent questions to help develop points further
    B. close his office door during the talk to block noisy distractions
    C. allow sufficient time to complete the discussion with the subordinate
    D. take over the conversation so the employee won't be embarrassed

28.____

29. Suppose that one of your goals as a supervisor is to foster good working relationships between yourself and your employees, without undermining your supervisory effectiveness by being too friendly.
Of the following, the BEST way to achieve this goal when dealing with employees' work problems is to

    A. discourage individual personal conferences by using regularly scheduled staff meetings to discuss work problems
    B. try to resolve work problems within a relatively short period of time

29.____

C. insist that employees put all work problems into writing before seeing you
D. maintain an open-door policy, allowing employees complete freedom of access to you without making appointments to discuss work problems

30. Of the following duties, the one that may be performed by a designated employee **instead** of the manager is   30._____

A. preparing work schedules for each job in the kitchen
B. placing all orders for food
C. checking, counting, and weighing supplies received
D. tasting all cooked foods, salads, sandwich and dessert mixtures

---

KEY (CORRECT ANSWERS)

1.	A	11.	A	21.	C
2.	C	12.	C	22.	D
3.	D	13.	B	23.	D
4.	C	14.	C	24.	B
5.	A	15.	D	25.	C
6.	C	16.	D	26.	B
7.	B	17.	B	27.	B
8.	D	18.	A	28.	D
9.	D	19.	C	29.	B
10.	C	20.	D	30.	C

EXAMINATION SECTION
TEST 1

DIRECTIONS: Each question or incomplete statement is followed by several suggested answers or completions. Select the one that BEST answers the question or completes the statement. *PRINT THE LETTER OF THE CORRECT ANSWER IN THE SPACE AT THE RIGHT.*

1.   The Federal and State grades of food are dependent upon

    A.   appearance and freedom from defects
    B.   maturity or freshness
    C.   variety
    D.   shape, color, and size
    E.   color, flavor, and size

1.____

2.   Select vegetables and fruits are

    A.   wilted or withered
    B.   ripe and well-colored
    C.   picked over
    D.   plump, well-colored, and ripe, firm without decay
    E.   well-colored, plump, firm, and top grade

2.____

3.   All perishable vegetables need to be

    A.   refrigerated
    B.   washed and wrapped
    C.   washed, wrapped, and refrigerated
    D.   stored at room temperature
    E.   stored in a special compartment in the refrigerator

3.____

4.   Fresh fruits, apples, pears, and peaches should be

    A.   washed and wrapped separately
    B.   refrigerated
    C.   wrapped and stored, unwashed, in the refrigerator or other cool place
    D.   kept at room temperature
    E.   purchased just as they are needed

4.____

5.   Dried vegetables are

    A.   equal to fresh vegetables of the same variety in mineral and cellulose
    B.   low-cost sources of protein and energy food
    C.   good main dish foods
    D.   usually cheaper than fresh vegetables
    E.   all of the above

5.____

6.   Commercially canned foods are

    A.   economical
    B.   convenient
    C.   easy to store

6.____

D. available
E. important to family food supply because of economy, convenience, and availability

7. Modern frozen foods are prepared   7.____

    A. by lowering the temperature slowly to freezing
    B. by lowering the temperature of a food rapidly to freezing
    C. from average grade food products
    D. at the peak of the seasonal supply
    E. at the sacrifice of vitamins

8. To insure color retention and prevent the spoilage action of bacteria, yeasts, and molds,   8.____
frozen foods should be kept at _____ degrees F.

    A. 10   B. 0   C. just under 32
    D. 20   E. 25-30

9. The grade stamp on beef, veal, calf, lamb, and mutton is one's guide to   9.____

    A. fat content
    B. leanness
    C. freedom from disease
    D. wholesomeness and quality characteristics
    E. price

10. Identity of the cuts of meat is helpful because of   10.____

    A. economy   B. method of cooking
    C. tenderness   D. all of the above
    E. none of the above

11. One will become a more economical shopper if cost of food is figured in terms of   11.____

    A. pounds
    B. quarts
    C. servings
    D. weight or measurement
    E. unit by which food is sold

12. The word poultry is applied to   12.____

    A. chickens and turkeys
    B. geese and ducks
    C. guineas and pigeons
    D. any wild bird used for food
    E. all domesticated birds used as food

13. Eggs are graded according to   13.____

    A. quality of white
    B. quality of yolk
    C. appearance of shell
    D. size
    E. size and quality of white and yolk

14. Coffee and tea contain   14.____

    A. vitamins   B. nutrients   C. stimulants
    D. all of the above   E. none of the above

15. With higher incomes and larger food budgets, Americans are using   15.____

    A. smaller amounts of cereal products
    B. more bread
    C. less fruits and vegetables
    D. more meat and less poultry
    E. greater amounts of cereal products

16. Prepared mixes   16.____

    A. are convenient
    B. are timesaving
    C. always cost more than homemade products
    D. should be firmly packaged
    E. are convenient and timesaving, and sometimes are economical

17. The well-planned kitchen includes areas for   17.____

    A. storage   B. cleanup   C. preparation
    D. service   E. all of the above

18. The selection of kitchen equipment considers   18.____

    A. materials
    B. construction
    C. design
    D. cost
    E. items well-constructed of durable materials in pleasing designs at reasonable costs

19. One of the MOST important things to remember about the kitchen is   19.____

    A. to keep everything immaculately clean
    B. to keep everything in its place
    C. to get as many labor-saving devices as possible
    D. to use all safety precautions - the kitchen can be a dangerous place
    E. that a great deal of the homemaker's time is spent here

20. Meal patterns vary as to   20.____

    A. cost
    B. kinds of foods
    C. amount of time and skill required for preparation
    D. all of the above
    E. none of the above

21. A distinctive menu includes   21.____

    A. flavor and texture contrast
    B. pleasing colors
    C. basic nutrients

D. family likes and dislikes
E. nutrients in pleasing flavor, texture, and color contrasts

22. The trend in modern meal service is toward 22.____

   A. very casual service
   B. traditional service
   C. more casual service with some meals served traditionally
   D. elaborate service
   E. a relaxed atmosphere with a hope that all service turns out well

23. The term flatware refers to 23.____

   A. pitchers
   B. trays and flat dishes
   C. knives, forks, and spoons
   D. anything made from stainless steel or silver
   E. teapots

24. A good design for dishes, glassware, and other service should be 24.____

   A. functional
   B. ornate
   C. simple
   D. an expression of the hostess' personality
   E. both beautiful and functional

25. The MOST practical choice for every day dinnerware for the family with several small 25.____
children would be

   A. earthenware
   B. high-silicate porcelain china
   C. semi-vitrified china
   D. durable molded plastic
   E. pottery

—————————

KEY (CORRECT ANSWERS)

1.	D	11.	C
2.	D	12.	E
3.	C	13.	E
4.	C	14.	C
5.	E	15.	A
6.	E	16.	E
7.	B	17.	E
8.	B	18.	E
9.	D	19.	D
10.	D	20.	D

21. E
22. C
23. C
24. E
25. D

TEST 2

DIRECTIONS: Each question or incomplete statement is followed by several suggested answers or completions. Select the one that BEST answers the question or completes the statement. *PRINT THE LETTER OF THE CORRECT ANSWER IN THE SPACE AT THE RIGHT.*

1. The MOST suitable choice for cake and frosting combination is   1.____

    A. angel food cake with thick buttery frosting
    B. buttery frosting on a simple economy cake
    C. light fluffy cooked frosting on a simple cake
    D. angel food cake with a heavy cooked frosting
    E. a simple chocolate cake with a chewy boiled frosting

2. Cookies   2.____

    A. are good with most meals
    B. can be frozen, raw, or baked
    C. are usually inexpensive and easy to store
    D. are easy to prepare
    E. all of the above

3. Hot water and *stir and roll* are nonconventional methods of making   3.____

    A. cake   B. cream puffs   C. bread
    D. pie crust   E. cookies

4. Nutmeats and bits of fruit are coated with flour before mixing them into cakes or cookies to   4.____

    A. help them sink to the bottom of the dough
    B. keep them evenly distributed throughout the dough
    C. keep them on top of the dough
    D. make them more attractive
    E. hold in their flavor

5. Poultry may be safely prepared by   5.____

    A. stuffing and freezing it
    B. stuffing it just before cooking
    C. leaving the stuffing in the cooked bird for a long time
    D. refrigerating poultry and stuffing separately two days before cooking
    E. none of the above

6. Cooked leftover meat, poultry, or fish may be used for   6.____

    A. casseroles
    B. salads
    C. sandwiches
    D. ingredients for main dishes, salads, or sandwiches
    E. none of the above

7. Every person who prepares or serves food should   7.____

    A. know and use ways to prevent food contamination or poisoning
    B. be especially clean and healthy
    C. keep foods very hot or very cold
    D. observe all of the above
    E. observe none of the above

8. A recent trend in entertaining with food service is   8.____

    A. buffet   B. cafeteria
    C. out-of-doors meals   D. teas
    E. coffees

9. The school lunch should be   9.____

    A. attractive, nutritious, and have variety
    B. made up of sandwiches
    C. providing half of the day"s calories
    D. packed in any sort of container
    E. given little planning time

10. Diets for the overweight are made up of   10.____

    A. foods high in calories, vitamins, and minerals
    B. foods low in calories, high in protein, vitamins, and minerals
    C. smaller servings of the regular family meals
    D. foods high in cellulose
    E. foods prepared with plenty of seasoning

11. Mental activity takes   11.____

    A. many calories   B. few calories
    C. much energy   D. more protein
    E. more fat in the diet

12. If the breadwinner works as a factory worker or farmer, he may need   12.____

    A. less food
    B. more iron
    C. more calories, perhaps as snacks
    D. more riboflavin
    E. a greater variety of food

13. In middle life, more _____ are needed to protect the body.   13.____

    A. fruits   B. vegetables
    C. calories   D. proteins
    E. fruits and vegetables

14. Older people need decreased numbers of calories and increased amounts of protein, vitamins, and minerals because   14.____

    A. the metabolic rate has slowed
    B. they are not so active
    C. their incomes are less

D. shopping for food is more difficult
E. their bodies are less active and the metabolic rate is slowed

15. It is wise to divide foods fairly evenly among three meals a day for   15.____

    A. older people   B. middle-aged people
    C. teenagers   D. children
    E. all ages

16. Consideration and thoughtfulness is the MOST important part of   16.____

    A. adjusting to special diets
    B. reactions to income increases
    C. reactions to income losses
    D. appreciation of unusual foods
    E. learning to cook

17. The healthier a child is between the years of six and twelve,   17.____

    A. the better adult health he will have
    B. the better teeth he will have
    C. the taller he will grow
    D. the better adjustments he will make in adolescence
    E. will not affect his future health

18. Pre-adolescent children need   18.____

    A. extra calcium and protein for growth
    B. iodine to help regulate the use of food
    C. quick-acting foods for extra energy
    D. minerals and vitamins for body regulation, protein for growth, and extra foods for
       quick energy
    E. starches and extras between meals

19. One of the MOST important events in the daily dietary life of each family member is   19.____

    A. breakfast   B. lunch
    C. dinner or supper   D. snack time
    E. the coffee break

20. It is good to remember to give a small child   20.____

    A. large servings
    B. small servings with seconds if he desires
    C. a wide variety of foods at the same meal
    D. several foods which are new to him
    E. food which he must eat

21. Children enjoy   21.____

    A. highly spiced foods
    B. very cold foods
    C. rough textures
    D. very hot foods
    E. warm foods of smooth texture and mild flavor

22. An infant should be fed   22.____

    A. in a relaxed atmosphere
    B. when he is hungry
    C. with a balanced diet
    D. on a definite schedule
    E. in a relaxed way, a balanced diet when he is hungry

23. When meat and low-acid vegetables are canned, it is necessary to use a temperature of   23.____
    _____ to kill bacteria.

    A. 100° F   B. 144° F
    C. 200° F   D. 400° F
    E. higher than boiling

24. Foods satisfactorily preserved by a concentration of sugar are   24.____

    A. meats
    B. fruits
    C. vegetables
    D. fruits and some vegetables
    E. whole fruits, or fruit and vegetable juices

25. It may be necessary to add _____ to fruit pulp or juice to make jelly.   25.____

    A. commercial pectin
    B. apple juice
    C. gelatin
    D. alcohol
    E. commercial pectin or apple juice

26. Good food packaging for freezing   26.____

    A. prevents freezer *burn*
    B. prevents transfer of flavor
    C. prevents transfer of odor
    D. need not be leakproof
    E. prevents loss of flavor, odor, color, and moisture

27. Scalding of vegetables before freezing helps   27.____

    A. retain color
    B. retard enzyme growth
    C. destroys some bacteria
    D. may soften and shrink the vegetables
    E. to do all of the above

28. Overscalding of vegetables before freezing   28.____

    A. causes an increase of sugar
    B. absorbs food values soluble in hot water
    C. destroys vitamins
    D. makes the product too soft
    E. does no harm

29. Darkening of color from enzyme action will take place in _____ unless ascorbic acid is used.   29.____

    A. vegetables
    B. fruits
    C. peaches, apples, and pears
    D. tomatoes
    E. meat

30. Before freezing, remove excess _____ from meat, fish, or poultry.   30.____

    A. fat
    B. bone
    C. skin
    D. membranes
    E. materials which will become rancid or waste space

KEY (CORRECT ANSWERS)

1.	B	11.	B	21.	E
2.	E	12.	C	22.	E
3.	D	13.	E	23.	E
4.	B	14.	E	24.	D
5.	B	15.	E	25.	E
6.	D	16.	A	26.	E
7.	D	17.	A	27.	E
8.	C	18.	D	28.	B
9.	A	19.	A	29.	C
10.	B	20.	B	30.	E

TEST 3

DIRECTIONS: Each question or incomplete statement is followed by several suggested answers or completions. Select the one that BEST answers the question or completes the statement. *PRINT THE LETTER OF THE CORRECT ANSWER IN THE SPACE AT THE RIGHT.*

1. Americans became nutrition-conscious approximately seventy years ago with the isolation of   1.____

    A. carbohydrates   B. fats   C. proteins
    D. minerals   E. vitamins

2. A family food plan should include   2.____

    A. sufficient foods from each basic group
    B. choices which meet all the likes of the family
    C. carbohydrates which are less expensive
    D. an abundance of protein
    E. foods containing delicious fats

3. A food plan made a week in advance   3.____

    A. allows one to shop ahead
    B. makes certain that all nutrients will be included
    C. shows how family needs will be met, amount of food needed, and something of cost
    D. is time consuming
    E. allows one to buy foods at bargain prices

4. A simplified food selection guide for healthful living builds meals around   4.____

    A. dairy foods   B. meats
    C. breads and cereals   D. vegetables and fruits
    E. all of the above

5. If thought is used in the family menu planning, an adequate supply of protein at a *low* cost may be secured from   5.____

    A. beef and veal
    B. pork and lamb
    C. poultry and fish
    D. dry beans, peas, and nuts
    E. meats and protein substitutes

6. Teenagers, pregnant women, and nursing mothers need LARGER amounts of _____ than do other family members.   6.____

    A. dairy foods   B. fruits and vegetables
    C. meats   D. breads and cereals
    E. all of the above

7. _____ servings of fruits and vegetables, and, breads and cereals should be included for adequate food intake.   7.____

A. Two   B. Three   C. One
D. Five   E. At least four or more

8. Research studies show the diets of teenagers are *likely* to be   8.____

    A. well-balanced
    B. poorly balanced
    C. lacking in protein and vitamins and minerals
    D. high in vitamins and minerals
    E. adequate in fruits and vegetables

9. When the daily caloric requirement is exceeded, that not used is   9.____

    A. excreted as waste
    B. stored as muscle protein
    C. stored as fat
    D. used for energy
    E. used for heat

10. The MAIN job of _____ is to build and repair body tissue.   10.____

    A. carbohydrates   B. proteins   C. minerals
    D. vitamins   E. fats

11. A unit used to measure the warmth and energy value of a food is the   11.____

    A. amino acid   B. calorie   C. kilogram
    D. ounce   E. atom

12. Individual caloric requirements depend upon   12.____

    A. age and sex
    B. temperature and kind of food eaten
    C. type and amount of exercise
    D. proportion of one's nonfat body weight
    E. all of the above

13. _____ creates bulk which helps to keep the digestive tract working smoothly.   13.____

    A. Water   B. Cellulose
    C. Protein   D. Fat
    E. Carbohydrate

14. _____ cups of liquid should be included in the daily food intake to promote body regula-   14.____
tion and elimination.

    A. Four   B. Five   C. Six   D. Seven   E. Eight

15. Good nutrition requires that one be able to   15.____

    A. discriminate between fact and fallacy in fad diets of today
    B. spend money for *health foods* and *health aids*
    C. purchase highly advertised brands of foods
    D. all of the above
    E. none of the above

16. One's nutritional health depends not only on the selection of a balanced diet but upon   16._____

     A. how this food has been stored before its use
     B. how it has been prepared
     C. how the body is able to use the nutrients
     D. all of the above
     E. none of the above

17. The MOST important factor in development of malnutrition is   17._____

     A. lack of sleep
     B. too little fresh air and sunshine
     C. fatigue
     D. faulty diet
     E. pressure of social life

18. The FIRST step in a weight-control project is to   18._____

     A. begin a program of strenuous exercise
     B. go on a diet to lose or gain weight
     C. try special diets advertised
     D. go on as one has been doing
     E. have a physical check-up by a doctor

19. Food requires a larger portion of the family income than any other item, using _____   19._____
percent of the income varying with the amount of income.

     A. 25-50   B. 50-75   C. 33   D. 20   E. 60

20. It is possible to have a nutritionally adequate diet on less money than the average family   20._____
spends by

     A. gaining more knowledge about nutrition
     B. considering more economical shopping procedures
     C. developing an interest in nutrition, consumer practices, and food habits
     D. changing food habits
     E. altering food habits and buying habits after studying nutrition

21. Good food management is essential to   21._____

     A. help economize while replenishing stored food supplies
     B. alter *expensive* food tastes
     C. develop greater numbers of food likes and fewer dislikes
     D. control meals eaten away from home
     E. meet the rise in the cost of staple goods

22. When one shops for food, it is wise to   22._____

     A. compare the market order with the Basic Four
     B. compare food prices and quality
     C. figure the food budget closely in advance
     D. be a careful, ethical shopper
     E. shop carefully and wisely with a good market order which was made considering
        the Basic Four, prices, and quality

23. State and Federal laws protect consumers from adulterated foods including   23.____

    A. food that may be injurious to health or in such condition as to be unfit for human food
    B. food that has been packed, packaged, or stored under unsanitary conditions
    C. food that uses coal-tar dyes
    D. food that is falsely labeled or has substitutes
    E. foods or any ingredients that use harmful colors or substitutes, or that may be prepared or stored in unsanitary ways so as to injure humans

24. The Federal Food and Drug Act, created in 1906, helps to safeguard our food supply by   24.____

    A. prohibiting false advertising of food, drugs, and cosmetics
    B. requiring the package label to give weight, measure, and contents
    C. prohibiting the transportation in interstate commerce of adulterated or misbranded foods
    D. all of the above
    E. none of the above

25. The MOST important factors in buying food are   25.____

    A. quality and price
    B. price and convenience
    C. quality and convenience
    D. quality, price, and convenience
    E. price and services available

———

KEY (CORRECT ANSWERS)

1.	E		11.	B
2.	A		12.	E
3.	C		13.	B
4.	E		14.	E
5.	E		15.	A
6.	A		16.	D
7.	E		17.	D
8.	C		18.	E
9.	C		19.	A
10.	B		20.	E

21.	E
22.	E
23.	E
24.	D
25.	D

TEST 4

DIRECTIONS: Each question or incomplete statement is followed by several suggested answers or completions. Select the one that BEST answers the question or completes the statement. *PRINT THE LETTER OF THE CORRECT ANSWER IN THE SPACE AT THE RIGHT.*

1. Centerpieces 1.____

    A. require little time and thought to arrange attractively
    B. using very fragrant flowers are good
    C. are expensive
    D. made by careful application of design principles are best
    E. should be high

2. A convenient way to serve many people with the MINIMUM amount of assistance and space is _____ service. 2.____

    A. compromise   B. plate   C. American
    D. formal   E. buffet

3. For the family type meal service, all food is passed 3.____

    A. to the left
    B. to the right
    C. either right or left as the family decides
    D. the direction which gives the shortest distance
    E. as the hostess indicates

4. The person served FIRST at dinner is *usually* the 4.____

    A. hostess
    B. host
    C. gentleman guest
    D. person seated at the right of the host
    E. person seated at the right of the hostess

5. Cookery can be fascinating allowing for 5.____

    A. creativity
    B. observation
    C. concentration
    D. management skill
    E. keen observation, concentrated management, and unlimited creativity

6. To use recipes effectively, it is necessary to 6.____

    A. understand terms and measurements
    B. use standard measuring tools
    C. have a knowledge of how substitutions may be made
    D. use correct ingredient combinations
    E. all of the above

7. To prevent excessive shrinkage of meat, use _____ roasting temperatures.   7.____

    A. very low - below 275° F
    B. slow - about 325° F
    C. moderate - 350° F
    D. hot - 400° F
    E. very hot - 450° F

8. In conventional cooking, heat is applied to the surface of the food, but by electronic cook-   8.____
    ing the food is cooked

    A. by energy
    B. by agitation of molecules
    C. by absorption of microwave energy and the resulting heat
    D. a golden brown
    E. a long time

9. Seasonings are used to _____ natural flavors in foods.   9.____

    A. hide   B. overpower
    C. bring out   D. alter
    E. disguise unpleasant

10. All oven temperatures in recipes are   10.____

    A. set when the product is put in the oven
    B. preheated temperatures
    C. set after the product is mixed
    D. approximate temperatures
    E. double-checked by use of a separate oven thermometer

11. Extra time is allowed in addition to time for meat cookery to   11.____

    A. allow the meat to set
    B. make the gravy
    C. carve the meat
    D. make carving easier and prepare gravy
    E. be certain the meat is cooked

12. Eggs and cheese should be cooked at _____ temperatures.   12.____

    A. very high   B. high
    C. moderate   D. low to moderate
    E. very low

13. To cook vegetables BEST,   13.____

    A. use little water and cook quickly
    B. cook slowly
    C. use a generous amount of water
    D. pare generously
    E. pour off cooking liquid

14. For BEST results, cook frozen vegetables   14.____

    A. as you would fresh vegetables
    B. the same as fresh vegetables, but reduce the cooking time
    C. in a pressure pan
    D. after thawing completely
    E. in a cup of water

15. Fruit cooked in sugar syrup   15.____

    A. retains its natural raw flavor
    B. loses its shape
    C. loses its vitamin content
    D. does keep its shape, but has a changed flavor
    E. remains unchanged in shape or flavor

16. All-purpose flour is   16.____

    A. a blend of hard and soft wheat flours
    B. not desirable for pastries
    C. whole wheat flour
    D. enriched with gluten
    E. more expensive than other flour

17. The _____ in wheat flour makes it possible to develop an elastic dough from it.   17.____

    A. bran   B. germ   C. vitamin B   D. starch   E. gluten

18. Points to consider when evaluating commercial or homemade mixes with conventional   18.____
    mixing methods are

    A. cost
    B. time involved
    C. quality of resulting product
    D. convenience
    E. analyses of the quality of final products by cost, time, and convenience

19. Essentials for making a good cup of coffee or tea are   19.____

    A. fresh ingredients
    B. freshly cleaned containers
    C. plenty of beverage to be reheated
    D. good fresh coffee or tea, a clean container, and water of the correct temperature
    E. dated ingredients

20. The BEST time to satisfy the craving for sweets is   20.____

    A. with a dessert at mealtime
    B. by eating candy between meals
    C. by eating desserts between meals as snacks
    D. by eating candy just after a meal
    E. whenever the craving arises

21. To adjust a cake recipe for higher altitudes, it may be necessary to 21.____

    A. increase leavening and sugar
    B. decrease leavening or sugar or both
    C. increase liquid
    D. decrease leavening or sugar and increase liquid
    E. increase the shortening

22. Butter cakes are USUALLY made by the _____ methods. 22.____

    A. conventional   B. one bowl quick
    C. sponge   D. conventional or quick
    E. none of the above

23. The characteristics of good plain pastry are 23.____

    A. light, crisp, tender, flaky crust and golden brown color
    B. firm, smooth golden crust
    C. a tender crumbling crust
    D. shrunken edges
    E. a very pale crust

24. The temperature at which candy is cooked determines 24.____

    A. the texture
    B. the softness
    C. the hardness or brittleness
    D. the desired consistency
    E. flavor

25. The amount of handling candy receives after cooking determines 25.____

    A. the flavor
    B. the texture - crystalline or noncrystalline
    C. hardness
    D. softness
    E. texture and consistency

KEY (CORRECT ANSWERS)

1.	D		11.	D
2.	E		12.	D
3.	B		13.	A
4.	D		14.	B
5.	E		15.	D
6.	E		16.	A
7.	B		17.	E
8.	C		18.	E
9.	C		19.	D
10.	B		20.	A

21.	D
22.	D
23.	A
24.	D
25.	B

EXAMINATION SECTION
TEST 1

DIRECTIONS: Each question or incomplete statement is followed by several suggested answers or completions. Select the one that BEST answers the question or completes the statement. *PRINT THE LETTER OF THE CORRECT ANSWER IN THE SPACE AT THE RIGHT.*

1. Fuel value of foods is determined by use of a(n)   1.____

    A. caloric unit   B. calorific unit
    C. calciferol   D. calorimeter

2. Folacin is necessary for   2.____

    A. digestion of carbohydrates
    B. metabolism of sterols
    C. synthesis of chlorophyll
    D. hematopoiesis

3. Avidin is a(n)   3.____

    A. vitamin   B. protein   C. fiber   D. fabric

4. Baking powders are a mixture of cornstarch, baking soda, and a(n)   4.____

    A. acid   B. alkali   C. gas   D. neutralizer

5. The CORRECT method of cooking green-colored vegetables is to   5.____

    A. pressure cook
    B. add a small amount of baking soda
    C. release the steam occasionally while cooking in a covered saucepan
    D. keep the saucepan tightly covered

6. Popovers and cream puffs are PRINCIPALLY leavened by   6.____

    A. steam   B. air
    C. carbon dioxide   D. nitrous oxide

7. Compared with the recommended figure of 50%, the actual percentage of food calories   7.____
    derived from protective foods in the American diet is

    A. 20%   B. 25%   C. 33%   D. 45%

8. A bacteriostatic method of food preservation is   8.____

    A. open kettle canning   B. pressure canning
    C. dehydration   D. irradiation

9. For the average American, minerals of value as food supplements for the diet are cal-   9.____
    cium,

    A. phosphorus, sodium, and choline
    B. chlorine, magnesium, and iron
    C. phosphorus, iron, and iodine
    D. chlorine, iron, and manganese

10. For the average American, the vitamins of value as food supplements are thiamine, pyridoxine, riboflavin, calciferol, ascorbic acid, and   10._____

    A. niacin, B_{12}, A   B. B_6, B_{12}, folic acid
    C. B_{12}, K and A   D. B_{12}, A and E

11. The critical temperatures for eggs in storage are   11._____

    A. 28° and 68° B. 32° and 75°
    C. 38° and 60° D. 25° and 75°

12. When they are to form an ingredient in cake, eggs blend with the batter better if they are   12._____

    A. new laid
    B. chilled thoroughly
    C. brought to room temperature
    D. candled

13. Of the following, the HIGHEST in caloric value is 1 cupful   13._____

    A. strained honey   B. orange juice
    C. sugar   D. homogenized milk

14. Among the following, the BEST food source of thiamine is   14._____

    A. refined sugars   B. fats
    C. egg white   D. pork

15. In the list below, the BEST source of vitamin A is   15._____

    A. wheat germ   B. pork   C. milk   D. spinach

16. A disadvantage resulting from the intake of mineral oil is that it   16._____

    A. adds calories   B. reduces weight
    C. impairs the appetite   D. dissolves vitamin A

17. The leavening power of baking powders results from chemical action which releases   17._____

    A. carbon monoxide   B. carbon dioxide
    C. cream of tartar   D. lactic acid

18. The diet prescribed in diverticulitis is one that is   18._____

    A. high in calorie value   B. high in roughage content
    C. low residue, bland   D. high protein, bland

19. In typhoid fever, the diet should be   19._____

    A. *high* in calories and residue
    B. *low* in calories, high in residue
    C. *high* in calories, low in residue
    D. *high* in fruit juice content

20. Allspice is derived from   20.____

    A.   the berry of the pimento tree
    B.   a mixture of nutmeg, cinnamon and cloves
    C.   the root of the allspice tree
    D.   the bark of the cassia tree

21. Among the following food additives, the one which is used for the purpose of enhancing   21.____
the keeping quality of the food is

    A.   vitamin D in milk
    B.   bleaching agents in flour
    C.   ascorbic acid in cider
    D.   minerals and vitamins in cereals

22. An example of the bactericidal method of food preservation is   22.____

    A.   jam and jellies   B.   pickling
    C.   freezing   D.   refrigeration

23. The material which destroys the activity of biotin is   23.____

    A.   the protein found in uncooked egg white
    B.   fluorides in drinking water
    C.   iodides in medications
    D.   fluorescent substances found in milk

24. Egg whites beat BEST if they are   24.____

    A.   warm   B.   chilled thoroughly
    C.   at room temperature   D.   beaten by hand

25. The RICHEST food sources of folacin are   25.____

    A.   livers and green leafy vegetables
    B.   eggs and milk
    C.   cereals
    D.   fats

KEY (CORRECT ANSWERS)

1.	D		11.	A
2.	D		12.	C
3.	B		13.	A
4.	A		14.	D
5.	C		15.	D
6.	A		16.	D
7.	C		17.	B
8.	C		18.	C
9.	C		19.	C
10.	A		20.	A

21.	C
22.	A
23.	A
24.	C
25.	A

TEST 2

DIRECTIONS: Each question or incomplete statement is followed by several suggested answers or completions. Select the one that BEST answers the question or completes the statement. *PRINT THE LETTER OF THE CORRECT ANSWER IN THE SPACE AT THE RIGHT.*

1. Riboflavin is easily destroyed by

   A. alkalies and light
   C. heat and agitation
   B. acids and oxygen
   D. air and agitation

   1.____

2. Cretinism is a form of idiocy due to extreme deficiency of secretion by

   A. fat-soluble vitamins in the diet
   B. B-complex vitamins in the diet
   C. thyroid gland
   D. adrenal glands

   2.____

3. Nyctalopia results from a lack of

   A. vitamin A
   C. citric acid
   B. fluorine
   D. flavinoids

   3.____

4. The MAJOR influence in the decline of endemic goiter in the United States is the use of

   A. saffron oil
   C. iodized salt
   B. homogenized milk
   D. enriched cereals

   4.____

5. The Food Drug & Cosmetic Act of 1934 provides for

   A. retention of nutritive values
   B. fair pricing of goods
   C. purity of content
   D. accurate labeling

   5.____

6. The liver is the storage depot in the body for vitamin

   A. A   B. E   C. C   D. B

   6.____

7. The anti-xerophthalmia vitamin is vitamin

   A. A   B. B   C. E   D. K

   7.____

8. The pathway of excretion of the nitrogenous end products of protein metabolism is the

   A. lungs
   C. kidneys
   B. skin
   D. large intestine

   8.____

9. The term *trace elements* refers to

   A. minerals needed in very small amounts in nutrition
   B. substances which trace circulation in the body
   C. tools used in sewing
   D. potent drugs used as pain killer

   9.____

10. Flavinoids which are effective in human health are

    A. biotics   B. bioflavinoids
    C. neoflavinoids   D. vitamins

10.____

11. Uric acid results from

    A. vitamin deficiency
    B. metabolism of purines
    C. digestion of carbohydrates
    D. injection of nicotine

11.____

12. Studies comparing the desirability of feeding to premature infants formulas warmed to body temperature and those given directly on removal from the refrigerator show

    A. no significant difference
    B. disturbed sleep following intake of cold formula
    C. regurgitation following intake of cold formula
    D. slower weight gain with cold feeding

12.____

13. Hypoglycemia is a condition of

    A. diseased eyes   B. B, low blood sugar
    C. high blood sugar   D. low purin content

13.____

14. The normal source of insulin in the human body is the

    A. liver   B. thymus
    C. pancreas   D. pineal gland

14.____

15. One of the earliest symptoms of a thiamine deficiency is

    A. polyneuritis   B. anorexia
    C. nyctalopia   D. conjunctivitis

15.____

16. Air is used as a leavening agent in

    A. sponge cake   B. pound cake
    C. cookies   D. bread

16.____

17. Cheese originates in

    A. pasteurization   B. fermentation
    C. inversion   D. coagulation

17.____

18. In measuring vitamin A value in foods, the International Unit is defined as the activity of

    A. 5.0 mg. calciferol   B. 6.0 gm. tocopherol
    C. 6.0 gm. carotene   D. 0.6 meg. betacarotene

18.____

19. In the last fifty years, the proportion of calories from milk, cheese, fruits, and vegetables in the American diet has

    A. remained the same   B. doubled
    C. tripled   D. quadrupled

19.____

20. Interference with absorption of vitamin A may result from

    A. a diet heavy with bulk foods
    B. overconsumption of salad oils
    C. mineral oil in salad dressings
    D. low cholesterol diet

20.____

21. Vitamin A food value is

    A. lacking in yams
    B. fairly constant in dairy products
    C. closely related to green coloring in vegetables
    D. closely related to sun available during growing time

21.____

22. The passage of digested substances into the villi for distribution through the body is called

    A. absorption   B. metabolism
    C. anabolism   D. peristalsis

22.____

23. Of the following, the RICHEST source of vitamin E is

    A. liver   B. green leafy vegetables
    C. wheat germ oil   D. egg yolk

23.____

24. Of the following, the number of calories which MOST NEARLY approximates the daily fuel needs of a moderately active 25-year-old woman is

    A. 1500   B. 2000   C. 2500   D. 3500

24.____

25. A deficiency of riboflavin results in

    A. xerophthalmia   B. polyneuritis
    C. cutaneous lesions   D. chielosis

25.____

KEY (CORRECT ANSWERS)

1.	A	11.	B
2.	C	12.	A
3.	A	13.	B
4.	C	14.	C
5.	D	15.	B
6.	A	16.	A
7.	A	17.	B
8.	C	18.	D
9.	A	19.	B
10.	B	20.	C

21.	C
22.	A
23.	C
24.	C
25.	B

———

EXAMINATION SECTION
TEST 1

DIRECTIONS: Each question or incomplete statement is followed by several suggested answers or completions. Select the one that BEST answers the question or completes the statement. *PRINT THE LETTER OF THE CORRECT ANSWER IN THE SPACE AT THE RIGHT.*

1. For creamed vegetables, the proportion of cream sauce to vegetables is   1._____

    A. one to one   B. one-half to one
    C. two to one   D. three to one

2. The BEST dessert to provide additional protein in a meal is   2._____

    A. apple pie   B. baked custard
    C. fruit jello   D. apricot whip

3. An appropriate first course for a hearty dinner might include   3._____

    A. cream of tomato soup   B. clear consomme
    C. split pea soup   D. puree of potato soup

4. For HIGHEST nutritive value at least cost, of the following choose   4._____

    A. meat, loaf, soy beans, and vegetables
    B. round steak with brown rice
    C. meatballs and spaghetti
    D. braised mushrooms and liver steak

5. The extractives in meat are valuable because they   5._____

    A. provide energy   B. are a source of iron
    C. supply vitamins   D. aid digestion

6. Whole grain cereals are preferred because they   6._____

    A. have flavor   B. are easily prepared
    C. contain vitamins   D. provide calories

7. The outside leaves of salad greens   7._____

    A. contain more vitamin A and iron
    B. make the salad crispy
    C. are more tender
    D. contain more roughage

8. Yeasts and molds are destroyed by   8._____

    A. decreasing the moisture content of the foods in which they rest
    B. one-hour exposure to sub-zero F.
    C. exposure of the container to infra-red light
    D. high temperature in a pressure cooker

9. Of the following, the process which adds NO food value to milk is   9.____

   A. irradiation   B. condensation with sugar
   C. fortification   D. homogenization

10. To store salad greens in the refrigerator, wash them and   10.____

   A. place on a china plate
   B. place in an air-tight container
   C. wrap in a brown paper bag
   D. wrap in a plastic bag with air holes

11. To increase vitamin A in the diet, eat   11.____

   A. cream cheese with chopped nuts on whole wheat toast
   B. tuna fish and celery on enriched white bread
   C. chicken and celery on rye bread
   D. shredded carrot and pineapple on white bread

12. Cream of tartar is used in taffy recipes to   12.____

   A. prevent hardening before pulling
   B. neutralize hard water
   C. cut the flat, sweet flavor
   D. initiate the change of sucrose to glucose

13. In comparison with regular cocoa, instant cocoa is   13.____

   A. more nutritious   B. less digestible
   C. less costly   D. more costly

14. To provide the basis for building red blood corpuscles, feed   14.____

   A. cream tapioca   B. buttered toast
   C. yolk of egg   D. white of egg

15. Salt water fish, as compared with fresh water fish, contain more   15.____

   A. iodine   B. calcium   C. copper   D. magnesium

16. As an aid to make up the daily quota of calcium and phosphorus, serve   16.____

   A. water at mealtime
   B. milk puddings as desserts
   C. pineapple juice as an appetizer
   D. peanut butter on white bread

17. Potatoes are superior in nutritive value when   17.____

   A. cut in strips and fried
   B. cut up and boiled
   C. baked whole
   D. boiled whole without skins

18. An excellent source of fibrous material is   18.____

   A. puréed potato soup   B. cream of wheat cereal
   C. mozzarella cheese   D. escarole

19. Sulfuring dried fruits   19._____

    A. promotes retention of vitamin B
    B. prevents darkening
    C. activates vitamin C
    D. increases tenderness

20. A skim milk cheese is   20._____

    A. parmesan   B. Cheddar
    C. fromage de Brie   D. camenbert

21. Tapioca is prepared   21._____

    A. by hydrolyzing fructose
    B. by hydrolyzing starch
    C. from the root of the cassava
    D. from the root of the glycerriza

22. The freshness of an egg is recognizable by   22._____

    A. the size of the air cell
    B. absence of blood spots
    C. light color of the yolk
    D. the thickness of the shell

23. Frozen meat is BEST preserved when stored   .   23._____

    A. in cheesecloth at 20° F
    B. unwrapped at 0° F
    C. in moisture-proof material at 0° F
    D. unwrapped at -20° F

24. Boiled milk cannot be used for preparing junket because boiling 24._____

    A. coagulates casein
    B. makes the calcium salts insoluble
    C. kills the lactic acid bacteria
    D. decreases the amount of important lactose

25. For a fluffy omelet, before cooking   25._____

    A. beat eggs thoroughly
    B. whip egg yolks; whip egg whites; fold together
    C. stiffen egg whites with cream of tartar
    D. mix egg whites with lemon juice

_____

KEY (CORRECT ANSWERS)

1.	B	11.	D
2.	B	12.	D
3.	B	13.	D
4.	A	14.	C
5.	D	15.	A
6.	C	16.	B
7.	A	17.	C
8.	D	18.	D
9.	D	19.	B
10.	D	20.	A

21.	C
22.	A
23.	C
24.	B
25.	B

TEST 2

DIRECTIONS: Each question or incomplete statement is followed by several suggested answers or completions. Select the one that BEST answers the question or completes the statement. *PRINT THE LETTER OF THE CORRECT ANSWER IN THE SPACE AT THE RIGHT.*

1. To reduce expense in recipes calling for more than one egg as a leavener, for one egg substitute

   A. 1/2 teaspoon cornstarch
   B. 1/2 teaspoon baking powder
   C. 1 teaspoon soda
   D. 1 teaspoon cream of tartar

   1._____

2. In preparing soft custard, cook until

   A. stiff
   B. starch is gone
   C. it coats the spoon
   D. curds have disappeared

   2._____

3. Sugar added to stiffly beaten egg whites produces

   A. custard
   B. glace
   C. junket
   D. meringue

   3._____

4. To lard meat,

   A. coat with flour and oil
   B. baste with oil and drippings
   C. insert strips of fat
   D. dredge with flour

   4._____

5. For roasting turkey, the temperature of the oven should be

   A. 500° F
   B. 425° F
   C. 375° F
   D. 325° F

   5._____

6. Puréed fruits and vegetables are served during convalescence because they

   A. require no chewing
   B. are highly nutritive
   C. do not irritate the digestive tract
   D. appeal to the appetite

   6._____

7. Hot, home-prepared cereals as compared with dry cereal

   A. provide more energy
   B. cost less
   C. contain more minerals
   D. contain more vitamins

   7._____

8. When baking, place a pan of water under the custard in order to

   A. prevent burning
   B. maintain a steady low temperature
   C. help it brown on top
   D. keep the custard moist

   8._____

9. The principle of operation in a mechanical refrigerator is that when

   A. liquid evaporates, heat is absorbed
   B. gas is liquified, heat is absorbed

   9._____

C. gas is liquified, heat is static
D. liquid evaporates, heat is given off

10. Milk, when placed in the refrigerator, should not be placed in the freezing unit but should be kept on the shelf that is 　　　　　10.____

    A. lowest
    C. coolest
    B. most accessible
    D. highest

11. Dried fruits do not spoil easily because 　　　　　11.____

    A. the container has been exposed to ultra-violet rays
    B. acid is present in the fruits
    C. microorganisms require moisture to flourish
    D. the rinds protect them

12. To provide vitamin C, serve 　　　　　12.____

    A. apricots
    C. whole wheat bread
    B. cole slaw
    D. cocoa

13. Soy sauce is made from soy beans and 　　　　　13.____

    A. lotus root
    C. brine and wheat
    B. rice
    D. mushrooms

14. When the main course is finished, the knife and fork should be placed 　　　　　14.____

    A. so that they lean on the edge of the dinner plate
    B. on the bread and butter plate
    C. on the table
    D. across the center of the dinner plate

15. The purpose of the gasket on a pressure cooker is to 　　　　　15.____

    A. control the gauge
    C. seal the vessel
    B. act as a steam valve
    D. indicate temperature

16. To prevent the demulsification of French dressing, add 　　　　　16.____

    A. gum arable
    C. gelatin
    B. agar
    D. gum trogacanth

17. In Mexico, a very common food item is 　　　　　17.____

    A. pemal　　B. cocoles　　C. tortilla　　D. habas

18. In Puerto Rico, rice and kidney beans are served as a(n) 　　　　　18.____

    A. main course
    C. dessert
    B. appetizer
    D. salad

19. An important meat used in preparing Italian meals is 　　　　　19.____

    A. truffles　　B. liver　　C. veal　　D. scallops

20. Kebabs are popular in the diet in 　　　　　20.____

    A. Germany　　B. Italy　　C. Egypt　　D. Armenia

21. It is generally conceded that salads originated with the people of   21.____

    A. Portugal   B. Italy   C. Spain   D. France

22. Pot roast is also known as   22.____

    A. weiner schnitzel   B. sauerbraten
    C. bratwurst   D. hackfleisch

23. Of the following, the BEST for growth and general health is   23.____

    A. orange juice, oatmeal, buttered toast, coffee
    B. roll with butter, eggs, coffee
    C. cornflakes, fried eggs, muffins, milk
    D. pancakes, syrup, bacon, milk

24. For ordinary use, the Fahrenheit temperature of the refrigerator should be   24.____

    A. 20° - 25° B. 35° - 40° C. 45° - 50° D. 55° - 60°

25. An underweight child should be fed   25.____

    A. more bread
    B. greater quantities of all foods eaten
    C. starchy desserts
    D. fatty meat cuts

KEY (CORRECT ANSWERS)

1.	B	11.	C
2.	C	12.	B
3.	D	13.	C
4.	C	14.	D
5.	D	15.	C
6.	C	16.	D
7.	B	17.	C
8.	B	18.	A
9.	A	19.	C
10.	C	20.	D

21.	B
22.	B
23.	A
24.	B
25.	B

EXAMINATION SECTION
TEST 1

DIRECTIONS: Each question or incomplete statement is followed by several suggested answers or completions. Select the one that BEST answers the question or completes the statement. *PRINT THE LETTER OF THE CORRECT ANSWER IN THE SPACE AT THE RIGHT.*

1. The item that acts as a catalytic agent for the assimilation of calcium and phosphorus is   1._____

    A. vitamin D   B. fat   C. vitamin B   D. protein

2. Contributing MOST to the weight of the living human body is   2._____

    A. copper   B. sodium   C. calcium   D. iron

3. Before cooking, the vegetable that MUST be soaked in water is   3._____

    A. string beans   B. Brussels sprouts
    C. turnips   D. celery

4. Amino acids are absorbed MAINLY in the   4._____

    A. stomach   B. liver   C. pancreas   D. intestine

5. Little spoilage occurs in stored, sun-dried fruits because the   5._____

    A. microorganisms have been destroyed
    B. moisture content is low
    C. pectin is inactive
    D. yeasts do not flourish in the absence of light

6. In pickling, the concentrated brine   6._____

    A. softens the cellulose
    B. preserves the original color
    C. retards the growth of microorganisms
    D. increases the acid content

7. Cheese is rich in   7._____

    A. calcium   B. iron   C. sodium   D. potassium

8. Tenderized dried fruits have been   8._____

    A. sulphurized, dried, then partially cooked
    B. dried, partially cooked, then partially dried
    C. partially·cooked, dried, then partially cooked
    D. dried, sulphurized, then partially cooked

9. The MOST tender cuts of beef are from the   9._____

    A. loin and rib   B. leg and rib
    C. shoulder and loin   D. rump and neck

10. In anabolism, the number of calories yielded by one gram of carbohydrates is 10.____

    A. two   B. four   C. six   D. eight

11. When making yeast rolls, the milk is scalded to 11.____

    A. improve the flavor of the product
    B. reduce the size of the air holes
    C. destroy the microorganisms
    D. encourage development of the yeast

12. Deterioration of dried vegetables is retarded by 12.____

    A. marinating before drying
    B. storage in metal boxes
    C. pre-cooking before drying
    D. infra-red light treatment before packaging

13. The LARGEST percentage of gluten is found in flour made from 13.____

    A. rye   B. barley   C. oats   D. wheat

14. A bed roll is a support for the patient's 14.____

    A. head   B. knees   C. back   D. feet

15. One pound of dried eggs is equivalent to _____ eggs. 15.____

    A. 50-60   B. 30-40   C. 20-25   D. 15-18

16. To store eggs at home, 16.____

    A. keep them exposed on the cupboard
    B. wash and place them in the refrigerator
    C. do not wash and place them in the refrigerator
    D. place them in a moderately cool place

17. Disease is MOST commonly spread through 17.____

    A. clothing   B. dishes   C. food   D. contact

18. For everyday use, the Fahrenheit temperature of the refrigerator should be 18.____

    A. $20°-25°$ B. $35°-40°$ C. $45°-50°$ D. $55°-60°$

19. To retard spoilage of bread, baking companies may add sodium 19.____

    A. benzoate   B. propionate
    C. sulphathionate   D. hypophosphate

20. Essential to jelly-making is 20.____

    A. proto-pectin   B. pectin
    C. pectic acid   D. pectoral liquor

KEY (CORRECT ANSWERS)

1.	A	11.	D
2.	C	12.	C
3.	B	13.	D
4.	D	14.	B
5.	B	15.	B
6.	C	16.	C
7.	A	17.	D
8.	B	18.	B
9.	A	19.	B
10.	B	20.	B

———

TEST 2

DIRECTIONS: Each question or incomplete statement is followed by several suggested answers or completions. Select the one that BEST answers the question or completes the statement. *PRINT THE LETTER OF THE CORRECT ANSWER IN THE SPACE AT THE RIGHT.*

1. A MAJOR source of riboflavin is

   A. meat
   C. fruits
   B. whole grains
   D. milk

   1.____

2. In wheat, the vitamin B complex is in the

   A. endosperm
   C. bran
   B. aleuron layer
   D. germ

   2.____

3. The duration of infectious colds has been materially diminished by dosages of vitamin

   A. A
   B. B_1
   C. B_2
   D. E

   3.____

4. Yeast plants grow BEST at the Fahrenheit temperature of

   A. 70°-75°
   B. 80°-85°
   C. 90°-95°
   D. 100°-105°

   4.____

5. A characteristic of riboflavin deficiency is

   A. cheilosis
   B. catarrh
   C. otitis
   D. pellagra

   5.____

6. Anemia responds to

   A. ascorbic acid
   C. niacin
   B. folic acid
   D. carotene

   6.____

7. Legumes and nuts provide much

   A. thiamine
   B. calcium
   C. niacin
   D. sodium

   7.____

8. Rich in thiamine is

   A. orange juice
   C. polished rice
   B. cheese
   D. brewer's yeast

   8.____

9. Carbohydrate stored in the liver is

   A. galleasss
   C. liepstarch
   B. glycogen
   D. galactose

   9.____

10. The antihemmorhagic is

    A. riboflavin
    C. vitamin K
    B. vitamin A
    D. niacin

    10.____

11. At the end of one year, the weight of an infant in relation to its birth weight should be

    A. an increase of 12 oz. monthly
    B. double
    C. 20 pounds more
    D. triple

    11.____

12. Pellagra indicates a deficiency of 12.____

    A. ascorbic acid   B. niacin
    C. thiamine   D. riboflavin

13. Provitamin A is 13.____

    A. ergosterol   B. carotene
    C. lysine   D. pyrodoxine

14. The nutritionally important minerals are 14.____

    A. sodium, iodine, potassium, copper
    B. iron, iodine, phosphorus, calcium
    C. iron, potassium, sulphur, copper
    D. sodium, phosphorus, sulphur, calcium

15. Root vegetables are BEST stored in atmosphere that is maintained 15.____

    A. at 36° F   B. dehumidified
    C. at 30° F   D. at 75% humidity

16. The government stamp on meats indicates 16.____

    A. date when slaughtered   B. point of origin
    C. nutritional value   D. quality

17. Whole grain products, in contrast with enriched products, possess more 17.____

    A. hydrocarbons   B. carbohydrates
    C. vitamins   D. proteins

18. In anabolism, the number of calories yielded by one gram of hydrocarbon is 18.____

    A. six   B. seven   C. eight   D. nine

19. In the digestion of starch, the intermediate product is 19.____

    A. dextrin   B. fibrinogen   C. cerine   D. maltine

20. Egg whites whip more quickly at the Fahrenheit temperature of 20.____

    A. 0°   B. 30°   C. 70°   D. 85°

KEY (CORRECT ANSWERS)

1.	D	11.	D
2.	D	12.	B
3.	A	13.	B
4.	B	14.	B
5.	A	15.	A
6.	B	16.	D
7.	A	17.	D
8.	D	18.	D
9.	B	19.	A
10.	C	20.	C

———

EXAMINATION SECTION
TEST 1

DIRECTIONS: Each question or incomplete statement is followed by several suggested answers or completions. Select the one that BEST answers the question or completes the statement. *PRINT THE LETTER OF THE CORRECT ANSWER IN THE SPACE AT THE RIGHT.*

1. An effective method for tenderizing meats that are tough is   1.____

    A. braising   B. broiling   C. frying   D. roasting

2. Mutton is obtained from   2.____

    A. lamb   B. hog   C. sheep   D. calf

3. The fibrous material in fruits and vegetables is   3.____

    A. connective tissue   B. pith
    C. cellulose   D. mineral matter

4. When sugar is used in cooking,   4.____

    A. acids soften cellulose
    B. alkalies invert sugar
    C. acids invert sugar
    D. dry heat changes sucrose to glucose

5. Fuel is saved by a   5.____

    A. coal range   B. pressure cooker
    C. gas stove   D. thermos bottle

6. A temperature higher than that of boiling water is obtained in a   6.____

    A. fireless cooker   B. double boiler
    C. steamer   D. pressure cooker

7. RICHEST vitamin D food for a one-year-old child is   7.____

    A. egg yolk   B. homogenized milk
    C. spinach   D. cod liver oil

8. Vitamin A is used in the body to   8.____

    A. stimulate the appetite   B. maintain nerve tissue
    C. resist infection   D. grow bone

9. In making white sauce,   9.____

    A. melt the butter, add flour, then add milk
    B. add butter to hot milk, then add dry flour
    C. mix the flour with hot milk, then add butter
    D. combine fat, flour, and milk simultaneously

10. Baking powder consists of
        A. baking soda, an acid salt, and a starch
        B. iron, carbon dioxide, and fat
        C. baking soda, salt, and starch
        D. carbohydrate, protein, and fat

10._____

11. Green vegetables should be
        A. cooked in large amount of boiling salted water uncovered
        B. cooked covered in small amount of boiling water and served at once
        C. started in cold water and brought quickly to boil covered
        D. cooked in small amount of water with addition of soda

11._____

12. MOST of the body's vitamin A is in the
        A. lungs   B. kidneys   C. liver   D. muscles

12._____

13. A food rich in vitamin C is
        A. plums   B. celery
        C. green pepper   D. watermelon

13._____

14. The duration of infectious colds has been measurably diminished by administering additional amounts of vitamin
        A. A   B. B_1 C. B_2 D. E

14._____

15. Carbohydrate stored in the liver is
        A. galleass   B. glycogen   C. heptarch   D. galactose

15._____

16. A quart of milk provides an amount of riboflavin equal to that supplied by lean meat weighing _____ pound(s).
        A. 1/2   B. 1   C. 2   D. 3

16._____

17. The number of tablespoonfuls of lemon juice to be added to each cup of sweet milk for a sour milk recipe is
        A. 1/2   B. 1   C. 1 1/2   D. 2

17._____

18. When buying boneless meat for one meal, a family of six will need _____ pounds.
        A. 1 1/2   B. 2   C. 2 1/2   D. 3

18._____

19. Enamel forming cells of the teeth are sensitive to a deficiency of vitamin
        A. A   B. B   C. C   D. D

19._____

20. When invited out to a meal, at the close of the meal
        A. fold your napkin   B. leave it unfolded
        C. fold it in a roll   D. leave it on the chair

20._____

KEY (CORRECT ANSWERS)

1.	A		11.	B
2.	C		12.	C
3.	C		13.	C
4.	C		14.	A
5.	B		15.	B
6.	D		16.	C
7.	D		17.	C
8.	C		18.	A
9.	A		19.	A
10.	A		20.	B

———

TEST 2

DIRECTIONS: Each question or incomplete statement is followed by several suggested answers or completions. Select the one that BEST answers the question or completes the statement. *PRINT THE LETTER OF THE CORRECT ANSWER IN THE SPACE AT THE RIGHT.*

1. When buying fish for one meal, a family of six will need _____ pounds.   1.____

    A. 1 1/2   B. 2   C. 2 1/2   D. 3

2. Molasses is rich in   2.____

    A. potassium   B. iron   C. vitamin C   D. niacin

3. The leavening agent in popovers is   3.____

    A. baking powder   B. steam
    C. baking soda   D. sour milk and soda

4. A leavening agent used in baking is   4.____

    A. baking soda and sweet milk
    B. sour milk and baking soda
    C. cream of tartar and sour milk
    D. cream of tartar and cornstarch

5. Thiamine is found in   5.____

    A. macaroni   B. rice   C. pork   D. suet

6. In baking a cake, the amount of baking powder needed depends on the   6.____

    A. kind of flour   B. amount of flour and egg
    C. amount of liquid   D. acidity of the liquid

7. Vitamin A is MOST concentrated in   7.____

    A. cream   B. whole milk
    C. skim milk   D. certified milk

8. HIGHEST in vitamin C is   8.____

    A. egg yolk   B. soft cooked egg
    C. beef juice   D. tomato juice

9. Vitamins are lacking in   9.____

    A. butter   B. fruit   C. egg   D. sugar

10. The oil RICHEST in vitamin D is   10.____

    A. mineral oil   B. olive oil
    C. Crisco   D. cod liver oil

11. RICHEST in vitamin A is(are)   11.____

    A. beans   B. onions
    C. Irish potatoes   D. spinach

12. Chuck steak should be   12.____

    A. pan fried   B. broiled   C. roasted   D. braised

13. Sugar in conventional cake method is   13.____

    A. sifted with dry ingredients
    B. added to creamed fat
    C. added alternately with flour
    D. added alternately with milk

14. Milk is heated in a double boiler to prevent   14.____

    A. curdling   B. burning
    C. coagulation of the protein   D. dehomogenization

15. Soft dough is used for   15.____

    A. pie   B. biscuits (baking powder)
    C. cake (butter)   D. muffins

16. Basal metabolism determines   16.____

    A. calories in food
    B. carbon dioxide in food
    C. calories required for internal activity of body
    D. ratio of energy to exertion

17. Overweight people have less   17.____

    A. need for relaxation
    B. resistance to infection
    C. danger of heart disease
    D. inclination to diabetes

18. A person's weight stays the same if he   18.____

    A. eats only enough to supply the energy he uses
    B. exercises daily
    C. rests more
    D. eats more fruits and vegetables

19. Enriched white flour contains   19.____

    A. niacin, thiamine, and iron
    B. ascorbic acid and vitamin D
    C. vitamin A and niacinamide
    D. folic acid

20. Pellagra is caused by   20.____

    A. bacteria   B. deficiency of niacin
    C. deficiency of iron   D. a virus

KEY (CORRECT ANSWERS)

1. D	11. D
2. B	12. D
3. B	13. B
4. B	14. B
5. C	15. B
6. B	16. C
7. A	17. B
8. D	18. A
9. D	19. A
10. D	20. B

———

EXAMINATION SECTION
TEST 1

DIRECTIONS: Each question or incomplete statement is followed by several suggested answers or completions. Select the one that BEST answers the question or completes the statement. *PRINT THE LETTER OF THE CORRECT ANSWER IN THE SPACE AT THE RIGHT.*

1. Spinach should be cooked   1._____

   A. in boiling water, without a cover
   B. dry, in an open pot
   C. dry, in a covered pot
   D. in boiling water with a cover

2. For cookies, one may use melted _____ fat.   2._____

   A. beef   B. ham   C. chicken   D. lamb

3. Baking powder is used in proportion to the   3._____

   A. flour   B. egg   C. liquid   D. shortening

4. To prevent curdling of soft custard, cook   4._____

   A. over boiling water   B. and stir constantly
   C. over a low flame   D. over water about to boil

5. In dressings, an example of a *permanent emulsion* is   5._____

   A. French dressing   B. mineral oil
   C. mayonnaise dressing   D. olive oil

6. Eggs stored in the home should be   6._____

   A. uncovered in the refrigerator
   B. washed
   C. in a cool place but not in the refrigerator
   D. in a refrigerator in a covered container

7. Meat should be stored in the refrigerator overnight for use on the next day   7._____

   A. loosely covered with patapar in the freezing unit
   B. tightly covered with aluminum foil in a cool part
   C. covered with aluminum foil in the freezing unit
   D. loosely covered with wax paper in a cool part

8. The MOST tender cuts of beef come from the   8._____

   A. loin and rib   B. leg and rib
   C. shoulder and loin   D. rump and neck

9. To preserve vitamin C in cooking frozen vegetables,   9._____

   A. cook before thawing in a small amount of boiling water
   B. thaw first and cook quickly

C. thaw and cook in a small amount of water
D. keep just below boiling point

10. Calcium and phosphorus are catalytic agents for use of   10.____

    A. vitamin D   B. fat   C. vitamin B   D. protein

11. Yeast plants grow BEST at a temperature of _____ F.   11.____

    A. 70°-75°   B. 80°-85°   C. 90°-95°   D. 100°-105°

12. Tunnels in plain muffins are due to   12.____

    A. overheating
    B. underbeating
    C. using too much shortening
    D. using too little shortening

13. For each cup of sour milk in a recipe, add soda in the amount of _____ teaspoon(s).   13.____
    A. 2   B. 1   C. 1/2   D. 1/4

14. Incompletely cooked pork, if eaten, may result in   14.____

    A. botulism   B. ptomaine
    C. trichinosis   D. typhoid

15. In cooked frostings, cream of tartar is added to   15.____

    A. provide a tang
    B. accelerate crystallization
    C. minimize the size of crystals
    D. increase viscosity

16. When substituting sodium aluminum sulphate-phosphate baking powder in a recipe calling for a tartrate baking powder, use _____ of the former per cup of flour   16.____

    A. one-half as much   B. one-half more
    C. the same amount   D. one-quarter

17. The MOST appropriate poultry to buy for a chicken fricassee is the   17.____

    A. broiler   B. guinea hen
    C. capon   D. fowl

18. Artichokes are scarce because they   18.____

    A. are in slight demand   B. are difficult to digest
    C. do not keep well   D. require special cultivatior

19. Less tender cuts of meat may be tenderized by   19.____

    A. quick cooking   B. the addition of tomatoes
    C. pan frying   D. broiling

20. The official grades for canned fruits which have been set up by the U.S. Department of Agriculture are A, (Fancy);   20.____

A. B, (Choice); C, (Standard)
B. B, (Choice)
C. B, (Choice); C, (Substandard)
D. C, (Standard)

21. If both starch and egg are used for thickening a mixture, the egg should be   21.____

    A. thoroughly beaten before it is added to the mixture
    B. added to the mixture after the starch is thoroughly cooked
    C. combined with the liquid ingredients
    D. combined with the dry ingredients

22. For everyday use, it is BEST to maintain the temperature of the refrigerator at _____ F.   22.____

    A. 20°-25°   B. 35°-40°   C. 45°-50°   D. 55°-60°

23. As to pork, the federal meat inspection law should be amended to require examination   23.____
    for

    A. botulism   B. trichina   C. tetanus   D. fastigium

24. When all-purpose flour is used in a recipe calling for pastry flour, for each cup of flour in   24.____
    the recipe _____ tablespoonsful.

    A. add two   B. subtract two
    C. add one   D. subtract one

25. Federal law regulates foods sold in   25.____

    A. cities   B. rural areas
    C. states   D. interstate commerce

KEY (CORRECT ANSWERS)

1.	D	11.	D
2.	C	12.	A
3.	A	13.	C
4.	B	14.	C
5.	C	15.	C
6.	D	16.	A
7.	C	17.	A
8.	A	18.	D
9.	A	19.	B
10.	A	20.	A

21.	B
22.	B
23.	B
24.	B
25.	D

TEST 2

DIRECTIONS: Each question or incomplete statement is followed by several suggested answers or completions. Select the one that BEST answers the question or completes the statement. *PRINT THE LETTER OF THE CORRECT ANSWER IN THE SPACE AT THE RIGHT.*

1. Goiters are caused by lack of   1.____

    A.   iodine in the food
    B.   iron in food
    C.   chlorine in the water supply
    D.   vitamins in vegetables

2. Of the following, the MOST inexpensive source of nutritive food is   2.____

    A.   soybean   B.   cereal   C.   eggs   D.   meats

3. In international units per pound, the vitamin A level of butter is *approximately*   3.____

    A.   9,000   B.   15,000   C.   3,000   D.   5,000

4. Vitamin <u>A</u> value of carrots is HIGHEST when they are   4.____

    A.   harvested as baby carrots
    B.   harvested later as mature carrots
    C.   selected on the basis of variety
    D.   planted in rich loam

5. Calciferol and viosterol are produced by irradiation of   5.____

    A.   ergosterol   B.   cholesterol
    C.   ascorbic acid   D.   leucosin

6. Provitamin A is   6.____

    A.   ergosterol   B.   carotene
    C.   lysine   D.   pyrodoxine

7. Breast feeding   7.____

    A.   is unimportant
    B.   is a drain on the mother
    C.   increases infant development
    D.   provides temporary immunity

8. A roast shrinks LEAST if   8.____

    A.   cooked at 300° - 350° F.
    B.   first seared
    C.   cooked at 500° F.
    D.   cooked in a small amount of water

9. When making yeast rolls, the milk is scalded in order to 9.____

    A. improve the flavor of the product
    B. reduce the size of the air holes
    C. destroy microorganisms
    D. encourage the development of yeast

10. When making medium white sauce, the ratio of fat to flour per cup of milk is 10.____

    A. 1 tsp. to 1 tsp.   B. 2 tbsp.to 2 tbsp.
    C. 1 tbsp, to 1 tbsp.   D. 1 tbsp.to 2 tbsp.

11. The four nutritionally important minerals are iron, 11.____

    A. iodine, potassium, and calcium
    B. iodine, phosphorus, and calcium
    C. potassium, phosphorus, and calcium
    D. iodine, sulphur, and calcium

12. Normal peristalsis in the digestive tract is encouraged by 12.____

    A. niacin   B. vitamin A
    C. thiamine   D. ascorbic acid

13. A MAIN source of riboflavin is 13.____

    A. meat   B. whole grains
    C. fruits and vegetables   D. milk

14. Invert sugar is a mixture of equal parts of 14.____

    A. lactose and maltose   B. fructose and lactose
    C. fructose and glucose   D. maltose and glucose

15. Whole grain products differ from *enriched* products in possessing a GREATER content of 15.____

    A. niacin   B. carbohydrates
    C. riboflavin   D. protein

16. Nutritionists recommend that our yearly per capita intake of sugar be reduced from 100 pounds to 16.____

    A. 65   B. 50   C. 35   D. 20

17. Proteins are 17.____

    A. capable of precipitating copper in Fehling's solution
    B. chemically insolvent
    C. substitutes for starch in body functions
    D. precursors of body catalysts

18. An inexpensive source of vitamin C is 18.____

    A. cabbage   B. asparagus   C. broccoli   D. cucumbers

19. In international units per pound, the U.S. Department of Agriculture standard for vitamin A fortification of margarine is 19.____

    A. 15,000   B. 5,000   C. 9,000   D. 25,000

20. The vitamin C content of one cup of pineapple juice is equivalent to that found in _____ 20.____
cup of orange juice.

    A. 1   B. 3/4   C. 1/2   D. 1/4

21. Pellagra indicates a deficiency of   21.____

    A. ascorbic acid   B. niacin
    C. thiamine   D. riboflavin

22. A growing child should NOT drink coffee because it   22.____

    A. acts as a stimulant   B. is habit-forming
    C. reduces milk intake   D. spoils the appetite

23. The PRINCIPAL food source of calcium is   23.____

    A. meats   B. nuts
    C. milk and milk products   D. vegetables

24. Legumes and nuts provide a RICH source of   24.____

    A. thiamine   B. calcium   C. niacin   D. sodium

25. Since 1850, the per capita consumption of sugar in the United States has increased   25.____

    A. 900%   B. 150%   C. 500%   D. 300%

KEY (CORRECT ANSWERS)

1.	A		11.	C
2.	A		12.	C
3.	B		13.	D
4.	A		14.	C
5.	A		15.	A
6.	B		16.	B
7.	C		17.	D
8.	A		18.	A
9.	B		19.	A
10.	B		20.	C

21.	B
22.	C
23.	C
24.	A
25.	D

EXAMINATION SECTION
TEST 1

DIRECTIONS: Each question or incomplete statement is followed by several suggested answers or completions. Select the one that BEST answers the question or completes the statement. *PRINT THE LETTER OF THE CORRECT ANSWER IN THE SPACE AT THE RIGHT.*

1. The state agency that is PRIMARILY responsible for purchasing goods in the state is   1._____

    A. Audit and Control
    B. Office of General Services
    C. Division of Fiscal Services
    D. Department of Purchasing and Regulations

2. If an item an agency wishes to purchase is listed in the Index of Commodities, this means that the item   2._____

    A. must be put out to bid
    B. can be obtained from a minority contractor
    C. is under contract and should be purchased from a particular vendor
    D. is made in the state

3. It is BEST for a purchasing assistant to   3._____

    A. order from the vendor with the lowest prices
    B. be as thorough as if the money he or she is spending is his or her own money
    C. always order everything in large quantities, as this saves money
    D. encourage program units to split orders over $100 whenever possible to save time

4. Which of the following considerations is MOST important in determining who should get a bid?   4._____

    A. Delivery date
    B. Quality of service or product
    C. Whether or not a price discount is available
    D. Whether or not the service or product is produced in the state by a state firm

5. An agency must seek three telephone quotes when a(n)   5._____

    A. purchase requisition is between $500 and $1,000
    B. item is not under contract
    C. purchase requisition is between $1,000 and $1,500
    D. purchase requisition is between $1,500 and $2,500

6. Five written bids are required in an agency when   6._____

    A. a purchase requisition is between $1,500 and $2,500
    B. a purchase requisition is over $1,500
    C. the Index of Commodities cannot be used
    D. the agency has not wisely split its orders

7. The *Notice of Contract Awards* should be consulted when　　　　　7.____

    A. quotes from minority vendors are desired
    B. an agency wishes to have input into vendor selection
    C. an order is less than $1,500
    D. buying commodities from vendors under contract

8. When a vendor quotes a price that states *FOB shipping point,*　　　　8.____

    A. the price of delivery is included
    B. half of the price of delivery is included
    C. the price of delivery is not included
    D. the agency must make arrangements with the Department of Transportation to have the supplies delivered

9. If an item is not under contract, but less than $1,000,　　　　　9.____

    A. the purchasing assistant may order the item without always first securing three quotes
    B. the purchase order must first be sent to audit and control for approval
    C. three quotes must be obtained before the item can be ordered
    D. every effort should be made by the purchasing assistant to obtain a contract for that item

10. The Bill of Lading is commonly referred to as the　　　　　10.____

    A. packing slip　　　　　B. receipt
    C. sealed bid　　　　　D. purchase order

11. A service contract is required　　　　　11.____

    A. when the performance of a service is required by a state agency
    B. when the cost of service by an outside vendor is over $1,000 annually
    C. whenever a unique service is performed by an outside vendor
    D. whenever the cost of service by an outside vendor exceeds $2,500 annually

12. You need to purchase 60 dozen pens at a cost of $1.25 per box. Eighteen pens come in each box.
The TOTAL cost would be　　　　　12.____

    A. $60　　　　　B. $50　　　　　C. $86　　　　　D. $65

13. An agency engaged in repair work uses a small electrical device which costs 45¢ each. During the year, the agency's total expenditure for this device was $3,060.
How many of these devices were purchased by this agency during the year?　　　　　13.____

    A. 7,460　　　　　B. 5,400　　　　　C. 1,377　　　　　D. 6,800

14. An order with a firm under contract for envelopes totals $855. The terms of the contract state that there is a 1% discount if payment is received within 15 days.
If payment is received within 15 days, the order would total　　　　　14.____

    A. $850　　　　　B. $846.45　　　　　C. $769.50　　　　　D. $828.50

15. Firm A quotes an order for birdfeed at $473, FOB destination, with a 2% discount if pay-   15.____
    ment is received within 15 days. Firm B quotes a price of $461, FOB destination, for the
    same quantity of birdfeed, with no discount.
    There is no contract for birdfeed.
    It would be BEST to

    A. select Firm A as their quote is $3.06 less
    B. select Firm B as their quote is $2.54 less
    C. secure five written bids for birdfeed
    D. select Firm B as their quote is $12 less

———————

KEY (CORRECT ANSWERS)

1.	B		6.	A
2.	C		7.	D
3.	B		8.	C
4.	B		9.	A
5.	C		10.	A

11.	B
12.	B
13.	D
14.	B
15.	B

———————

EXAMINATION SECTION
TEST 1

DIRECTIONS: Each question or incomplete statement is followed by several suggested
answers or completions. Select the one that BEST answers the question or
completes the statement. *PRINT THE LETTER OF THE CORRECT ANSWER
IN THE SPACE AT THE RIGHT.*

1. When all of her employees are assigned to perform identical routine tasks, a supervisor   1.____
    would PROBABLY find it most difficult to differentiate among these employees as to the

    A.   amount of work each completed
    B.   initiative each one shows in doing the work
    C.   number of errors in each one"s work
    D.   number of times each one is absent or late

2. The one of the following guiding principles to which a supervisor should give the GREAT-   2.____
    EST weight when it becomes necessary to discipline an employee is that the

    A.   discipline should be of such a nature as to improve the future work of the employee
    B.   main benefit gained in disciplining one employee is that all employees are kept
         from breaking the same rule
    C.   morale of all the employees should be improved by the discipline of the one
    D.   rules should be applied in a fixed and unchanging manner

3. In using praise to encourage employees to do better work, the supervisor should realize   3.____
    that praising an employee too often is not good MAINLY because the

    A.   employee will be resented by her fellow employees
    B.   employee will begin to think she's doing too much work
    C.   praise will lose its value as an incentive
    D.   supervisor doesn't have the time to praise an employee frequently

4. A supervisor notices that one of her best employees has apparently begun to loaf on the   4. -___
    job.
    In this situation, the supervisor should FIRST

    A.   allow the employee a period of grace in view of her excellent record
    B.   change the employee's job assignment
    C.   determine the reason for the change in the employee's behavior
    D.   take disciplinary action immediately as she would with any other employee

5. A supervisor who wants to get a spirit of friendly cooperation from the employees in her   5.____
    unit is MOST likely to be successful if she

    A.   makes no exceptions in strictly enforcing department procedures
    B.   shows a cooperative spirit herself
    C.   tells them they are the best in the department
    D.   treats them to coffee once in a while

6. *Accidents do not just happen.*
   In view of this statement, it is important for the supervisor to realize that

   6._____

   A. accidents are sometimes deliberate
   B. combinations of unavoidable circumstances cause accidents
   C. she must take the blame for each accident
   D. she should train her employees in accident prevention

7. Suppose your superior points out to you several jobs that were poorly done by the employees under your supervision. As the supervisor of these employees, you should

   7._____

   A. accept responsibility for the poor work and take steps to improve the work in the future
   B. blame the employees for shirking on the job while you were busy on other work
   C. defend the employees since up to this time they were all good workers
   D. explain that the poor work was due to circumstances beyond your control

8. If a supervisor discovers a situation which is a possible source of grievance, it would be BEST for her to

   8._____

   A. be ready to answer the employees when they make a direct complaint
   B. do nothing until the employees make a direct complaint
   C. tell the employees, in order to keep them from making a direct complaint, that nothing can be done
   D. try to remove the cause before the employees make a direct complaint

9. Suppose there is a departmental rule that requires supervisors to prepare reports of unusual incidents by the end of the tour of duty in which the incident occurs.
   The MAIN reason for requiring such prompt reporting is that

   9._____

   A. a quick decision can be made whether the employee involved was neglectful of her duty
   B. other required reports cannot be made out until this one is turned in
   C. the facts are recorded before they are forgotten or confused by those involved in the incident
   D. the report is submitted before the supervisor required to make the report may possibly leave the department

10. A good practical method to use in determining whether an employee is doing his job properly is to

    10._____

    A. assume that if he asks no questions, he knows the work
    B. question him directly on details of the job
    C. inspect and follow-up the work which is assigned to him
    D. ask other employees how this employee is making out

11. If an employee continually asks how he should do his work, you should

    11._____

    A. dismiss him immediately
    B. pretend you do not hear him unless he persists
    C. explain the work carefully but encourage him to use his own judgment
    D. tell him not to ask so many questions

12. You have instructed an employee to complete a job in a certain area.   12.____
    To be sure that the employee understands the instructions you have given him, you
    should

    A. ask him to repeat the instructions to you
    B. check with him after he has done the job
    C. watch him while he is doing the job
    D. repeat the instructions to the employee

13. One of your men disagrees with your evaluation of his work.   13.____
    Of the following, the BEST way to handle this situation would be to

    A. explain that you are in a better position to evaluate his work than he is
    B. tell him that since other men are satisfied with your evaluation, he should accept
       their opinions
    C. explain the basis of your evaluation and discuss it with him
    D. refuse to discuss his complaint in order to maintain discipline

14. Of the following, the one which is NOT a quality of leadership desirable in a supervisor is   14.____

    A. intelligence   B. integrity
    C. forcefulness   D. partiality

15. Of the following, the one which LEAST characterizes the grapevine is that it   15.____

    A. consists of a tremendous amount of rumor, conjecture, information, advice, predic-
       tion, and even orders
    B. seems to rise spontaneously, is largely anonymous, spreads rapidly, and changes
       in unpredictable directions
    C. can be eliminated without any great effort
    D. commonly fills the gaps left by the regular organizational channels of communica-
       tion

16. When a superintendent delegates authority to a foreman, of the following, it would be   16.____
    MOST advisable for the superintendent to

    A. set wide limits of such authority to allow the foreman considerable leeway
    B. define fairly closely the limits of the authority delegated to the foreman
    C. wait until the foreman has some experience in the assignment before setting limits
       to his authority
    D. inform him that it is the foreman's ultimate basic responsibility to get the work done

17. One of the hallmarks of a good supervisor is his ability to use many different methods of   17.____
    obtaining information about the status of work in progress.
    Which one of the following would *probably* indicate that a supervisor does NOT have
    this ability?

    A. Holding specified staff meetings at specified intervals
    B. Circulating among his subordinates as often as possible
    C. Holding staff meetings only when absolutely necessary
    D. Asking subordinates to come in and discuss the progress of their work and their
       problems

18. Of the following, the one which is the LEAST important factor in deciding that additional   18._____
    training is necessary for the men you supervise is that

    A. the quality of work is below standard
    B. supplies are being wasted
    C. too much time is required to do specific jobs
    D. the absentee rate has declined

19. To promote proper safety practices in the operation of power tools and equipment, you   19._____
    should emphasize in meetings with the staff that

    A. every accident can be prevented through proper safety regulations
    B. proper safety practices will probably make future safety meetings unnecessary
    C. when safety rules are followed, tools and equipment will work better
    D. safety rules are based on past experience with the best methods of preventing
       accidents

20. Employee morale is the way employees feel about each other and their job.   20._____
    To a supervisor, it should be a sign of good morale if the employees

    A. are late for work
    B. complain about their work
    C. willingly do difficult jobs
    D. take a long time to do simple jobs

21. A supervisor who encourages his workers to make suggestions about job improvement   21._____
    shows his workers that he

    A. is not smart enough to improve the job himself
    B. wants them to take part in making improvements
    C. does not take the job seriously
    D. is not a good supervisor

22. Suppose that your supervisor tells you that a procedure which has been followed for   22._____
    years is going to be changed. It is your job to make sure the workers you supervise
    understand and accept the new procedure.
    What would be the BEST thing for you to do in this situation?

    A. Give a copy of the new procedure to each worker with orders that it must be fol-
       lowed.
    B. Explain the new procedure to one worker and have him explain it to the others.
    C. Ask your supervisor to explain the new procedure since he has more authority.
    D. Call your workers together to explain and discuss the new procedure.

23. One of the foundations of scientific management of an organization is the proper use of   23._____
    control measures.
    Of the following, the BEST way, in general, to implement control measures is to

    A. develop suitable procedures, systems, and guidelines for the organization
    B. evaluate the actual employees' job performance realistically and reasonably
    C. set standards which are designed to increase productivity
    D. publish a set of rules and insist upon strict compliance with these rules

24. A district superintendent would MOST likely be justified in taking up a matter with his borough superintendent when the problem involved   24.____

    A. a dispute among different factions in his district
    B. a section foreman's difficulties with his assistant foreman
    C. his own men and others not under his control
    D. methods of doing the work and the amount of production

25. The superintendent has the authority to recommend disciplinary action. He can BEST use this authority to   25.____

    A. demonstrate his authority as a superintendent
    B. improve a man's work
    C. make it less difficult for other superintendents to maintain order
    D. punish the men for wrong-doing

KEY (CORRECT ANSWERS)

1.	B		11.	C
2.	A		12.	A
3.	C		13.	C
4.	C		14.	D
5.	B		15.	C
6.	D		16.	B
7.	A		17.	B
8.	D		18.	D
9.	C		19.	D
10.	C		20.	C

21.	B
22.	D
23.	C
24.	B
25.	B

TEST 2

DIRECTIONS: Each question or incomplete statement is followed by several suggested answers or completions. Select the one that BEST answers the question or completes the statement. *PRINT THE LETTER OF THE CORRECT ANSWER IN THE SPACE AT THE RIGHT.*

1. From the standpoint of equal opportunity, the MOST critical item that a superintendent should focus on is

   A. assigning only minority workers to supervisory positions
   B. helping minority employees to upgrade their knowledge so they may qualify for higher positions
   C. placing minority workers in job categories above their present level of ability so that they can *sink or swim*
   D. disregarding merit system principles

   1.____

2. After careful deliberation, you have decided that one of your workers should be disciplined.
   It is MOST important that the

   A. discipline be severe for best results
   B. discipline be delayed as long as possible
   C. worker understands why he is being disciplined
   D. other workers be consulted before the discipline is administered

   2.____

3. Of the following, the MOST important qualities of an employee chosen for a supervisory position are

   A. education and intelligence
   B. interest in the objectives and activities of the agency
   C. skill in performing the type of work to be supervised
   D. knowledge of the work and leadership ability

   3.____

4. Of the following, the CHIEF characteristic which distinguishes a good supervisor from a poor supervisor is the good supervisor's

   A. ability to favorably impress others
   B. unwillingness to accept monotony or routine
   C. ability to deal constructively with problem situations
   D. strong drive to overcome opposition

   4.____

5. Of the following, the MAIN disadvantage of on-the-job training is that, *generally,*

   A. special equipment may be needed
   B. production may be slowed down
   C. the instructor must maintain an individual relationship with the trainee
   D. the on-the-job instructor must be better qualified than the classroom instructor

   5.____

6. If it becomes necessary for you, as a supervisor, to give a subordinate employee confidential information, the MOST effective of the following steps to take to make sure the information is kept confidential by the employee is to

   6.____

A. tell the employee that the information is confidential and is not to be repeated
B. threaten the employee with disciplinary action if the information is repeated
C. offer the employee a merit increase as an incentive for keeping the information confidential
D. remind the employee at least twice a day that the information is confidential and is not to be repeated

7. Three new men have just been assigned to work under your supervision. Every time you give them an assignment, one of these men asks you several questions.
Of the following, the MOST advisable action for you to take is to

    7.____

A. assure him of your confidence in his ability to carry out the assignment correctly without asking so many questions
B. have all three men listen to your answers to these questions
C. point out that the other two men do the job without asking so many questions
D. tell him to see if he can get the answers from other workers before coming to you

8. Two of your subordinates suggest that you recommend a third man for an above-standard service rating because of his superior work.
You should

    8.____

A. ask the two subordinates whether the third man knows that they intended to discuss this matter with you
B. explain to the two subordinates that an above-standard service rating for one man would have a detrimental effect on many of the other men
C. recommend the man for an above-standard service rating if there is sufficient justification for it
D. tell the two subordinates that the matter of service ratings is not their concern

9. All of the following are indications of good employee morale EXCEPT

    9.____

A. the number of grievances are lowered
B. labor turnover is decreased
C. the amount of supervision required is lowered
D. levels of production are lowered

10. All of the following statements regarding the issuance of direct orders are true EXCEPT

    10.____

A. use direct orders only when necessary
B. make sure that the receiver of the direct order is qualified to carry out the order
C. issue direct orders in clear, concise words
D. give direct orders only in writing

11. In order to achieve the BEST results in on-the-job training, supervisors should

    11.____

A. allow frequent coffee breaks during the training period
B. be in a higher salary range than that of the individuals they are training
C. have had instructions or experience in conducting such training
D. have had a minimum of five years of experience in the job

12. Of the following, the LEAST important quality of a good supervisor is

    12.____

A. technical competence   B. teaching ability
C. ability to communicate with others   D. ability to socialize with subordinates

13. One of your usually very hard working, reliable employees brings in a bottle of whiskey to   13.____
     celebrate his birthday during the rest period.
     Which one of the following actions should you take?

     A.   Offer to pay for the cost of the whiskey
     B.   Confiscate the bottle
     C.   Tell him to celebrate after working hours
     D.   Pretend that you have not seen the bottle of whiskey

14. Assume that you find it necessary to discipline two subordinates, Mr. Tate and Mr. Saw-   14.____
     yer, for coming to work late on several occasions. Their latenesses have had disruptive
     effects on the work schedule, and you have given both of them several verbal warnings.
     Mr. Tate has been in your work unit for many years, and his work has always been satis-
     factory. Mr. Sawyer is a probationary employee, who has had some problems in learning
     your procedures. You decide to give Mr. Tate one more warning, in private, for his late-
     nesses.
     According to good supervisory practice, which one of the following disciplinary actions
     should you take with regard to Mr. Sawyer?

     A.   Give him a reprimand in front of his co-workers, to make a lasting impression.
     B.   Recommend dismissal since he has not yet completed his probationary period.
     C.   Give him one more warning, in private, for his latenesses.
     D.   Recommend a short suspension or payroll deduction to impress on him the impor-
          tance of coming to work on time.

15. Assume that you have delegated a very important work assignment to Johnson, one of   15.____
     your most experienced subordinates. Prior to completion of the assignment, your supe-
     rior accidentally discovers that the assignment is being carried out incorrectly, and tells
     you about it. Which one of the following responses is MOST appropriate for you to give to
     your superior?

     A.   *I take full responsibility, and I will see to it that the assignment is carried out cor-
          rectly.*
     B.   *Johnson has been with us for many years now and should know better.*
     C.   *It really isn't Johnson's fault, rather it is the fault of the ancient equipment we have
          to do the job.*
     D.   *I think you should inform Johnson since he is the one at fault, not I.*

16. Assume that you observe that one of your employees is talking excessively with other   16.____
     employees, quitting early, and taking unusually long rest periods. Despite these abuses,
     she is one of your most productive employees, and her work is usually of the highest
     quality.
     Of the following, the MOST appropriate action to take with regard to this employee is to

     A.   ignore these infractions since she is one of your best workers
     B.   ask your superior to reprimand her so that you can remain on the employee's good
          side
     C.   reprimand her since not doing so would lower the morale of the other employees
     D.   ask another of your subordinates to mention these infractions to the offending
          employee and suggest that she stop breaking rules

17. Assume that you have noticed that an employee whose attendance had been quite satis-   17._____
factory is now showing marked evidence of a consistent pattern of absences.
Of the following, the BEST way to cope with this problem is to

    A. wait several weeks to see whether this pattern continues
    B. meet with the employee to try to find out the reasons for this change
    C. call a staff meeting and discuss the need for good attendance
    D. write a carefully worded warning to the employee

18. It is generally agreed that the successful supervisor must know how to wisely delegate   18._____
work to her subordinates since she cannot do everything herself.
Which one of the following practices is MOST likely to result in ineffective delegation by
a supervisor?

    A. Establishment of broad controls to assure feedback about any deviations from
       plans
    B. Willingness to let subordinates use their own ideas about how to get the job done,
       where appropriate
    C. Constant observance of employees to see if they are making any mistakes
    D. Granting of enough authority to make possible the accomplishment of the dele-
       gated work

19. Suppose that, in accordance with grievance procedures, an employee brings a complaint   19._____
to you, his immediate supervisor.
In dealing with his complaint, the one of the following which is MOST important for you
to do is to

    A. talk to the employee's co-workers to learn whether the complaint is justified
    B. calm the employee by assuring him that you will look into the matter as soon as
       possible
    C. tell your immediate superior about the employee's complaint
    D. give the employee an opportunity to tell the full story

20. Holding staff meetings at regular intervals is generally considered to be a good supervi-   20._____
sory practice.
Which one of the following subjects is LEAST desirable for discussion at such a meeting?

    A. Revisions in agency personnel policies
    B. Violation of an agency rule by one of the employees present
    C. Problems of waste and breakage in the work area
    D. Complaints of employees about working conditions

21. Suppose that you are informed that your staff is soon to be reduced by one-third due to   21._____
budget problems.
Which one of the following steps would be LEAST advisable in your effort to maintain a
quality service with the smaller number of employees?

    A. Directing employees to speed up operations
    B. Giving employees training or retraining
    C. Rearranging the work area
    D. Revising work methods

22. Of the following, which action on the part of the supervisor is LEAST likely to contribute to upgrading the skills of her subordinates?

    A. Providing appropriate training to subordinates
    B. Making periodic evaluations of subordinates and discussing the evaluations with the subordinates
    C. Consistently assigning subordinates to those tasks with which they are familiar
    D. Giving increased responsibility to appropriate subordinates

22.____

23. Suppose that a new employee on your staff has difficulty in performing his assigned tasks after having been given training.
Of the following courses of action, the one which would be BEST for you, his supervisor, to take FIRST is to

    A. change his work assignment
    B. give him a poor evaluation since he is obviously unable to do the work
    C. give him the training again
    D. have him work with an employee who is more experienced in the tasks for a short while

23.____

24. Several times, an employee has reported to work unfit for duty because he had been drinking. He refused to get counseling for his emotional problems when this was suggested by his supervisor. Last week, his supervisor warned him that he would face disciplinary action if he again reported to work unfit for duty because of drinking. Now, the employee has again reported to work in that condition.
Of the following, the BEST action for the supervisor to take now would be to

    A. arrange to have the employee transferred to another work location
    B. give the employee one more chance by pretending to not notice his condition this time
    C. start disciplinary action against the employee
    D. warn him that he will face disciplinary action if he reports for work in that condition again

24.____

25. An employee has been calling in sick repeatedly, and these absences have disrupted the work schedule. To try to make sure that the employee use sick leave only on days when he is actually sick, which of the following actions would be the BEST for his supervisor to take?

    A. Telephone the employee's home on days when he is out on sick leave
    B. Require the employee to obtain a note from a physician explaining the reason for his absence whenever he uses sick leave in the future
    C. Require that he get a complete physical examination and have his doctor send a report to the supervisor
    D. Warn the employee that he will face disciplinary action the next time he stays out on sick leave

25.____

KEY (CORRECT ANSWERS)

1.	B		11.	C
2.	C		12.	D
3.	D		13.	C
4.	C		14.	C
5.	B		15.	A
6.	A		16.	C
7.	B		17.	B
8.	C		18.	C
9.	D		19.	D
10.	D		20.	B

21.	A
22.	C
23.	D
24.	C
25.	B

TEST 3

DIRECTIONS: Each question or incomplete statement is followed by several suggested answers or completions. Select the one that BEST answers the question or completes the statement. *PRINT THE LETTER OF THE CORRECT ANSWER IN THE SPACE AT THE RIGHT.*

1. Suppose that, as a supervisor, you have an idea for changing the way a certain task is performed by your staff so that it will be less tedious and get done faster. Of the following, the MOST advisable action for you to take regarding this idea is to

   A. issue a written memorandum explaining the new method and giving reasons why it is to replace the old one
   B. discuss it with your staff to get their reactions and suggestions
   C. set up a training class in the new method for your staff
   D. try it out on an experimental basis on half the staff

   1.____

2. A troubled subordinate privately approaches his supervisor in order to talk about a problem on the job.
   In this situation, the one of the following actions that is NOT desirable on the part of the supervisor is to

   A. ask the subordinate pertinent questions to help develop points further
   B. close his office door during the talk to block noisy distractions
   C. allow sufficient time to complete the discussion with the subordinate
   D. take over the conversation so the employee won't be embarrassed

   2.____

3. Suppose that one of your goals as a supervisor is to foster good working relationships between yourself and your employees, without undermining your supervisory effectiveness by being too friendly.
   Of the following, the BEST way to achieve this goal when dealing with employees' work problems is to

   A. discourage individual personal conferences by using regularly scheduled staff meetings to discuss work problems
   B. try to resolve work problems within a relatively short period of time
   C. insist that employees put all work problems into writing before seeing you
   D. maintain an open-door policy, allowing employees complete freedom of access to you without making appointments to discuss work problems

   3.____

4. An employee under your supervision complains that he is assigned to work late more often than any of the other employees. You check the records and find that this isn't so. You should

   A. advise this employee not to worry about what the other employees do but to see that he puts in a full day's work himself
   B. explain to this employee that you get the same complaint from all the other employees
   C. inform this employee that you have checked the records and the complaint is not justified
   D. not assign this employee to work late for a few days in order to keep him satisfied

   4.____

5. An employee has reported late for work several times. His supervisor should   5.____

    A. give this employee less desirable assignments
    B. overlook the lateness if the employee's work is otherwise exceptional
    C. recommend disciplinary action for habitual lateness
    D. talk the matter over with the employee before doing anything further

6. In choosing a man to be in charge in his absence, the supervisor should select FIRST   6.____
the employee who

    A. has ability to supervise others
    B. has been longest with the organization
    C. has the nicest appearance and manner
    D. is most skilled in his assigned duties

7. An employee under your supervision comes to you to complain about a decision you   7.____
have made in assigning the men. He is excited and angry. You think what he is complain-
ing about is not important, but it seems very important to him. The BEST way for you to
handle this is to

    A. let him talk until *he gets it off his chest* and then explain the reasons for your deci-
sion
    B. refuse to talk to him until he has cooled off
    C. show him at once how unimportant the matter is and how ridiculous his arguments
are
    D. tell him to take it up with your superior if he disagrees with your decision

8. Suppose that a new employee has been appointed and assigned to your supervision.   8.____
When this man reports for work, it would be BEST for you to

    A. ask him questions about different problems connected with his line of work and see
if he answers them correctly
    B. check him carefully while he carries out some routine assignment that you give him
    C. explain to him the general nature of the work he will be required to do
    D. make a careful study of his previous work record before coming to your department

9. *The competent supervisor will be friendly with the employees under his supervision but*   9.____
will avoid close familiarity.
This statement is justified MAINLY because

    A. a friendly attitude on the part of the supervisor toward the employee is likely to
cause suspicion on the part of the employee
    B. a supervisor can handle his employees better if he doesn't know their personal
problems
    C. close familiarity may interfere with the discipline needed for good supervisor-subor-
dinate relationships
    D. familiarity with the employees may be a sign of lack of ability on the part of the
supervisor

10. An employee disagrees with the instructions that you, his supervisor, have given him for   10.____
carrying out a certain assignment.
The BEST action for you to take is to tell this employee that

A. he can do what he wants but you will hold him responsible for failure
B. orders must be carried out or morale will fall apart
C. this job has been done in this way for many years with great success
D. you will be glad to listen to his objections and to his suggestions for improvement

11. As a supervisor, it is LEAST important for you to use a new employee's probationary period for the purpose of

    11.____

    A. carefully checking how he performs the work you assign him
    B. determining whether he can perform the duties of his job efficiently
    C. preparing him for promotion to a higher position
    D. showing him how to carry out his assigned duties properly

12. Suppose you have just given an employee under your supervision instructions on how to carry out a certain assignment.
The BEST way to check that he has understood your instructions is to

    12.____

    A. ask him to repeat your instructions word for word
    B. check the progress of his work the first chance you get
    C. invite him to ask questions if he has any doubts
    D. question him briefly about the main points of the assignment

13. Suppose you find it necessary to change a procedure that the men under your supervision have been following for a long time.
A good way to get their cooperation for this change would be to

    13.____

    A. bring them together to talk over the new procedure and explain the reasons for its adoption
    B. explain to the men that if most of them still don't approve of the change after giving it a fair try, you will consider giving it up
    C. give them a few weeks' notice of the proposed change in procedure
    D. not enforce the new procedure strictly at the beginning

14. An order can be given by a supervisor in such a way as to make the employee want to obey it.
According to this statement, it is MOST reasonable to suppose that

    14.____

    A. a person will be glad to obey an order if he realizes that he must
    B. if an order is given properly, it will be obeyed more willingly
    C. it is easier to obey an order than to give one correctly
    D. supervisors should inspire confidence by their actions as well as by their words

15. If one of the men you supervise disagrees with how you rate his work, the BEST way for you to handle this is to

    15.____

    A. advise him to appeal to your superior about it
    B. decline to discuss the matter with him in order to keep discipline
    C. explain why you rate him the way you do and talk it over with him
    D. tell him that you are better qualified to rate his work than he is

16. A supervisor should be familiar with the experience and abilities of the employees under his supervision MAINLY because   16.____

    A. each employee's work is highly important and requires a person of outstanding ability
    B. it will help him to know which employees are best fitted for certain assignments
    C. nearly all men have the same basic ability to do any job equally well
    D. superior background shortly shows itself in superior work quality, regardless of assignment

17. The competent supervisor will try to develop respect rather than fear in his subordinates. This statement is justified MAINLY because   17.____

    A. fear is always present and, for best results, respect must be developed to offset it
    B. it is generally easier to develop respect in the men than it is to develop fear
    C. men who respect their supervisor are more likely to give more than the required minimum amount and quality of work
    D. respect is based on the individual, and fear is based on the organization as a whole

18. If one of the employees you supervise does outstanding work, you should   18.____

    A. explain to him how his work can still be improved so that he will not become self-satisfied
    B. mildly criticize the other men for not doing as good a job as this man
    C. praise him for his work so that he will know it is appreciated
    D. say nothing or he might become conceited

19. A supervisor can BEST help establish good morale among his employees if he   19.____

    A. confides in them about his personal problems in order to encourage them to confide in him
    B. encourages them to become friendly with him but discourages social engagements with them
    C. points out to them the advantages of having a cooperative spirit in the department
    D. sticks to the same rules that he expects them to follow

20. The one of the following situations which would seem to indicate poor scheduling of work by the supervisor is   20.____

    A. everybody seeming to be very busy at the same time
    B. re-assignment of a man to other work because of breakdown of a piece of equipment
    C. two employees on vacation at the same time
    D. two operators waiting to use the same equipment at the same time

KEY (CORRECT ANSWERS)

1.	B		11.	C
2.	D		12.	D
3.	B		13.	A
4.	C		14.	B
5.	D		15.	C
6.	A		16.	B
7.	A		17.	C
8.	C		18.	C
9.	C		19.	D
10.	D		20.	D

PHILOSOPHY, PRINCIPLES, PRACTICES AND TECHNICS
OF
SUPERVISION, ADMINISTRATION, MANAGEMENT AND ORGANIZATION

TABLE OF CONTENTS

TABLE OF CONTENTS (CONTINUED)

PHILOSOPHY, PRINCIPLES, PRACTICES, AND TECHNICS
OF
SUPERVISION, ADMINISTRATION, MANAGEMENT AND ORGANIZATION

I. MEANING OF SUPERVISION

The extension of the democratic philosophy has been accompanied by an extension in the scope of supervision. Modern leaders and supervisors no longer think of supervision in the narrow sense of being confined chiefly to visiting employees, supplying materials, or rating the staff. They regard supervision as being intimately related to all the concerned agencies of society, they speak of the supervisor's function in terms of "growth", rather than the "improvement," of employees.

This modern concept of supervision may be defined as follows:

Supervision is leadership and the development of leadership within groups which are cooperatively engaged in inspection, research, training, guidance and evaluation.

II. THE OLD AND THE NEW SUPERVISION

TRADITIONAL
1. Inspection
2. Focused on the employee
3. Visitation
4. Random and haphazard
5. Imposed and authoritarian
6. One person usually

MODERN
1. Study and analysis
2. Focused on aims, materials, methods, supervisors, employees, environment
3. Demonstrations, intervisitation, workshops, directed reading, bulletins, etc.
4. Definitely organized and planned (scientific)
5. Cooperative and democratic
6. Many persons involved (creative)

III THE EIGHT (8) BASIC PRINCIPLES OF THE NEW SUPERVISION

1. *PRINCIPLE OF RESPONSIBILITY*
   Authority to act and responsibility for acting must be joined.
   a. If you give responsibility, give authority.
   b. Define employee duties clearly.
   c. Protect employees from criticism by others.
   d. Recognize the rights as well as obligations of employees.
   e. Achieve the aims of a democratic society insofar as it is possible within the area of your work.
   f. Establish a situation favorable to training and learning.
   g. Accept ultimate responsibility for everything done in your section, unit, office, division, department.
   h. Good administration and good supervision are inseparable.

2. PRINCIPLE OF AUTHORITY

The success of the supervisor is measured by the extent to which the power of authority is not used.

    a. Exercise simplicity and informality in supervision.
    b. Use the simplest machinery of supervision.
    c. If it is good for the organization as a whole, it is probably justified.
    d. Seldom be arbitrary or authoritative.
    e. Do not base your work on the power of position or of personality.
    f. Permit and encourage the free expression of opinions.

3. PRINCIPLE OF SELF-GROWTH

The success of the supervisor is measured by the extent to which, and the speed with which, he is no longer needed.

    a. Base criticism on principles, not on specifics.
    b. Point out higher activities to employees.
    c. Train for self-thinking by employees, to meet new situations.
    d. Stimulate initiative, self-reliance and individual responsibility.
    e. Concentrate on stimulating the growth of employees rather than on removing defects.

4. PRINCIPLE OF INDIVIDUAL WORTH

Respect for the individual is a paramount consideration in supervision.

    a. Be human and sympathetic in dealing with employees.
    b. Don't nag about things to be done.
    c. Recognize the individual differences among employees and seek opportunities to permit best expression of each personality.

5. PRINCIPLE OF CREATIVE LEADERSHIP

The best supervision is that which is not apparent to the employee.

    a. Stimulate, don't drive employees to creative action.
    b. Emphasize doing good things.
    c. Encourage employees to do what they do best.
    d. Do not be too greatly concerned with details of subject or method.
    e. Do not be concerned exclusively with immediate problems and activities.
    f. Reveal higher activities and make them both desired and maximally possible.
    g. Determine procedures in the light of each situation but see that these are derived from a sound basic philosophy.
    h. Aid, inspire and lead so as to liberate the creative spirit latent in all good employees.

6. PRINCIPLE OF SUCCESS AND FAILURE

There are no unsuccessful employees, only unsuccessful supervisors who have failed to give proper leadership.

    a. Adapt suggestions to the capacities, attitudes, and prejudices of employees.
    b. Be gradual, be progressive, be persistent.
    c. Help the employee find the general principle; have the employee apply his own problem to the general principle.
    d. Give adequate appreciation for good work and honest effort.
    e. Anticipate employee difficulties and help to prevent them.
    f. Encourage employees to do the desirable things they will do anyway.
    g. Judge your supervision by the results it secures.

7. *PRINCIPLE OF SCIENCE*
Successful supervision is scientific, objective, and experimental. It is based on facts, not on prejudices.
>a. Be cumulative in results.
>b. Never divorce your suggestions from the goals of training.
>c. Don't be impatient of results.
>d. Keep all matters on a professional, not a personal level.
>e. Do not be concerned exclusively with immediate problems and activities.
>f. Use objective means of determining achievement and rating where possible.

8. *PRINCIPLE OF COOPERATION*
Supervision is a cooperative enterprise between supervisor and employee.
>a. Begin with conditions as they are.
>b. Ask opinions of all involved when formulating policies.
>c. Organization is as good as its weakest link.
>d. Let employees help to determine policies and department programs.
>e. Be approachable and accessible - physically and mentally.
>f. Develop pleasant social relationships.

IV. WHAT IS ADMINISTRATION?

Administration is concerned with providing the environment, the material facilities, and the operational procedures that will promote the maximum growth and development of supervisors and employees. (Organization is an aspect, and a concomitant, of administration.)

There is no sharp line of demarcation between supervision and administration; these functions are intimately interrelated and, often, overlapping. They are complementary activities.

1. *PRACTICES COMMONLY CLASSED AS "SUPERVISORY"*
>a. Conducting employees conferences
>b. Visiting sections, units, offices, divisions, departments
>c. Arranging for demonstrations
>d. Examining plans
>e. Suggesting professional reading
>f. Interpreting bulletins
>g. Recommending in-service training courses
>h. Encouraging experimentation
>i. Appraising employee morale
>j. Providing for intervisitation

2. *PRACTICES COMMONLY CLASSIFIED AS "ADMINISTRATIVE"*
>a. Management of the office
>b. Arrangement of schedules for extra duties
>c. Assignment of rooms or areas
>d. Distribution of supplies
>e. Keeping records and reports
>f. Care of audio-visual materials
>g. Keeping inventory records
>h. Checking record cards and books
>i. Programming special activities
>j. Checking on the attendance and punctuality of employees

3. *PRACTICES COMMONLY CLASSIFIED AS BOTH "SUPERVISORY" AND "ADMINISTRATIVE"*
    a. Program construction
    b. Testing or evaluating outcomes
    c. Personnel accounting
    d. Ordering instructional materials

V. RESPONSIBILITIES OF THE SUPERVISOR

A person employed in a supervisory capacity must constantly be able to improve his own efficiency and ability. He represents the employer to the employees and only continuous self-examination can make him a capable supervisor.

Leadership and training are the supervisor's responsibility. An efficient working unit is one in which the employees work with the supervisor. It is his job to bring out the best in his employees. He must always be relaxed, courteous and calm in his association with his employees. Their feelings are important, and a harsh attitude does not develop the most efficient employees.

VI. COMPETENCIES OF THE SUPERVISOR

1. Complete knowledge of the duties and responsibilities of his position.
2. To be able to organize a job, plan ahead and carry through.
3. To have self-confidence and initiative.
4. To be able to handle the unexpected situation and make quick decisions.
5. To be able to properly train subordinates in the positions they are best suited for.
6. To be able to keep good human relations among his subordinates.
7. To be able to keep good human relations between his subordinates and himself and to earn their respect and trust.

VII. THE PROFESSIONAL SUPERVISOR-EMPLOYEE RELATIONSHIP

There are two kinds of efficiency: one kind is only apparent and is produced in organizations through the exercise of mere discipline; this is but a simulation of the second, or true, efficiency which springs from spontaneous cooperation. If you are a manager, no matter how great or small your responsibility, it is your job, in the final analysis, to create and develop this involuntary cooperation among the people whom you supervise. For, no matter how powerful a combination of money, machines, and materials a company may have, this is a dead and sterile thing without a team of willing, thinking and articulate people to guide it.

The following 21 points are presented as indicative of the exemplary basic relationship that should exist between supervisor and employee:

1. Each person wants to be liked and respected by his fellow employee and wants to be treated with consideration and respect by his superior.
2. The most competent employee will make an error. However, in a unit where good relations exist between the supervisor and his employees, tenseness and fear do not exist. Thus, errors are not hidden or covered up and the efficiency of a unit is not impaired.
3. Subordinates resent rules, regulations, or orders that are unreasonable or unexplained.
4. Subordinates are quick to resent unfairness, harshness, injustices and favoritism.
5. An employee will accept responsibility if he knows that he will be complimented for a job well done, and not too harshly chastised for failure; that his supervisor will check the cause of the failure, and, if it was the supervisor's fault, he will assume the blame therefore. If it was the employee's fault, his supervisor will explain the correct method or means of handling the responsibility.

6. An employee wants to receive credit for a suggestion he has made, that is used. If a suggestion cannot be used, the employee is entitled to an explanation. The supervisor should not say "no" and close the subject.
7. Fear and worry slow up a worker's ability. Poor working environment can impair his physical and mental health. A good supervisor avoids forceful methods, threats and arguments to get a job done.
8. A forceful supervisor is able to train his employees individually and as a team, and is able to motivate them in the proper channels.
9. A mature supervisor is able to properly evaluate his subordinates and to keep them happy and satisfied.
10. A sensitive supervisor will never patronize his subordinates.
11. A worthy supervisor will respect his employees' confidences.
12. Definite and clear-cut responsibilities should be assigned to each executive.
13. Responsibility should always be coupled with corresponding authority.
14. No change should be made in the scope or responsibilities of a position without a definite understanding to that effect on the part of all persons concerned.
15. No executive or employee, occupying a single position in the organization, should be subject to definite orders from more than one source.
16. Orders should never be given to subordinates over the head of a responsible executive. Rather than do this, the officer in question should be supplanted.
17. Criticisms of subordinates should, whoever possible, be made privately, and in no case should a subordinate be criticized in the presence of executives or employees of equal or lower rank.
18. No dispute or difference between executives or employees as to authority or responsibilities should be considered too trivial for prompt and careful adjudication.
19. Promotions, wage changes, and disciplinary action should always be approved by the executive immediately superior to the one directly responsible.
20. No executive or employee should ever be required, or expected, to be at the same time an assistant to, and critic of, another.
21. Any executive whose work is subject to regular inspection should, whever practicable, be given the assistance and facilities necessary to enable him to maintain an independent check of the quality of his work.

VIII. MINI-TEXT IN SUPERVISION, ADMINISTRATION, MANAGEMENT, AND ORGANIZATION

A. BRIEF HIGHLIGHTS

Listed concisely and sequentially are major headings and important data in the field for quick recall and review.

1. LEVELS OF MANAGEMENT
Any organization of some size has several levels of management. In terms of a ladder the levels are:

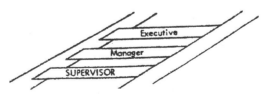

The first level is very important because it is the beginning point of management leadership.

2. WHAT THE SUPERVISOR MUST LEARN
A supervisor must learn to:
(1) Deal with people and their differences
(2) Get the job done through people
(3) Recognize the problems when they exist
(4) Overcome obstacles to good performance
(5) Evaluate the performance of people
(6) Check his own performance in terms of accomplishment

3. A DEFINITION OF SUPERVISOR
The term supervisor means any individual having authority, in the interests of the employer, to hire, transfer, suspend, lay-off, recall, promote, discharge, assign, reward, or discipline other employees or responsibility to direct them, or to adjust their grievances, or effectively to recommend such action, if, in connection with the foregoing, exercise of such authority is not of a merely routine or clerical nature but requires the use of independent judgment.

4. ELEMENTS OF THE TEAM CONCEPT
What is involved in teamwork? The component parts are:
(1) Members   (3) Goals   (5) Cooperation
(2) A leader   (4) Plans   (6) Spirit

5. PRINCIPLES OF ORGANIZATION
(1) A team member must know what his job is.
(2) Be sure that the nature and scope of a job are understood.
(3) Authority and responsibility should be carefully spelled out.
(4) A supervisor should be permitted to make the maximum number of decisions affecting his employees.
(5) Employees should report to only one supervisor.
(6) A supervisor should direct only as many employees as he can handle effectively.
(7) An organization plan should be flexible.
(8) Inspection and performance of work should be separate.
(9) Organizational problems should receive immediate attention.
(10) Assign work in line with ability and experience.

6. THE FOUR IMPORTANT PARTS OF EVERY JOB
(1) Inherent in every job is the *accountability* for results.
(2) A second set of factors in every job is *responsibilities*.
(3) Along with duties and responsibilities one must have the *authority* to act within certain limits without obtaining permission to proceed.
(4) No job exists in a vacuum. The supervisor is surrounded by key *relationships*.

7. PRINCIPLES OF DELEGATION
Where work is delegated for the first time, the supervisor should think in terms of these questions:
(1) Who is best qualified to do this?
(2) Can an employee improve his abilities by doing this?
(3) How long should an employee spend on this?
(4) Are there any special problems for which he will need guidance?
(5) How broad a delegation can I make?

8. PRINCIPLES OF EFFECTIVE COMMUNICATIONS
(1) Determine the media
(2) To whom directed?
(3) Identification and source authority
(4) Is communication understood?

9. PRINCIPLES OF WORK IMPROVEMENT
(1) Most people usually do only the work which is assigned to them
(2) Workers are likely to fit assigned work into the time available to perform it
(3) A good workload usually stimulates output
(4) People usually do their best work when they know that results will be reviewed or inspected
(5) Employees usually feel that someone else is responsible for conditions of work, workplace layout, job methods, type of tools/equipment, and other such factors
(6) Employees are usually defensive about their job security
(7) Employees have natural resistance to change
(8) Employees can support or destroy a supervisor
(9) A supervisor usually earns the respect of his people through his personal example of diligence and efficiency

10. AREAS OF JOB IMPROVEMENT
The areas of job improvement are quite numerous, but the most common ones which a supervisor can identify and utilize are:

(1) Departmental layout
(2) Flow of work
(3) Workplace layout
(4) Utilization of manpower
(5) Work methods
(6) Materials handling
(7) Utilization
(8) Motion economy

11. SEVEN KEY POINTS IN MAKING IMPROVEMENTS
(1) Select the job to be improved
(2) Study how it is being done now
(3) Question the present method
(4) Determine actions to be taken
(5) Chart proposed method
(6) Get approval and apply
(7) Solicit worker participation

12. CORRECTIVE TECHNIQUES OF JOB IMPROVEMENT

Specific Problems	General Improvement	Corrective Techniques
(1) Size of workload	(1) Departmental layout	(1) Study with scale model
(2) Inability to meet schedules	(2) Flow of work	(2) Flow chart study
(3) Strain and fatigue	(3) Work plan layout	(3) Motion analysis
(4) Improper use of men and skills	(4) Utilization of manpower	(4) Comparison of units produced to standard allowance
(5) Waste, poor quality, unsafe conditions	(5) Work methods	(5) Methods analysis
(6) Bottleneck conditions that hinder output	(6) Materials handling	(6) Flow chart & equipment study
(7) Poor utilization of equipment and machine	(7) Utilization of equipment	(7) Down time vs. running time
(8) Efficiency and productivity of labor	(8) Motion economy	(8) Motion analysis

13. A *PLANNING CHECKLIST*

(1) Objectives	(6) Resources	(11) Safety
(2) Controls	(7) Manpower	(12) Money
(3) Delegations	(8) Equipment	(13) Work
(4) Communications	(9) Supplies and materials	(14) Timing of improvements
(5) Resources	(10) Utilization of time	

14. *FIVE CHARACTERISTICS OF GOOD DIRECTIONS*

In order to get results, directions must be:

(1) Possible of accomplishment   (3) Related to mission   (5) Unmistakably clear
(2) Agreeable with worker interests   (4) Planned and complete

15. *TYPES OF DIRECTIONS*

(1) Demands or direct orders   (3) Suggestion or implication
(2) Requests   (4) Volunteering

16. *CONTROLS*

A typical listing of the overall areas in which the supervisor should establish controls might be:

(1) Manpower   (3) Quality of work   (5) Time   (7) Money
(2) Materials   (4) Quantity of work   (6) Space   (8) Methods

17. *ORIENTING THE NEW EMPLOYEE*

(1) Prepare for him   (3) Orientation for the job
(2) Welcome the new employee   (4) Follow-up

18. *CHECKLIST FOR ORIENTING NEW EMPLOYEES*   Yes   No

(1) Do your appreciate the feelings of new employees when they
    first report for work?   ____ ____

(2) Are you aware of the fact that the new employee must make
    a big adjustment to his job?   ____ ____

(3) Have you given him good reasons for liking the job and the
    organization?   ____ ____

(4) Have you prepared for his first day on the job?

(5) Did you welcome him cordially and make him feel needed?

(6) Did you establish rapport with him so that he feels free to talk
    and discuss matters with you?   ____ ____

(7) Did you explain his job to him and his relationship to you?   ____ ____

(8) Does he know that his work will be evaluated periodically on
    a basis that is fair and objective?   ____ ____

(9) Did you introduce him to his fellow workers in such a way that
    they are likely to accept him?   ____ ____

(10) Does he know what employee benefits he will receive?

(11) Does he understand the importance of being on the job
     and what to do if he must leave his duty station?   ____ ____

(12) Has he been impressed with the importance of accident
     prevention and safe practice?   ____ ____

(13) Does he generally know his way around the department?   ____ ____

(14) Is he under the guidance of a sponsor who will teach the
     right ways of doing things?   ____ ____

(15) Do you plan to follow-up so that he will continue to adjust
     successfully to his job?   ____ ____

- 9 -

19. *PRINCIPLES OF LEARNING*
      (1) Motivation   (2) Demonstration or explanation   (3) Practice

20. *CAUSES OF POOR PERFORMANCE*
(1) Improper training for job
(2) Wrong tools
(3) Inadequate directions
(4) Lack of supervisory follow-up
(5) Poor communications
(6) Lack of standards of performance
(7) Wrong work habits
(8) Low morale
(9) Other

21. *FOUR MAJOR STEPS IN ON-THE-JOB INSTRUCTION*
(1) Prepare the worker
(2) Present the operation
(3) Tryout performance
(4) Follow-up

22. *EMPLOYEES WANT FIVE THINGS*
(1) Security (2) Opportunity (3) Recognition (4) Inclusion (5) Expression

23. *SOME DON'TS IN REGARD TO PRAISE*
(1) Don't praise a person for something he hasn't done
(2) Don't praise a person unless you can be sincere
(3) Don't be sparing in praise just because your superior withholds it from you
(4) Don't let too much time elapse between good performance and recognition of it

24. *HOW TO GAIN YOUR WORKERS' CONFIDENCE*
Methods of developing confidence include such things as:
(1) Knowing the interests, habits, hobbies of employees
(2) Admitting your own inadequacies
(3) Sharing and telling of confidence in others
(4) Supporting people when they are in trouble
(5) Delegating matters that can be well handled
(6) Being frank and straightforward about problems and working conditions
(7) Encouraging others to bring their problems to you
(8) Taking action on problems which impede worker progress

25. *SOURCES OF EMPLOYEE PROBLEMS*
On-the-job causes might be such things as:
(1) A feeling that favoritism is exercised in assignments
(2) Assignment of overtime
(3) An undue amount of supervision
(4) Changing methods or systems
(5) Stealing of ideas or trade secrets
(6) Lack of interest in job
(7) Threat of reduction in force
(8) Ignorance or lack of communications
(9) Poor equipment
(10) Lack of knowing how supervisor feels toward employee
(11) Shift assignments

Off-the-job problems might have to do with:
(1) Health (2) Finances (3) Housing (4) Family

26. *THE SUPERVISOR'S KEY TO DISCIPLINE*

There are several key points about discipline which the supervisor should keep in mind:
   (1) Job discipline is one of the disciplines of life and is directed by the supervisor.
   (2) It is more important to correct an employee fault than to fix blame for it.
   (3) Employee performance is affected by problems both on the job and off.
   (4) Sudden or abrupt changes in behavior can be indications of important employee problems.
   (5) Problems should be dealt with as soon as possible after they are identified.
   (6) The attitude of the supervisor may have more to do with solving problems than the techniques of problem solving.
   (7) Correction of employee behavior should be resorted to only after the supervisor is sure that training or counseling will not be helpful.
   (8) Be sure to document your disciplinary actions.
   (9) Make sure that you are disciplining on the basis of facts rather than personal feelings.
  (10) Take each disciplinary step in order, being careful not to make snap judgments, or decisions based on impatience.

27. *FIVE IMPORTANT PROCESSES OF MANAGEMENT*
   (1) Planning   (2) Organizing   (3) Scheduling
   (4) Controlling   (5) Motivating

28. *WHEN THE SUPERVISOR FAILS TO PLAN*
   (1) Supervisor creates impression of not knowing his job
   (2) May lead to excessive overtime
   (3) Job runs itself -- supervisor lacks control
   (4) Deadlines and appointments missed
   (5) Parts of the work go undone
   (6) Work interrupted by emergencies
   (7) Sets a bad example
   (8) Uneven workload creates peaks and valleys
   (9) Too much time on minor details at expense of more important tasks

29. *FOURTEEN GENERAL PRINCIPLES OF MANAGEMENT*
   (1) Division of work   (8) Centralization
   (2) Authority and responsibility   (9) Scalar chain
   (3) Discipline   (10) Order
   (4) Unity of command   (11) Equity
   (5) Unity of direction   (12) Stability of tenure of
   (6) Subordination of individual   personnel
       interest to general interest   (13) Initiative
   (7) Remuneration of personnel   (14) Esprit de corps

30. *CHANGE*

Bringing about change is perhaps attempted more often, and yet less well understood, than anything else the supervisor does. How do people generally react to change? (People tend to resist change that is imposed upon them by other individuals or circumstances.

Change is characteristic of every situation. It is a part of every real endeavor where the efforts of people are concerned.

A. Why do people resist change?
 People may resist change because of:
  (1) Fear of the unknown
  (2) Implied criticism
  (3) Unpleasant experiences in the past
  (4) Fear of loss of status
  (5) Threat to the ego
  (6) Fear of loss of economic stability

B. How can we best overcome the resistance to change?
 In initiating change, take these steps:
  (1) Get ready to sell
  (2) Identify sources of help
  (3) Anticipate objections
  (4) Sell benefits
  (5) Listen in depth
  (6) Follow up

B. BRIEF TOPICAL SUMMARIES

I. WHO/WHAT IS THE SUPERVISOR?

1. The supervisor is often called the "highest level employee and the lowest level manager."
2. A supervisor is a member of both management and the work group. He acts as a bridge between the two.
3. Most problems in supervision are in the area of human relations, or people problems.
4. Employees expect: Respect, opportunity to learn and to advance, and a sense of belonging, and so forth.
5. Supervisors are responsible for directing people and organizing work. Planning is of paramount importance.
6. A position description is a set of duties and responsibilities inherent to a given position.
7. It is important to keep the position description up-to-date and to provide each employee with his own copy.

II. THE SOCIOLOGY OF WORK

1. People are alike in many ways; however, each individual is unique.
2. The supervisor is challenged in getting to know employee differences. Acquiring skills in evaluating individuals is an asset.
3. Maintaining meaningful working relationships in the organization is of great importance.
4. The supervisor has an obligation to help individuals to develop to their fullest potential.
5. Job rotation on a planned basis helps to build versatility and to maintain interest and enthusiasm in work groups.
6. Cross training (job rotation) provides backup skills.
7. The supervisor can help reduce tension by maintaining a sense of humor, providing guidance to employees, and by making reasonable and timely decisions. Employees respond favorably to working under reasonably predictable circumstances.
8. Change is characteristic of all managerial behavior. The supervisor must adjust to changes in procedures, new methods, technological changes, and to a number of new and sometimes challenging situations.
9. To overcome the natural tendency for people to resist change, the supervisor should become more skillful in initiating change.

III. PRINCIPLES AND PRACTICES OF SUPERVISION
1. Employees should be required to answer to only one superior.
2. A supervisor can effectively direct only a limited number of employees, depending upon the complexity, variety, and proximity of the jobs involved.
3. The organizational chart presents the organization in graphic form. It reflects lines of authority and responsibility as well as interrelationships of units within the organization.
4. Distribution of work can be improved through an analysis using the "Work Distribution Chart."
5. The "Work Distribution Chart" reflects the division of work within a unit in understandable form.
6. When related tasks are given to an employee, he has a better chance of increasing his skills through training.
7. The individual who is given the responsibility for tasks must also be given the appropriate authority to insure adequate results.
8. The supervisor should delegate repetitive, routine work. Preparation of recurring reports, maintaining leave and attendance records are some examples.
9. Good discipline is essential to good task performance. Discipline is reflected in the actions of employees on the job in the absence of supervision.
10. Disciplinary action may have to be taken when the positive aspects of discipline have failed. Reprimand, warning, and suspension are examples of disciplinary action.
11. If a situation calls for a reprimand, be sure it is deserved and remember it is to be done in private.

IV. DYNAMIC LEADERSHIP
1. A style is a personal method or manner of exerting influence.
2. Authoritarian leaders often see themselves as the source of power and authority.
3. The democratic leader often perceives the group as the source of authority and power.
4. Supervisors tend to do better when using the pattern of leadership that is most natural for them.
5. Social scientists suggest that the effective supervisor use the leadership style that best fits the problem or circumstances involved.
6. All four styles -- telling, selling, consulting, joining -- have their place. Using one does not preclude using the other at another time.
7. The theory X point of view assumes that the average person dislikes work, will avoid it whenever possible, and must be coerced to achieve organizational objectives.
8. The theory Y point of view assumes that the average person considers work to be as natural as play, and, when the individual is committed, he requires little supervision or direction to accomplish desired objectives.
9. The leader's basic assumptions concerning human behavior and human nature affect his actions, decisions, and other managerial practices.
10. Dissatisfaction among employees is often present, but difficult to isolate. The supervisor should seek to weaken dissatisfaction by keeping promises, being sincere and considerate, keeping employees informed, and so forth.
11. Constructive suggestions should be encouraged during the natural progress of the work.

V. PROCESSES FOR SOLVING PROBLEMS
1. People find their daily tasks more meaningful and satisfying when they can improve them.
2. The causes of problems, or the key factors, are often hidden in the background. Ability to solve problems often involves the ability to isolate them from their backgrounds. There is some substance to the cliché that some persons "can't see the forest for the trees."
3. New procedures are often developed from old ones. Problems should be broken down into manageable parts. New ideas can be adapted from old ones.

4. People think differently in problem-solving situations. Using a logical, patterned approach is often useful. One approach found to be useful includes these steps:

    (a) Define the problem   (d) Weigh and decide
    (b) Establish objectives   (e) Take action
    (c) Get the facts   (f) Evaluate action

VI. TRAINING FOR RESULTS

1. Participants respond best when they feel training is important to them.
2. The supervisor has responsibility for the training and development of those who report to him.
3. When training is delegated to others, great care must be exercised to insure the trainer has knowledge, aptitude, and interest for his work as a trainer.
4. Training (learning) of some type goes on continually. The most successful supervisor makes certain the learning contributes in a productive manner to operational goals.
5. New employees are particularly susceptible to training. Older employees facing new job situations require specific training, as well as having need for development and growth opportunities.
6. Training needs require continuous monitoring.
7. The training officer of an agency is a professional with a responsibility to assist supervisors in solving training problems.
8. Many of the self-development steps important to the supervisor's own growth are equally important to the development of peers and subordinates. Knowledge of these is important when the supervisor consults with others on development and growth opportunities.

VII. HEALTH, SAFETY, AND ACCIDENT PREVENTION

1. Management-minded supervisors take appropriate measures to assist employees in maintaining health and in assuring safe practices in the work environment.
2. Effective safety training and practices help to avoid injury and accidents.
3. Safety should be a management goal. All infractions of safety which are observed should be corrected without exception.
4. Employees' safety attitude, training and instruction, provision of safe tools and equipment, supervision, and leadership are considered highly important factors which contribute to safety and which can be influenced directly by supervisors.
5. When accidents do occur they should be investigated promptly for very important reasons, including the fact that information which is gained can be used to prevent accidents in the future.

VIII. EQUAL EMPLOYMENT OPPORTUNITY

1. The supervisor should endeavor to treat all employees fairly, without regard to religion, race, sex, or national origin.
2. Groups tend to reflect the attitude of the leader. Prejudice can be detected even in very subtle form. Supervisors must strive to create a feeling of mutual respect and confidence in every employee.
3. Complete utilization of all human resources is a national goal. Equitable consideration should be accorded women in the work force, minority-group members, the physically and mentally handicapped, and the older employee. The important question is: "Who can do the job?"
4. Training opportunities, recognition for performance, overtime assignments, promotional opportunities, and all other personnel actions are to be handled on an equitable basis.

IX. IMPROVING COMMUNICATIONS

1. Communications is achieving understanding between the sender and the receiver of a message. It also means sharing information -- the creation of understanding.
2. Communication is basic to all human activity. Words are means of conveying meanings; however, real meanings are in people.
3. There are very practical differences in the effectiveness of one-way, impersonal, and two-way communications. Words spoken face-to-face are better understood. Telephone conversations are effective, but lack the rapport of person-to-person exchanges. The whole person communicates.
4. Cooperation and communication in an organization go hand in hand. When there is a mutual respect between people, spelling out rules and procedures for communicating is unnecessary.
5. There are several barriers to effective communications. These include failure to listen with respect and understanding, lack of skill in feedback, and misinterpreting the meanings of words used by the speaker. It is also common practice to listen to what we want to hear, and tune out things we do not want to hear.
6. Communication is management's chief problem. The supervisor should accept the challenge to communicate more effectively and to improve interagency and intra-agency communications.
7. The supervisor may often plan for and conduct meetings. The planning phase is critical and may determine the success or the failure of a meeting.
8. Speaking before groups usually requires extra effort. Stage fright may never disappear completely, but it can be controlled.

X. SELF-DEVELOPMENT

1. Every employee is responsible for his own self-development.
2. Toastmaster and toastmistress clubs offer opportunities to improve skills in oral communications.
3. Planning for one's own self-development is of vital importance. Supervisors know their own strengths and limitations better than anyone else.
4. Many opportunities are open to aid the supervisor in his developmental efforts, including job assignments; training opportunities, both governmental and non-governmental -- to include universities and professional conferences and seminars.
5. Programmed instruction offers a means of studying at one's own rate.
6. Where difficulties may arise from a supervisor's being away from his work for training, he may participate in televised home study or correspondence courses to meet his self-develop- ment needs.

XI. TEACHING AND TRAINING

A. The Teaching Process

Teaching is encouraging and guiding the learning activities of students toward established goals. In most cases this process consists in five steps: preparation, presentation, summarization, evaluation, and application.

1. Preparation

Preparation is twofold in nature; that of the supervisor and the employee.

Preparation by the supervisor is absolutely essential to success. He must know what, when, where, how, and whom he will teach. Some of the factors that should be considered are:

(1) The objectives	(5) Employee interest
(2) The materials needed	(6) Training aids
(3) The methods to be used	(7) Evaluation
(4) Employee participation	(8) Summarization

Employee preparation consists in preparing the employee to receive the material. Probably the most important single factor in the preparation of the employee is arousing and maintaining his interest. He must know the objectives of the training, why he is there, how the material can be used, and its importance to him.

2. Presentation

In presentation, have a carefully designed plan and follow it.
The plan should be accurate and complete, yet flexible enough to meet situations as they arise. The method of presentation will be determined by the particular situation and objectives.

3. Summary

A summary should be made at the end of every training unit and program. In addition, there may be internal summaries depending on the nature of the material being taught. The important thing is that the trainee must always be able to understand how each part of the new material relates to the whole.

4. Application

The supervisor must arrange work so the employee will be given a chance to apply new knowledge or skills while the material is still clear in his mind and interest is high. The trainee does not really know whether he has learned the material until he has been given a chance to apply it. If the material is not applied, it loses most of its value.

5. Evaluation

The purpose of all training is to promote learning. To determine whether the training has been a success or failure, the supervisor must evaluate this learning.
In the broadest sense evaluation includes all the devices, methods, skills, and techniques used by the supervisor to keep him self and the employees informed as to their progress toward the objectives they are pursuing. The extent to which the employee has mastered the knowledge, skills, and abilities, or changed his attitudes, as determined by the program objectives, is the extent to which instruction has succeeded or failed.
Evaluation should not be confined to the end of the lesson, day, or program but should be used continuously. We shall note later the way this relates to the rest of the teaching process.

B. Teaching Methods

A teaching method is a pattern of identifiable student and instructor activity used in presenting training material.
All supervisors are faced with the problem of deciding which method should be used at a given time.
As with all methods, there are certain advantages and disadvantages to each method.

1. Lecture

The lecture is direct oral presentation of material by the supervisor. The present trend is to place less emphasis on the trainer's activity and more on that of the trainee.

2. Discussion

Teaching by discussion or conference involves using questions and other techniques to arouse interest and focus attention upon certain areas, and by doing so creating a learning situation. This can be one of the most valuable methods because it gives the employees 'an opportunity to express their ideas and pool their knowledge.

3. Demonstration

The demonstration is used to teach how something works or how to do something. It can be used to show a principle or what the results of a series of actions will be. A well-staged demonstration is particularly effective because it shows proper methods of performance in a realistic manner.

4. Performance

Performance is one of the most fundamental of all learning techniques or teaching methods. The trainee may be able to tell how a specific operation should be performed but he cannot be sure he knows how to perform the operation until he has done so.

5. Which Method to Use

Moreover, there are other methods and techniques of teaching. It is difficult to use any method without other methods entering into it. In any learning situation a combination of methods is usually more effective than anyone method alone.

Finally, evaluation must be integrated into the other aspects of the teaching-learning process.
It must be used in the motivation of the trainees; it must be used to assist in developing understanding during the training; and it must be related to employee application of the results of training.

This is distinctly the role of the supervisor.

———

CONTENTS

TRAINING PROGRAM FOR
FOOD SERVICE WORKER

Developing Course Plans

The following suggestions are for training persons who are to be employed by health or welfare institutions for supervised work in the preparation and serving of food. Supervised work implies supervision on the job by someone with formal training in quantity food production. In this training guide the title Supervised Food Service Worker is used.

Teachers must adjust and adapt the suggestions in this guide to the needs of the particular group they are teaching because the duties expected of the Supervised Food Service Worker may differ from community to community, and the trainees will vary in education, experience, and ability. In addition to having first-hand information concerning job requirements, the individual teacher must secure as much information as possible about the trainees from testing service of the Employment Office or the guidance staff of the school. The specific objectives, teaching methods, and time allotted to each aspect of the training can then be adjusted to the local situation and to the trainees.

Job Functions

The Supervised Food Service Worker prepares and serves foods, under the direction of the Food Service Supervisor, in institutions such as hospitals, nursing homes, homes for the aged, children's institutional homes, and child day-care centers.

Program Objectives

To prepare trainees:

1. To assist the head cook in preparing and cooking food in institutions, or serve as the only cook in small institutions;
2. To learn the correct methods of preparing and cooking all types of food served in hospitals or welfare institutions;
3. To follow time- and energy-saving methods in assembling and arranging utensils and supplies needed for each job;
4. To learn how to plan the sequence and interrelation of the work to be done each day;
5. To learn how to fill the containers, get the food to diet kitchens, and serve food on trays for patients;
6. To learn how to set up a hot food table and serve food;
7. To follow sanitary and time-saving procedures
   a. preparing dishes and cooking utensils for washing
   b. cleaning stoves, work tables, and sinks.

Teacher Qualifications

A qualified teacher is a person with a baccalaureate degree in Institutional Management who has had successful experience in teaching adults. She should also have had experience in institutional food service, including supervision and training of personnel.

Background of Trainee

A trainee should be a person with manual dexterity and the ability to read, speak, write, and follow oral and written directions. She should be in sound physical and mental health and be willing to have a physical examination.

Length of Course and Course Units

A course of 240 hours is suggested for training. The following suggested time in hours for each of the five units can be used as a guide for planning a course to meet trainee and community needs.

Course Unit	Title	Hours
I	Orientation to the Nature of the Work and Desirable Personal Qualities for Job Success	5
II	Safe Food Handling, Essential Health Practices, and Sanitation	10
III	Care and Use of Equipment and Safety Requirements	10
IV	Basic Skills in Management of Work and in Preparation and Service of Food	210
V	Adequate Storage of Food	5
	Total	240

COURSE UNIT I

ORIENTATION TO THE NATURE OF THE WORK AND DESIRABLE PERSONAL QUALITIES FOR JOB SUCCESS

<u>Suggested Training Time</u>   5 Hours

<u>Objectives</u>

   To orient trainees to the nature of the work of a Supervised Food Service Worker in hospitals, nursing homes, homes for the aged, children's institutional homes, and child day-care centers. This course unit will also help trainees to cultivate personal qualities needed for job success.

<u>Course Unit Outline</u>

   A. Work of the Supervised Food Service Worker
       1. Importance and purpose of the job
       2. Employment opportunities
           a. Hospitals and nursing homes
           b. Homes for the aged
           c. Children's homes and child day-care centers
       3. Kinds of work and work situations
           a. Types of work involved in preparing and serving food
           b. Typical work areas—food preparation, receiving and storage, and serving counters
           c. Assistance is given by the trained food supervisor in making a work schedule, interpreting large quantity recipes, setting standards for acceptable food standards, and selecting and using appropriate equipment
       4. Employment policies
           a. Hours of work
           b. Compensation
           c. Sick leave; procedures for reporting absence
           d. Social Security and laws affecting employment

   B. Desirable personal qualities to cultivate
       1. Reasons for importance of such personal qualities as honesty, dependability, promptness, and courtesy, cooperative attitude toward coworkers and people to be served, willingness to follow directions, good grooming, good health, and acceptable behavior on job
       2. Some ways to improve or develop desirable personal qualities
           a. Dramatization of situations which illustrate use of desirable personal qualities
           b. Discussions of ways to work on personal improvement

4

COURSE UNIT II

SAFE FOOD HANDLING, ESSENTIAL HEALTH
PRACTICES, AND SANITATION

<u>Suggested Training Time</u>   10 Hours

<u>Objectives</u>
   To help trainees develop the skills and knowledge they will need to handle food safely, to develop essential health practices, and to use sanitary housekeeping methods.

<u>Course Unit Outline</u>
   A. Safe handling of food
      1. State and local food service regulations
         a. State and local ordinances
         b. Importance of physical examinations, testing, and other ordinances for food service workers
      2. Hygiene and health
         a. Essential institutional facilities, equipment, and supplies
            (1) For the care of food—refrigerators and storerooms
            (2) For the use of employees—hand soap, hot water, toilet facilities
         b. Essential hygienic and health practices
            (1) Personal cleanliness, good grooming
            (2) Care of hair (wearing a hair net)
            (3) Habits which avoid spreading colds
            (4) Sanitary practices related to tasting food, dishwashing, food storage, and care of work area
      3. Importance of and reasons for strict sanitary control in handling food
         a. Prevention of spoilage and contamination
            (1) Temperatures for safe refrigeration
            (2) Temperatures for keeping foods hot
            (3) Techniques for handling food
         b. Food-borne diseases
            (1) Types—ptomaine poisoning
            (2) Methods of prevention

   B. Sanitation and housekeeping practices
      1. Definition of terms commonly used in housekeeping
         a. Procedures—scrub, rinse, scald, dry, dust
         b. Materials—detergents, soap, scouring materials, brooms, brushes, mops, pails, sponges, disinfectants
      2. Follow cleaning schedule and procedures developed by Food Service Supervisor for care of
         a. Storeroom
         b. Kitchen—walls, floors, working surfaces
         c. Equipment—refrigerators, ranges, ovens, garbage cans

COURSE UNIT III

CARE AND USE OF EQUIPMENT AND SAFETY REQUIREMENTS

Suggested Training Time   10 Hours

Objectives
    To help trainees develop understanding and ability in the selection and use of appropriate equipment for specific tasks, and to work safely in an institutional kitchen.

Course Unit Outline
    A. Selection and use of equipment
        1. Select piece of equipment most appropriate to use for the job
            a. Steam equipment—steam jacket kettle for cooking potatoes
            b. Power equipment—potato peeler, mixer for mashing potatoes and mixing cakes
            c. Miscellaneous equipment
                (1) Cutlery—correct knife for job as slicing knife – slicing cold meats; utility knife – cutting large vegetables; french knife – chopping vegetables and cutting sandwiches
                (2) Measuring equipment
        2. Demonstrate use and care of major pieces of equipment used in institution kitchens—trainees practice
        3. Understand precautions in operating equipment for
            a. Protection of worker
            b. Protection of equipment
        4. Needed adjustment or repair of equipment
        5. Storage of equipment

    B. Safety—accident prevention
        1. Common accidents in food service area—burns, falls, cuts, strains, splinters
        2. Causes of accidents
            a. Personal—carelessness, hurrying
            b. Mechanical—malfunction or incorrect use of equipment
        3. Safety precautions
            a. Alert to hazards—broken glass, damp floor, highly polished floor
            b. Avoid plugging in electric equipment when hands are wet
            c. Check electric cords and connections
        4. Procedures in case of injuries
        5. Safety regulations required by local ordinances

COURSE UNIT IV

BASIC SKILLS IN MANAGEMENT OF WORK AND IN PREPARATION AND SERVICE OF FOOD

<u>Suggested Training Time</u>   210 Hours

<u>Objectives</u>

   To help trainee develop skills in large-quantity food preparation—management of work; correct procedures in preparing food in large quantities; acceptable standards for furnished products; and suitable ways to serve food in hospitals or institutional homes for older people or children.

<u>Course Unit Outline</u>
   A. Conditions for good work
      1. Some methods of simplifying work through arrangement of work space and equipment
      (Planning the arrangement of equipment is not the responsibility of the supervised food service worker, but an understanding of the reasons for good arrangement is important and helps the worker see ways to make adaptations to meet individual needs, particularly height of work surfaces.)
         a. Provide a fixed location for storage of all equipment and materials at point of first use
         b. Furnish sufficient work surface, of convenient height for the worker, adequate light, and circulation of air
         c. Place supplies in semicircle in front of and near worker
         d. Place all materials for best sequence of work before beginning a task
         e. Where hand equipment is used, choose pieces with handles which permit most of the hand to contact the handles
      2. Some methods of simplifying hand work
         a. Use both hands whenever possible
         b. Use continuous curved motions in preference to straightline motions
         c. Arrange for work to be done in a natural rhythmic sequence
            (1) Demonstrations of the influence of different arrangements of equipment on time required for a task. Follow demonstration with trainee practice in performing simple tasks
            (2) Demonstrate and direct trainees in practicing correct hand motions in doing a food-preparation task

B. Basic information for food preparation
1. Purposes and correct uses of recipes
   a. Weights and/or measures used in large-quantity cookery
   b. Interpreting and following directions in recipes
   c. Methods of making correct measurements
   d. Relation of accurate measurements and correct procedure to quality of product
2. Temperatures in food preparation
   a. Terms used to indicate temperature—low, medium, high, simmer, boil, rolling boil
   b. Ways to determine and control temperature
   c. Importance of correct temperature in securing standard products
3. Methods of combining ingredients
   a. Demonstrate and practice common methods for combining ingredients such as stirring, mixing, sifting, folding, beating, mincing
   b. Suitable equipment for each method
   c. Appropriate use of each method

C. Food preparation
1. Beverages—coffee, cocoa, hot or iced tea
   a. Methods of preparation
   b. Equipment required
   c. Standards for product
   d. Methods of serving at proper temperature
2. Soups
   a. Meat stock and vegetable stock base
   b. Cream soups
   c. Clear soups
   d. For each of the above types of soups: methods of preparation, standards for product, methods of serving at proper temperature
3. Protein foods—milk, eggs, cheese, meat, poultry, fish
   a. Principles of cookery of protein foods
   b. Correct temperature, moist or dry heat
   c. Recipes for different protein foods suitable to serve at each meal in the day
   d. Types of meat extenders for reducing cost
   e. Methods, other than frying, for preparing fish
4. Vegetables
   a. Demonstrations of methods of preparing fresh vegetables for cooking or salads
   b. Methods of cooking starchy vegetables
   c. Methods of cooking leafy or green vegetables
   d. Health reasons for proper cooking of vegetables
   e. Time guide for vegetable cookery
   f. Standards for different types of cooked vegetables

5. Baked foods
    a. Breads—yeast and quick breads
       (1) Standard recipes for different types of breads
       (2) Equipment used
       (3) Methods of preparation
       (4) Standards for finished products
    b. Cakes, cookies, and pastry
       (1) Standard recipes
       (2) Equipment used
       (3) Methods of preparation
       (4) Standards for products

6. Salads
    a. Tossed or cooked vegetable salads
    b. Fruit salads
    c. Meat and fish salads
       (1) Preparation of ingredients to insure acceptable product
       (2) Methods of making salads
       (3) Types of salad dressings
       (4) For each of the types of salads and dressings: methods of making; possible variations; standards for product

7. Desserts
    a. Custards—baked and soft
    b. Puddings—rice, tapioca, cornstarch, bread
    c. Gelatin desserts
    d. For each of the above types of desserts: standard recipes; methods of preparation; standards for product

8. Sandwiches
    a. Types of fillings
    b. Standards for finished product
    c. Work procedures for quantity production

D. Food service in hospital or institutional home
    1. Method of keeping food at correct temperature to serve
    2. Safe length of time for keeping food at correct temperature for serving
    3. Methods of taking food from the kitchen to diet kitchens on different floors
    4. Tray setups for each meal of the day
    5. Arranging food on hot table to serve in a cafeteria
    6. Portions suitable to group to be served

E. Organization of work
    1. Plan work within space and time
    2. Assemble equipment
    3. Follow sequence of steps within basic tasks
    4. Keep work space orderly
    5. Follow time schedule

COURSE UNIT V

ADEQUATE STORAGE OF FOOD

<u>Suggested Training Time</u>   5 Hours

<u>Objectives</u>
To help trainees develop an understanding of adequate facilities for storage of food, and to acquire the ability to use and care for these facilities.

<u>Course Unit Outline</u>
A. Effects of storage on
  1. Nutritive value of food
  2. Quality of product
  3. Spoilage of food

B. Facilities for food storage
  1. Refrigerators
      a. Types of refrigerators—walk-in or upright
      b. Types of foods kept by refrigeration
      c. Preparation of food for refrigeration
      d. Placement of various foods in refrigerator, rotation of food
      e. Temperature requirement
      f. Length of time for keeping foods by refrigeration
      g. Cleaning refrigerator—schedule, method
  2. Freezers
      a. Types of food which can be kept by freezer
      b. Selection of containers
      c. Placement of food in freezer according to institution plan
      d. Temperature requirement
      e. Record of food placed in and removed from freezer
      f. Avoidance of refreezing foods
  3. Storeroom
      a. Types of foods stored in storeroom—perishables, staples, canned goods
      b. Desirable facilities
      c. Temperature and ventilation control
      d. Desirable location—proximity to kitchen, delivery entrance
      e. Length of time for keeping foods in storeroom
      f. Arrangement of food
      g. Cleaning—schedule and method
      h. Record of foods placed in and removed from storeroom

TEACHING THE COURSE

<u>Planning the Learning Experiences</u>

The objectives of a training program are achieved by learning experiences designed to help the trainees develop those behaviors and abilities designated in the objectives. Each experience should serve a definite function and should not be introduced because it is traditional or "modern" or because it is satisfying to the teacher.

A good teacher constantly reminds herself that "covering" the topics outlined for a course does not automatically result in learning. She knows that effective learning experiences should be planned by visualizing what the trainee must be able to do on the job. The job analysis will be an important guide, because the class experiences must be realistic and based on work situations for which the training is being given. Each trainee needs opportunity to apply her understandings and abilities to the different kinds of problems she may face.

A variety of learning experiences will be needed to develop the kinds of abilities required in home and community service occupations. Creativity is a key in providing meaningful experiences for a particular group. The successful teacher will see new ways to synthesize, adapt, and revise experiences to fit the unique characteristics of the group and fulfill the requirements of the job.

These are some planned experiences to be considered:

A. Experiences that will add to and enrich the background of trainees

1. Bringing employers to class to give information on nature of the job
2. Using persons from special fields such as mental health, geriatrics, nutrition or dietetics, child development, medicine, public health, and housing to extend basic knowledge and answer questions
3. Providing reading material appropriate to age and reading ability
4. Using movies, filmstrips, charts, tape recordings, or other audiovisual materials to present specific information (it will be necessary for teachers to preview films, filmstrips, and tapes for appropriateness of and familiarization with the content)

B. Experiences which help develop insight and desirable attitudes

1. Playing out roles of people who might be involved in a work situation
2. Visiting with prospective employers who are to benefit from services to be given by trainees
3. Comparing methods of doing a task by making simple time and motion studies
4. Reacting to situations illustrated in movies, cartoons, or short dramas
5. Making planned trips to representative places of employment

C. Experiences in analyzing work situations and solving problems

1. Considering a specific employment problem or work situation. The situation presented must be realistic. (If actual cases are studied, anonymity should be maintained.) The teacher should ask questions which lead trainees to recognize the problem, to decide what additional information might be needed, and to suggest and evaluate solutions.

   2. Developing step-by-step work schedules for some aspects of the job
   3. Working out typical problems in a laboratory situation

D. Experiences to develop specific skills and abilities

   1. Watching demonstration of a technique, with follow-up practice in class, laboratory, in own home, or in a situation provided by cooperating employer(s)
   2. Observing and participating in specific activities in places similar to those where trainee will be employed
   3. Experimenting with different arrangement or placement of equipment and supplies, or different techniques for completing a job
   4. Acting out situations such as interviewing a prospective employer, repeating directions given, or getting help from a supervisor

E. Some teaching methods which help trainees draw conclusions and summarize important ideas

   1. Circle discussion-each member tells of something she observed on a field trip or in a film that would be useful to an employee
   2. Buzz group--a small group of trainees applies a principle to new situations
   3. Summarizing panel- 2 to 5 members of the class review important ideas presented in a class session
   4. Summary sheets-brief summaries of major ideas, important facts, or steps in a work process, prepared by the teacher for distribution to trainees at the end of a lesson

Evaluating Achievement

Major functions of evaluation in a program designed to prepare individuals for wage-earning:

   1. Assessing basic abilities of persons desiring to enroll in the training program as a basis for selection
   2. Determining needs and backgrounds of trainees as one basis of setting up specific goals for the course
   3. Measuring the extent to which trainees achieve the goals

Evaluation made for these purposes also will give the teacher a basis for developing learning experiences, modifying course plans, and selecting appropriate references and teaching materials. The needs, backgrounds, and abilities of potential trainees can be assessed by teachers in informal interviews with each person. Personal data sheets and more formal measurement of reading ability and aptitudes for the job may be supplied by vocational counselors or employment service offices.

An integral part of planning a course is selecting some means for checking the progress of each trainee. The desired understandings, attitudes, and abilities are described in the objectives. Course plans must include:

   1. Ways of observing each trainee's progress toward achieving objectives
   2. Methods of recording observations so progress may be assessed

A teacher can obtain some clues to progress from the trainee's participation in class and from individual conferences. An "anecdotal record," which is a factual report of what the trainee says or does, needs to be written at frequent intervals. Evaluation of the anecdotes should not be attempted until a number of observations has been recorded and at a time when the teacher's feelings and emotions are least likely to influence her judgment.

A rating scale may be used to indicate the level or quality of trainee accomplishment. Three levels are commonly used such as "very good," "acceptable," "not acceptable." (An experienced teacher may use one with 5 to 7 levels, but those used by trainees should be less complex.) The accomplishments being evaluated should be stated specifically and the meaning of the different levels on the scale should be indicated clearly so that all persons using the scale have a common under standing of the meaning of each rating. A check-off type of list can be used by both teacher and trainee to record completion of learning activity or achievement of some measurable skill. Rating scales, sometimes called "score cards," may also be developed to rate a completed task.

Evidence of trainee accomplishments should be compiled throughout the training course. Since observations are more valid if made in realistic situations, much of the evaluation will usually take place in laboratory and practice sessions.

Planning the Lesson

The best guide or lesson plan is, of course, one that has been prepared by the individual teacher, based on personal experience and manner of teaching. Although teachers differ in their ways of organizing and coordinating important parts of their presentations, they agree that the purpose of a lesson is effective and meaningful classroom instruction.

Written plans may be very brief, but the good teacher will know before the class starts:

1. The goals or objectives of the lesson-the kind of learning desired
2. The outline and suggested time schedule for the lesson, including
    a. An interest approach--a way to introduce the lesson, to capture the interest of the trainees and to direct their attention to the lesson's goals or objectives
    b. Activities which will involve the trainees in discovering new facts and principles, solving realistic problems, or practicing skills
    c. A way to summarize the lesson--to help trainees arrive at some valid conclusions and /or to evaluate the extent to which lesson goals have been achieved
    d. Assignments of additional study or practice
3. The subject matter content-the facts and principles or main ideas to be brought out in the lesson
4. The teaching materials and references to be used

Teaching Facilities

The training center must provide equipment such as that used in small hospitals or large school lunchrooms. It must make possible large-quantity food preparation. There should be sufficient work stations and supplies to permit trainees repetitive experiences, both in food preparation and in serving food at a hot food counter or putting it in containers to be sent to diet kitchens. The arrangement of equipment should make possible the teaching of good work procedures.

Opportunities should be provided to observe institutional food-preparation facilities in actual use in order that the trainee may study acceptable procedures and techniques.

Criteria for Judging Trainee Readiness for Employment

The criteria which serve as guides in determining whether the trainee is ready for employment as a Supervised Food Service Worker will be more intangible than in some other occupations. However, some understanding of human frailties and needs, some insight into how to maintain effective working relationships with people, and an ability to follow supervision are of such importance that every attempt should be made to evaluate trainee progress.

The use of various evaluative devices is necessary for the teacher and the trainee to accumulate objective information about the growth of the trainee. The following competencies should be developed or strengthened during the training program:

A. Personal qualities

   1. Courtesy, friendliness, and tact in dealing with supervisors, coworkers, and people being served
   2. Acceptable appearance-good grooming, cleanliness, and neatness in dress
   3. Good personal habits-dependability, promptness, cleanliness, and honesty
   4. Understanding of own role and that of others

B. Activities showing knowledge, understanding, and skills

   1. Works effectively under supervision-understands and conforms to institution's requirements; understands and carries out instructions or directions given by supervisors
   2. Demonstrates knowledge of basic food preparation techniques
   3. Demonstrates ability to prepare and serve nutritious meals
   4. Demonstrates understanding of safety in work areas-basic precautions, procedures in case of accidents
   5. Demonstrates care and use of equipment-refrigerators, stoves, storage spaces, serving areas, utensils
   6. Demonstrates acceptable methods or techniques for care and storage of food-refrigeration, room storage
   7. Demonstrates understanding of methods and materials for keeping work and storage spaces clean and sanitary
   8. Understands importance of personal hygiene and sanitation in handling foods-preparation, cooking, storing, and serving

Kitchen Layouts
RECOMMENDATIONS FOR THE LAYOUT OF RESTAURANT KITCHENS

1. The floor area of a kitchen should include:

    A. The area occupied by the equipment.
    B. The spaces between equipment and the walls, and the spaces between equipment exclusive of aisle space.
    C. Aisle space.

2. Spacing of equipment:

    A. Aisle space should be a dequate for the operation and not less than 30" wide.
    B. All stoves, ovens, fryers, refrigerators, kitchen and food preparation and food service equipment should be spaced sufficiently from the wall so as to allow access for cleaning and inspection of all equipment. Inaccessible spaces which would become potential insect and rodent harborages should not be permitted. Distances of 12"-24" from the wall are recommended. If such space is not available, then the equipment should be sealed to the wall and floor.
    C. Stationary, tied-in units such as fountain, counter, and back bar units should be sealed to each other, thus eliminating crevices and open spaces.
    D. Dish and glass-washing machines should be spaced away from the wall to permit complete access for cleaning and repair.

3. Walls and ceilings in the kitchen and other food preparation rooms shall be constructed of a hard material and shall have a smooth finish. When the use of the premises results in the presence of steam or vapor, such as in dishwashing rooms or rooms containing steam kettles, and when required by the Department, the walls and ceilings shall be constructed of smooth cement, glazed tile, glazed brick, or other non-absorbent material. Walls and ceilings should be kept clean and in good repair.

4. The use of a metal covering on a wall or ceiling should be discouraged and permitted only where it can be installed in such a manner that all joints can be welded or soldered tight and smooth. Futhermore, the metal should be of sufficient gauge to prevent buckling and should be non-corrosive.

5. The use of wooden walls in kitchens and food preparation rooms is not desirable. The wall should be free of any pits, cracks, crevices, or protruding ledges. Baseboards or molding should be flush with the wall.

6. No paper or oilcloth coverings should be used on walls or restaurant kitchens of food preparation rooms.

7. The need for a tile-finished wall or an enamel paint-finished wall should be judged on the basis of the accessibility of the wall for cleaning purposes. If the equipment is placed in such proximity to the wall as to make it impossible to hand-brush or mop, then a tile wall is preferred so that it may be hosed down. If, on the other hand, there is adequate aisle space for a worker to clean the wall by hand, then an enamel-painted wall would be adequate, since repairs or repainting could be easily accomplished if necessary.

8. All defects in the walls behind the fixtures should be repaired and holes filled before the installation of fixtures, so as to prevent possible rodent and insect harborage.

9. Kitchen floors should be constructed of water-tight, non-absorbent material, impervious to moisture or grease. These materials may include:

   A. Trowel-finished smooth cement
   B. Terrazzo stone
   C. Packing house brick tile
   D. Asbestos vinyl tile
   E. Hardwood water-tight floor
   F. Any other suitable material that is impervious and water-tight.
      When it is deemed necessary by the Department, because the type of operation will result in wet floors or require frequent flushing of walls and floors, then the construction should be limited to items a, b, and c, and such floor should be graded and drained to a properly trapped sewer-connected sanitary drain. The juncture of the wall and floor should be coved to a flush finish. The use of linoleum or similar floor coverings is not recommended in kitchens and food preparation rooms.

10. Adequate ventilation should be provided for the kitchen, dishwashing room, toilet, locker rooms, food preparation areas, storerooms, cellar areas, and particularly in all sections having gas-burning units.

11. All hoods and ducts which carry off to the outer air any steam, gases, odors, or smoke, or any apparatus used for air-conditioning shall be constructed, operated, and maintained in such a manner so as not to be objectionable, or create a nuisance.

12. Suitable means should be provided for the protection of food against condensation from suspended pipes and possible leaks from overhead waste or sewer pipes.

13. The walls of the cellar may be whitewashed, provided that such cellar is not used for food preparation purposes.

14. The garbage room walls and floor should be constructed of concrete, cement, or other watertight, non-absorbent materials, so graded and drained as to discharge all liquid matter into a properly trapped floor drain. The garbage room should be adequately ventilated and water-supplied, and provided with water connections for cleansing the garbage cans. Refrigeration of the garbage room is desirable.

15. The entire kitchen premises shall be lighted adequately by natural or artificial means so as to permit the activity for which the premises are used to be carried on safely and to permit effective inspection and cleaning of the premises. It is recommended that a minimum of 20 foot-candles of light be maintained in the general kitchen area, while a minimum of 40 foot-candles be maintained in the areas requiring accurate observation.

16. One or more grease traps adequate in size to handle the total flow of waste water from the water-supplied kitchen fixtures should be installed in the kitchen waste line in accordance with approved plumbing code requirements.

17. All shelving should be spaced at least 2" from the wall and so constructed as to be readily accessible for cleaning. Bottom shelves should be at least 6" to 10" off the floor and the underpart open for cleaning. Wooden shelves in kitchens or stockrooms should not be painted. All shelves must be kept free of any oilcloth, paper, or other covering.

18. All cutting boards and work boards should be constructed so as to be readily removable for cleaning.

19. A dipper-well with an "over-the-rim" inlet with fresh running water should be provided for the storage of ice cream scoops at each ice cream dispensing station.

20. Provisions shall be made for the sanitary handling of ice intended for human consumption. The use of some device for handling the ice is required. The handle end of such device or any part of the human hand must not be permitted to come in contact with the ice. It is suggested that the scoop or other ice-handling device be hung up after each use.

————

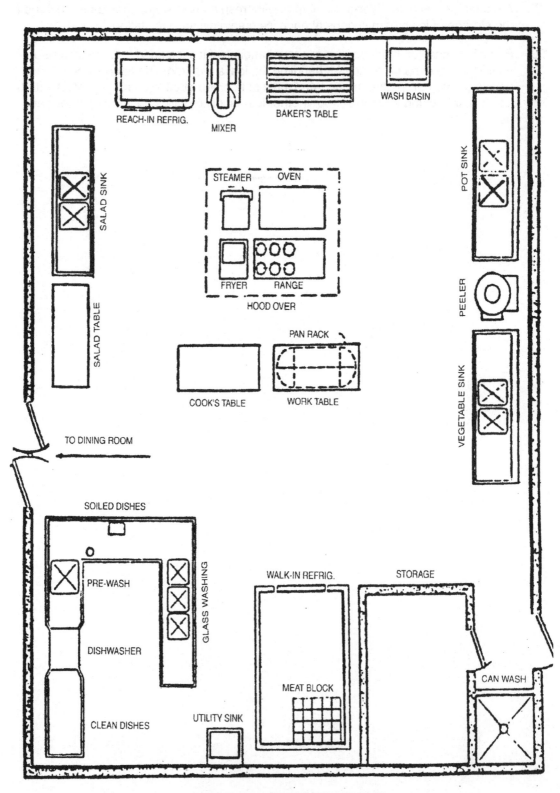

LAYOUT OF KITCHEN EQUIPMENT

COMPARISON OF KITCHEN LAY-OUTS

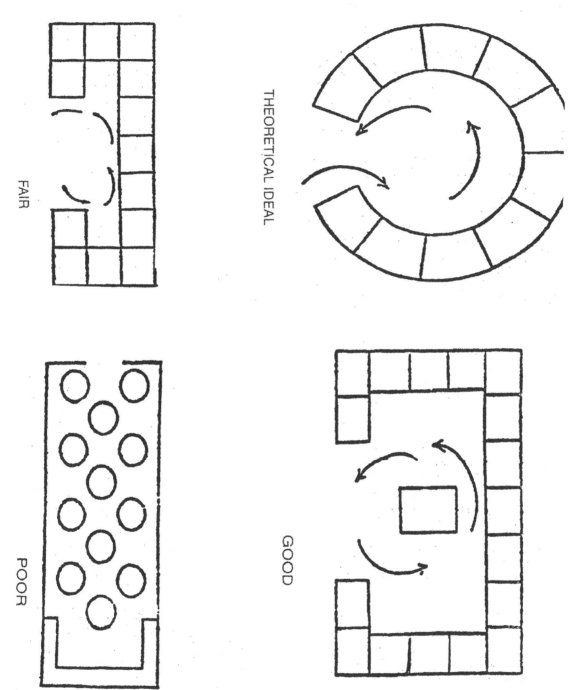

KITCHEN SAFETY
ACCIDENTS DON'T HAPPEN! THEY ARE CAUSED!

I. WHAT ARE THE COMMON ACCIDENTS?

1. Slips and Falls
2. Cuts
3. Burns
4. Bumps and Bruises
5. Electrical Shock
6. Overlifting

II. WHAT ARE THE CAUSES?

1. Inadequate Safety Instructions
2. Inadequate Maintenance
3. Carelessness
4. Haste
5. Employee Resistance to Training
6. Inadequate Equipment
7. Short Cuts
8. Improper Shoes
        SAFETY
    RULES AND
        REGULATIONS

III. HOW CAN THEY BE PREVENTED

1. Good Management Attitude
2. Proper Employee Training
3. Good Equipment
4. Proper Construction
5. Excellent Housekeeping
6. Correct Traffic Patterns

GOOD
    MAINTENANCE

HAVE FIRST AID FACILITIES AVAILABLE AND BE PREPARED TO PROVIDE AID!!

_____

FOOD PURCHASING GUIDE

TABLE OF CONTENTS

Page

FOOD PURCHASING GUIDE FOR GROUP FEEDING

INTRODUCTION

This food purchasing guide contains information useful in estimating the number of purchase units of foods to buy to serve a specific number of portions.

Foods have been listed by major groups in tables 1 through 21. Within each group the individual foods are arranged alphabetically. For each purchase unit specified, these data are given: Weight of the unit of purchase, yield from weight "as purchased" to weight "as served," size and description of portion, number of portions from each purchase unit, and the approximate number of purchase units needed for 25 and 100 portions. Table 22 presents an easy method for computing the number of purchase units needed for portions of sizes other than those given in tables 1 through 21. Table 23 gives an easy method for finding the cost of a portion of food.

The yields of edible meat from the carcass of wholesale cuts of beef, lamb, and pork given in tables 24 to 26 are useful to institutions that raise their own meat animals or purchase meat by the carcass or wholesale cuts. The yields of canned and frozen products from fresh vegetables and fruits given in table 27 are useful to institutions that produce and preserve their own vegetables and fruits.

Table 28 gives the common can and jar sizes, and on page 48 equivalents used frequently by food planners are given.

EXPLANATION OF TERMS USED

Food as purchased. Foods are described in the forms as purchased—fresh, frozen, canned, dried. Further descriptive information that would affect the yield is also given, such as: for meats—bone in, bone out; for carrots—with tops, without tops; and for potatoes—to be pared, ready-to-cook.

Unit of purchase. Sizes of cans, packages, or other containers and weights of units in common use in the wholesale and retail markets are given. Usually, data for the 1-pound unit are given; from these the yield of any weight purchase unit can be determined.

Weight per unit. Weights given for purchase units refer to weights as purchased on the market. Legal weights for contents of such units as bushels, lugs, crates, and boxes may vary in different States. The lowest of these weights is used to insure that the specified portions can be obtained.

Weights for canned goods are the same as those given as net weight on the label.

Yield as served. Yield as served refers to the weight of food "as served" as a percentage of weight "as purchased." Absence of information in this column means a weight yield was not used to determine the number of portions per purchase unit.

The same item "as purchased" may have more than one yield, depending on the way it is served.

For example, 1 pound of fresh carrots without tops will yield 0.75 pound cooked and 0.82 pound grated raw.

The yield does not always refer to a serving that is all edible. For example, because pork chops are usually served with bone, the yield given is the percentage of the "as purchased" weight represented by the cooked chop with the bone in. On the other hand, the yield of the chuck roast, usually served without bone, is, the percentage of the chuck "as purchased" that is, cooked and served without the bone. For meats, the yield of cooked lean is given in an additional column.

The amount of ready-to-serve food obtained from a given amount of food "as purchased" may vary widely, depending on the size, grade, and general condition of the food, discards in preparation, and the method and time of cooking. For yields given in this Handbook, it is assumed that the food used is in good condition (free of rot, insect infestation, bruising), that only usual amounts are discarded in preparation, and that usual cooking methods and time of cooking for the food specified are used.

For yields given, discard of inedible material such as bones, pits, and shells, except where otherwise specified, is assumed. Also assumed as discard are some foods that could be eaten but are usually discarded, such as potato parings and outer leaves of vegetables.

The yields presented in these tables were obtained from Agriculture Handbook No. 102, "Food Yields Summarized by Different Stages of Preparation," and unpublished data from the Agricultural Research Service of the U.S. Department of Agriculture and from the Fish and Wildlife Service of the U.S. Department of the Interior. Yields for commercially prepared meat combinations (table 2) are based on minimum meat requirements for meat food products packed for interstate shipment under Federal inspection. Contents of cooked poultry meat in poultry products are based on regulations governing the inspection of poultry and poultry products, effective January 1, 1965.

Size and description of portion. Weight or volume of portion commonly used is given. This portion for most foods refers to the amount served. For foods often used in combination with other foods, such as canned milk, nonfat dry milk, eggs, nuts, flour, and uncooked cereals, a portion refers to a measure commonly called for in institution recipes.

For meat, poultry, and fish, data for two sizes of portions are given. The larger portion may be appropriate for an adult serving; the smaller may be sufficient for a child's meal or a luncheon menu. The size of meat portions is given (1) in ounces of cooked meat as served including fat and, in some cases, bone; and (2) in ounces of conked lean only.

For vegetables and fruits, the portion size is generally the weight of 1/2 cup rounded to the nearest ounce. It is assumed that canned, cooked fresh, and cooked dried fruits are served with sirup, and that heated canned vegetables and cooked fresh and frozen vegetables are served drained. It is assumed that solid-pack fruits are served without liquid.

Institutions that use a different portion size than those given may adjust the amount to purchase by the method given in table 22.

Portions per purchase unit. In obtaining the portions per purchase unit or the yield of a purchase unit in portions, average quantities of refuse and usual weight losses in cooking are assumed. The number of portions may vary from that shown if the condition of the food purchased is poor or unusual waste occurs in preparation and cooking.

To obtain the number of units to purchase, the number of portions per purchase unit can be divided into the number of persons to be served. This may be the most practical method of computing the amount to purchase if the institution does not serve 25 or 100 persons or easy multiples of these numbers of persons.

For example, if 1 pound of meat will serve 2.57 portions of the size desired, the food manager of an institution serving 580 persons may divide 580 by 2.57 to get the amount of meat needed 226 pounds. It is because of such use of these figures, and not because the figures represent this degree of accuracy, that they have been carried to the nearest one-hundredth of a portion. Had the portions per pound of meat been rounded to the nearest number of portions per pound (3), the food manager would purchase only 193 pounds of meat—33 pounds short of the best estimate of his needs.

The number of portions per purchase unit can be used with the cost of the purchase unit and table 23 in obtaining the cost for one portion.

Approximate purchase units for 25 and 100 portions. These columns represent 25 and 100 divided by the number of portions per purchase unit in the preceding column. The resulting number of purchase units is always carried to the next even one-quarter (1/4) unit. Thus, the number of purchase units specified is always sufficient if the yield and portion size are as shown in the table. If the purchase units serve many portions, such as a bushel of apples or a No. 10 can of vegetables, this 1/4 purchase unit may be very significant. If the purchase unit serves few portions as in the case of a pound of meat, the 1/4 purchase unit is relatively unimportant.

QUANTITIES TO PURCHASE FOR 25 AND 100 PORTIONS

Table 1.—MEAT

Meat as purchased	Unit of purchase	Yield, cooked: As served	Yield, cooked: Lean only	Description of portion as served	Size of portion: As served	Size of portion: Lean only	Portions per purchase unit	Approximate purchase units for— 25 portions	Approximate purchase units for— 100 portions
BEEF, FRESH OR FROZEN									
		Percent	*Percent*		*Ounces*	*Ounces*	*Number*	*Number*	*Number*
Brisket: Corned, bone out	Pound	60	41	Simmered	4	2.8	2.40	10½	41¾
					3	2.1	3.20	8	31¼
Fresh: Bone in	do	52	36	Simmered, bone out	4	2.8	2.08	12¼	48¼
					3	2.1	2.77	9¼	36¼
Bone out	do	67	46	Simmered	4	2.8	2.68	9½	37½
					3	2.1	3.57	7¼	28¼
Ground beef: Lean	do	75	75	Broiled	3	3.0	4.00	6¼	25
					2	2.0	6.00	4¼	16¾
Regular	do	72	72	Pan-fried	3	3.0	3.84	6¾	26¼
					2	2.0	5.76	4½	17½
Heart	do	39	39		2	2.0	3.12	8¼	32¼
Kidney	do	39	39		2	2.0	3.12	8¼	32¼
Liver	do	69	69	Braised	3	3.0	3.68	7	27¼
					2	2.0	5.52	4¾	18¼
Oxtails	do	29	29		(1)	(1)	(1)	(1)	(1)
Roasts: **Chuck:** Bone in	do	52	42	Roasted, moist heat, bone out	4	3.2	2.08	12¼	48¼
					3	2.4	2.77	9¼	36¼
Bone out	do	67	54	Roasted, moist heat	4	3.2	2.68	9½	37½
					3	2.4	3.57	7¼	28¼
7-Rib (shortribs removed): Bone in	do	65	42	Roasted, dry heat, bone out	4	2.6	2.60	9¾	38½
					3	1.9	3.47	7¼	29
Bone out	do	73	47	Roasted, dry heat	4	2.6	2.92	8¾	34¼
					3	1.9	3.89	6½	25¾
Round: Bone in	do	69	56	Roasted, dry heat, medium, bone out	4	3.3	2.76	9¼	36¼
					3	2.5	3.68	7	27¼
Bone out	do	73	60	Roasted, dry heat, medium	4	3.3	2.92	8¾	34¼
					3	2.5	3.89	6½	25¾
Rump: Bone in	do	58	43	Roasted, dry heat, bone out	4	3.0	2.32	11	43¼
					3	2.2	3.09	8¼	32½
Bone out	do	73	55	Roasted, dry heat	4	3.0	2.92	8¾	34¼
					3	2.2	3.89	6½	25¾
Shortribs	do	67	32	Braised, bone in	6	2.9	1.79	14	56
					4	1.9	2.68	9½	37½

See footnotes at end of table.

TABLE 1.—MEAT—Continued

Meat as purchased	Unit of purchase	Yield, cooked: As served	Yield, cooked: Lean only	Description of portion as served	Size of portion: As served	Size of portion: Lean only	Portions per purchase unit	Approximate purchase units for— 25 portions	Approximate purchase units for— 100 portions
BEEF, FRESH OR FROZEN—Continued									
Steaks:									
Club:		*Percent*	*Percent*		*Ounces*	*Ounces*	*Number*	*Number*	*Number*
Bone in	Pound	73	33	Broiled, bone in	6	2.7	1.95	13	51½
					4	1.8	2.92	8¾	34¼
Bone out	do	73	42	Broiled	4	2.3	2.92	8¾	34¼
					3	1.7	3.89	6½	25¾
Flank	do	67	67	Braised	3	3.0	3.57	7¼	28¼
					2	2.0	5.36	4¾	18¾
Hip:									
Bone in	do	73	32	Broiled, bone in	6	2.6	1.95	13	51½
					4	1.8	2.92	8¾	34¼
Bone out	do	73	40	Broiled	4	2.2	2.92	8¾	34¼
					3	1.6	3.89	6½	25¾
Minute, cubed	do	75	75	Pan-fried	3	3.0	4.00	6¼	25
					2	2.0	6.00	4¼	16¾
Porterhouse:									
Bone in	do	73	36	Broiled, bone in	8	4.0	1.46	17¼	68½
					6	3.0	1.95	13	51½
					4	2.0	2.92	8¾	34¼
Bone out	do	73	42	Broiled	4	2.3	2.92	8¾	34¼
					3	1.7	3.89	6½	25¾
Round:									
Bone in	do	73	56	Broiled, bone in	4	3.1	2.92	8¾	34¼
					3	2.3	3.89	6½	25¾
Bone out	do	73	60	Broiled	4	3.3	2.92	8¾	34¼
					3	2.5	3.89	6½	25¾
Sirloin (wedge and round):									
Bone in	do	73	44	Broiled, bone in	6	3.6	1.95	13	51½
					4	2.4	2.92	8¾	34¼
Bone out	do	73	48	Broiled	4	2.6	2.92	8¾	34¼
					3	2.0	3.89	6½	25¾
T-bone:									
Bone in	do	73	34	Broiled, bone in	8	3.8	1.46	17¼	68½
					6	2.8	1.95	13	51½
					4	1.9	2.92	8¾	34¼
Bone out	do	73	41	Broiled	4	2.2	2.92	8¾	34¼
					3	1.7	3.89	6½	25¾
Stew meat (chuck), bone out	do	67	54	Cooked, moist heat	3	2.4	3.57	7¼	28¼
					2	1.6	5.36	4¾	18¾
Tongue:									
Fresh	do	59	59	do	3	3.0	3.15	8	31¾
					2	2.0	4.72	5½	21¼
Smoked	do	51	51	do	3	3.0	2.72	9¼	37
					2	2.0	4.08	6¼	24½

BEEF, CANNED[2]									
Beef, corned	do	100	100	Heated	3	3.0	5.33	4¾	19
					2	2.0	8.00	3¼	12½
	6-pound can	100	100	do	3	3.0	32.00	1	3¼
BEEF, DRIED									
Beef, chipped	Pound	125	125	Cooked, moist heat	3	3.0	6.67	3¾	15
					2	2.0	10.00	2½	10
LAMB, FRESH OR FROZEN									
Chops:									
Loin	do	76	41	Broiled, bone in	5.0	2.7	2.43	10½	41¼
Rib	do	76	34	do	5.0	2.2	2.43	10½	41¼
Shoulder	do	70	41	do	5.0	2.9	2.24	11¼	44¾
Ground lamb	do	68	68	Broiled patties	3.0	3.0	3.63	7	27¾
					2.0	2.0	5.44	4½	18½
Roasts:									
Leg:									
Bone in	do	54	45	Roasted, bone out	4.0	3.3	2.16	11½	46½
					3.0	2.5	2.88	8¾	34¾
Bone out	do	70	58	Roasted	4.0	3.3	2.80	9	35¾
					3.0	2.5	3.73	6¾	27
Shoulder:									
Bone in	do	55	41	Roasted, bone out	4.0	3.0	2.20	11½	45½
					3.0	2.2	2.93	8¾	34¼
Bone out	do	70	52	Roasted	4.0	3.0	2.80	9	35¾
					3.0	2.2	3.73	6¾	27
Stew meat,[3] bone out	do	66	----	Simmered	3.0	----	3.52	7¼	28½
					2.0	----	5.28	4¾	19
PORK, CURED (MILD)									
Bacon (24 slices per pound)	do	32	----	Fried or broiled	2 slices	----	12.00	2½	8½
Canadian bacon	do	63	63	Broiled, sliced	2	2.0	5.04	5	20
					1	1.0	10.08	2½	10
Ham:									
Bone in	do	67	54	Roasted, slices and pieces	4	2.9	2.68	9½	37½
					3	2.2	3.57	7¼	28¼
	do	56	44	Roasted, slices	4	2.4	2.24	11¼	44¾
					3	1.8	2.99	8½	33½
Bone out	do	77	72	Roasted, slices and pieces	4	2.9	3.08	8¼	32½
					3	2.2	4.11	6¼	24½
	do	64	60	Roasted, slices	4	2.4	2.56	10	39¼
					3	1.8	3.41	7½	29½
Ground	do	77	77	Patties	3	3.0	4.11	6¼	24½
					2	2.0	6.16	4¼	16¼
Shoulder, Boston butt:									
Bone in	do	67	52	Roasted, bone out	4	3.1	2.68	9½	37½
					3	2.3	3.57	7¼	28¼
Bone out	do	74	58	Roasted	4	3.1	2.96	8½	34
					3	2.3	3.95	6½	25½
Shoulder, picnic:									
Bone in	do	56	41	Roasted, bone out	4	3.9	2.24	11¼	44¾
					3	2.2	2.99	8½	33½
Bone out	do	74	53	Roasted	4	3.9	2.96	8½	34
					3	2.2	3.95	6½	25½

See footnotes at end of table.

TABLE 1.—MEAT—Continued

Meat as purchased	Unit of purchase	Yield, cooked		Description of portion as served	Size of portion		Portions per purchase unit	Approximate purchase units for—	
		As served	Lean only		As served	Lean only		25 portions	100 portions
PORK, FRESH		*Percent*	*Percent*		*Ounces*	*Ounces*	*Number*	*Number*	*Number*
Chops:									
Loin	Pound	69	42	Broiled, bone in	5	3.0	2.21	11½	45¼
					3	1.8	3.68	7	27¼
Rib	do	70	37	do	5	2.6	2.24	11¼	44¾
					3	1.6	3.73	6¾	27
Cutlet, tenderloin	do	75	75	Broiled	3	3.0	4.00	6¼	25
					2	2.0	6.00	4¼	16¾
Ground pork	do	57	57	do	3	3.0	3.04	8¼	33
					2	2.0	4.56	5½	22
Liver	do	60	60	Pan- or oven-fried	3	3.0	3.20	8	31¼
					2	2.0	4.80	5¼	21
Roasts:									
Ham:									
Bone in	do	54	40	Roasted, bone out	4	3.0	2.16	11¾	46½
					3	2.2	2.88	8¾	34¾
Bone out	do	68	50	Roasted	4	3.0	2.72	9¼	37
					3	2.2	3.63	7	27¾
Loin:									
Bone in	do	68	37	Roasted, bone in	5	2.8	2.18	11½	46
					4	2.2	2.72	9¼	37
	do	47	37	Roasted, bone out	4	3.2	1.88	13½	53¼
					3	2.4	2.51	10	40
Bone out	do	68	54	Roasted	4	3.2	2.72	9¼	37
					3	2.4	3.63	7	27¾
Shoulder, Boston butt:									
Bone in	do	62	49	Roasted, bone out	4	3.2	2.48	10¼	40½
					3	2.4	3.31	7¾	30¼
Bone out	do	68	54	Roasted	4	3.2	2.72	9¼	37
					3	2.4	3.63	7	27¾
Shoulder, picnic:									
Bone in	do	47	35	Simmered, bone out	4	3.0	1.88	13½	53¼
					3	2.2	2.51	10	40
Bone out	do	64	47	Simmered	4	3.0	2.56	10	39¼
					3	2.2	3.41	7½	29½
Sausage:									
Brown and serve	do	81	81	Heated	3	3.0	4.32	6	23¼
					2	2.0	6.48	4	15½
Bulk or link	do	48	48	Oven-fried	3	3.0	2.56	10	39¼
					2	2.0	3.84	6¾	26¼
Spareribs	do	66	26	Braised, bone in	6	[4] 2.3	1.76	14¼	57
					4	[4] 1.6	2.64	9½	38
PORK, CANNED [5]									
Ham, chopped	do	100	100	Sliced	3	3.0	5.33	4¾	19
					2	2.0	8.00	3¼	12½

Ham, smoked	do	77	75	Slices and pieces	3	2.9	4.11	6¼	24½
					2	1.9	6.16	4¼	16¼
	do	73	71	Slices	3	2.9	3.89	6½	25¾
					2	1.9	5.84	4¼	17¼
Pork luncheon meat (with natural juices).	do	89	89	Unheated	3	3.0	4.75	5½	21¼
					2	2.0	7.12	3¾	14¼
SAUSAGES									
Frankfurters:									
8 per pound	do	98		2 frankfurters			4.00	6¼	25
				1 frankfurter			8.00	3¼	12½
10 per pound	do	98		2 frankfurters			5.00	5	20
				1 frankfurter			10.00	2½	10
Luncheon meats (all meat varieties).	do	100	100		3	3.0	5.33	4¾	19
					2	2.0	8.00	3¼	12½
Vienna sausage (all meat)	Pound (drained weight).	100	100	About 4 sausages	2	2.0	8.00	3¼	12½
				About 2 sausages	1	1.0	16.00	1¾	6¼
VEAL, FRESH OR FROZEN									
Chops:									
Loin	Pound	78	47	Broiled, bone in	5	3.0	2.50	10	40
					3	1.8	4.16	6	24¼
Rib	do	69	38	do	5	2.8	2.21	11½	45¼
					3	1.6	3.68	7	27¼
Shoulder	do	66	40	do	5	3.0	2.11	12	47½
					3	1.8	3.52	7¼	28½
Cutlet, bone out	do	75	75	Broiled	4	3.0	3.00	8½	33½
					3	2.2	4.00	6¼	25
Ground	do	64	64	Oven- or pan-fried	3	3.0	3.41	7½	29½
					2	2.0	5.12	5	19¾
Heart	do	35	35	Braised	2	2.0	2.80	9	35¾
Liver, calf	do	58	58	Fried or braised	3	3.0	3.09	8¼	32½
					2	2.0	4.64	5½	21¾
Roasts:									
Chuck (shoulder):									
Bone in	do	46	40	Braised, bone out	4	3.4	1.84	13¾	54½
					3	2.6	2.45	10¼	41
Bone out	do	66	56	Braised	4	3.4	2.64	9½	38
					3	2.6	3.52	7¼	28½
Leg:									
Bone in	do	44	36	Roasted, bone out	4	3.3	1.76	14¼	57
					3	2.5	2.35	10¾	42¾
Bone out	do	66	54	Roasted	4	3.3	2.64	9½	38
					3	2.5	3.52	7¼	28½
Plate (breast):									
Bone in	do	45	33	Stewed, bone out	4	2.9	1.80	14	55¾
					3	2.2	2.40	10½	41¾
Bone out	do	66	48	Stewed	4	2.9	2.64	9½	38
					3	2.2	3.52	7¼	28½
Stew meat	do	66	48	do	4	2.9	2.64	9½	38
					3	2.2	3.52	7¼	28½

[1] Size of portion and number of portions per purchase unit are determined by use.
[2] For combination foods including beef, see p. 8.
[3] Breast, flank.
[4] Fat and lean.
[5] For combination foods including pork, see p. 8.

TABLE 2.—COMBINATION FOODS CONTAINING MEAT

Meat combinations, canned or frozen, as purchased	Unit of purchase	Weight per unit [1]	Cooked meat	Size of portion	Meat in portion	Portions per purchase unit	Approximate purchase units for— 25 portions	Approximate purchase units for— 100 portions
		Pounds	*Percent*	*Ounces*	*Ounces*	*Number*	*Number*	*Number*
Beans with frankfurters in sauce	Pound	1.00	20	8	1.6	2.00	12½	50
	No. 3 cylinder	3.12	20	8	1.6	6.24	4¼	16¼
	No. 10 can	6.75	20	8	1.6	13.50	2	7½
Beans with ham in sauce	Pound	1.00	12	8	1.0	2.00	12½	50
	No. 3 cylinder	3.19	12	8	1.0	6.38	4	15¾
Beans with meat in chili sauce	Pound	1.00	8	8	.6	2.00	12½	50
	No. 10 can	6.50	8	8	.6	13.00	2	7¾
Beef goulash:								
Canned	Pound	1.00	18	8	1.4	2.00	12½	50
	No. 3 cylinder	3.12	18	8	1.4	6.24	4¼	16¼
Frozen	Carton	5.00	18	8	1.4	10.00	2½	10
	do	6.75	18	9	1.6	12.00	2¼	8½
	do	8.25	18	11	2.0	12.00	2¼	8½
Beef stew	Pound	1.00	18	8	1.4	2.00	12½	50
	No. 3 cylinder	3.12	18	8	1.4	6.24	4¼	16¼
	No. 10 can	6.62	18	8	1.4	13.24	2	7¾
Beef with barbecue sauce	Pound	1.00	50	6	3.0	2.67	9½	37½
	No. 3 cylinder	3.25	50	6	3.0	8.67	3	11¾
	No. 10 can	6.50	50	6	3.0	17.33	1½	6
Beef with gravy	Pound	1.00	50	6	3.0	2.67	9½	37½
	No. 3 cylinder	3.00	50	6	3.0	8.00	3¼	12¾
	No. 10 can	6.50	50	6	3.0	17.33	1½	6
Brunswick stew	Pound	1.00	18	8	1.4	2.00	12½	50
	No. 10 can	6.62	18	8	1.4	13.24	2	7¾
Chili con carne	Pound	1.00	28	8	2.2	2.00	12½	50
	No. 3 cylinder	3.19	28	8	2.2	6.38	4	15¾
	No. 10 can	6.75	28	8	2.2	13.50	2	7½
Chili con carne with beans	Pound	1.00	18	8	1.4	2.00	12½	50
	No. 3 cylinder	3.19	18	8	1.4	6.38	4	15¾
	No. 10 can	6.75	18	8	1.4	13.50	2	7½
Chili mac	Pound	1.00	18	8	1.4	2.00	12½	50
	No. 3 cylinder	3.19	18	8	1.4	6.38	4	15¾
	No. 10 can	6.50	18	8	1.4	13.00	2	7¾

Chop suey or chow mein vegetables with meat:								
Canned	Pound	1.00	8	8	.6	2.00	12½	50
	No. 3 cylinder	3.06	8	8	.6	6.12	4¼	16½
Frozen	Carton	5.00	8	8	.6	10.00	2½	10
Hash, corn beef, roast beef, beef	Pound	1.00	35	7	2.4	2.29	11¼	44¼
	No. 3 cylinder	3.19	35	7	2.4	7.29	3½	14
	No. 10 can	6.50	35	7	2.4	14.86	1¾	7
Lamb stew	Pound	1.00	18	8	1.4	2.00	12½	50
	No. 3 cylinder	3.19	18	8	1.4	6.38	4	15¾
	No. 10 can	6.62	18	8	1.4	13.24	2	7¾
Macaroni and beef in tomato sauce	Pound	1.00	8	8	.6	2.00	12½	50
	No. 10 can	6.50	8	8	.6	13.00	2	7¾
Meatballs with gravy:								
Canned	Pound	1.00 (10 count)	38	6	2.3 (4 count)	2.67	9½	37½
	No. 10 can	6.50 (70 count)	38	6	2.3 (4 count)	17.33	1½	6
Frozen	Carton	8.00 (160 count)	38	6	2.3 (7½ count)	21.33	1¼	5
	do	10.00 (100 count)	38	6	2.3 (4 count)	26.67	1	4
Pork with barbecue sauce:								
Canned	Pound	1.00	50	6	3.0	2.67	9½	37½
	No. 3 cylinder	3.19	50	6	3.0	8.51	3	12
	No. 10 can	6.62	50	6	3.0	17.65	1½	5¾
In waxed tub (perishable)	4-pound tub	4.00	50	6	3.0	10.67	2⅜	9½
	5-pound tub	5.00	50	6	3.0	13.33	2	7¾
Pork with gravy	Pound	1.00	50	6	3.0	2.67	9½	37½
	No. 3 cylinder	3.12	50	6	3.0	8.32	3¼	12¼
	No. 10 can	6.50	50	6	3.0	17.33	1½	6
Ravioli with meat in sauce	Pound	1.00	7	8	.6	2.00	12½	50
	No. 3 cylinder	3.19	7	8	.6	6.38	4	15¾
		3.62	7	8	.6	7.24	3½	14
Spaghetti with meatballs and sauce	Pound	1.00	8	8	.6	2.00	12½	50
	No. 3 cylinder	3.19	8	8	.6	6.38	4	15¾
	No. 10 can	6.62	8	8	.6	13.24	2	7¾
Tamales, frozen	Pound	1.00 (4 tamales)	18	8 (2 tamales)	1.4	2.00	12½	50
	Carton	6.00 (24 tamales)	18	8 (2 tamales)	1.4	12.00	2¼	8½
	do	18.00	18	8	1.4	36.00	(2)	3
Tamales with gravy or sauce (Packed in sizes from 1½ oz. to 6 oz. per tamale).	Pound	1.00	14	8	1.1	2.00	12½	50
	No. 10 can	6.50	14	8	1.1	13.00	2	7¾

[1] Net weights of containers are not standardized and may vary depending on establishment preparing the product.
[2] Number of purchase units needed is less than one.

Table 3.—POULTRY

Poultry as purchased	Unit of purchase	Yield, as served	Description of portion as served	Size of portion: As served	Size of portion: Edible portion [1]	Portions per purchase unit	Approximate purchase units for—: 25 portions	Approximate purchase units for—: 100 portions
CHICKEN, FRESH OR FROZEN								
Live:		*Percent*		*Ounces*	*Ounces*	*Number*	*Number*	*Number*
Roasters	Pound	30	Boned, excludes neck and giblets.	3.0	3.0	1.60	15¾	62½
				2.0	2.0	2.40	10½	41¾
Stewers	do	34	Boned, includes neck and giblets.	3.0	3.0	1.81	14	55¼
				2.0	2.0	2.72	9¼	37
Ready-to-cook:								
Broilers	1½-pound bird	70	½ bird	8.3	5.4	2.00	12½	50
Fryers	Pound [2]	43	Boned	3.0	3.0	2.29	11	43¾
				2.0	2.0	3.44	7½	29¼
	2½-pound bird	65	¼ bird	5.8	3.9	4.00	6¼	25
			⅙ bird	3.9	2.6	6.00	4¼	16¾
			⅛ bird	2.9	1.9	8.00	3¼	12½
Parts (from 2½-pound bird):								
Breast half	Pound	67	With bone	3.2	2.6	3.35	7½	30
Drumstick	do	72	do	2.1	1.4	5.49	4¾	18¼
Thigh	do	68	do	2.2	1.6	4.95	5¼	20¼
Drumstick and thigh	do	70	do	4.3	3.1	2.60	9¾	38½
Wing	do	64	do	1.6	0.8	6.40	4	15¾
Back	do	49	do	2.5	1.3	3.14	8	32
Rib	do	65	do	2.5	1.3	4.16	6¼	24¼
Giblets:								
Gizzards	do	26		2	2	2.08	12¼	48¼
Hearts	do	38		2	2	3.04	8¼	33
Livers	do	65		2	2	5.20	5	19¼
Roasters	do	42	Boned, excludes neck and giblets.	3	3	2.24	11¼	44¾
				2	2	3.36	7½	30
Stewers	do	47	Boned, includes neck and giblets.	3	3	2.51	10	40
				2	2	3.76	6¾	26¾
CHICKEN, CANNED								
Boned	do	90	Meat	3	3	4.80	5¼	21
				2	2	7.20	3½	14
	Can (35 ounces)	90	do	3	3	10.50	2¼	9¾
				2	2	15.75	1¾	6½
Boned, solid pack	Pound	95	do	3	3	5.07	5	19¾
				2	2	7.60	3½	13¼

Boned, with broth	do	80	do	3	3	4.27	6	23½
				2	2	6.40	4	15¾
Whole	do	32	do	3	3	1.71	14¾	58½
				2	2	2.56	10	39¼
TURKEY, FRESH OR FROZEN								
Live	do	36	Excludes neck and giblets	3	3	1.92	13¼	52¼
				2	2	2.88	8¾	34¾
Ready-to-cook:								
Roasters	do	47	do	3	3	2.51	10	40
				2	2	3.76	6¾	26¾
Parts:								
Breasts, whole	do	60		3	3	3.20	8	31¼
				2	2	4.80	5¼	21
Legs (thigh and drumstick)	do	48		3	3	2.56	10	39¼
				2	2	3.84	6¾	26¼
Giblets:								
Gizzards	do	34		2	2	2.72	9¼	37
Hearts	do	38		2	2	3.04	8¼	33
Livers	do	67		2	2	5.36	4¾	18¾
TURKEY, FROZEN ONLY								
Stuffed, whole	do	33	Boned meat	3	3	1.76	14¼	57
				2	2	2.64	9½	38
Rolls, precooked	do	92	Meat	3	3	4.91	5¼	20½
				2	2	7.36	3½	13¾
Rolls, ready-to-cook	do	61	do	3	3	3.25	7¾	31
				2	2	4.88	5¼	20½
TURKEY, CANNED								
Boned	do	90	do	3	3	4.80	5¼	21
				2	2	7.20	3½	14
	Can (35 ounces)	90	do	3	3	10.50	2½	9¾
				2	2	15.75	1¾	6½
Boned, solid pack	Pound	95	do	3	3	5.07	5	19¾
				2	2	7.60	3½	13¼
Boned, with broth	do	80	do	3	3	4.27	6	23½
				2	2	6.40	4	15¾
OTHER POULTRY, FRESH OR FROZEN								
Duck, ready-to-cook	do	38	Boned, excludes neck and giblets.	3	3	2.03	12½	49½
				2	2	3.04	8¼	33
Goose, ready-to-cook	do	39	do	3	3	2.08	12¼	48¼
				2	2	3.12	8¼	32¼

[1] Includes edible skin.

[2] Based on 2½-pound bird as purchased; neck and giblets not served.

TABLE 4.—COMBINATION FOODS CONTAINING POULTRY

Poultry combinations, canned or frozen, as purchased	Unit of purchase [1]	Weight per unit	Cooked meat	Size of portion	Meat in portion	Portions per purchase unit	Approximate purchase units for—	
							25 portions	100 portions
		Pounds	Percent	Ounces	Ounces	Number	Number	Number
Chicken a la king	Pound	1.00	20	8	1.60	2.00	12½	50
Chickenburgers	do	1.00	100	3	3.00	5.33	4¾	19
Chicken cacciatore	do	1.00	20	8	1.60	2.00	12½	50
Chicken chop suey	do	1.00	4	8	.32	2.00	12½	50
Chicken chow mein	do	1.00	4	8	.32	2.00	12½	50
Chicken fricassee	do	1.00	20	8	1.60	2.00	12½	50
Chicken noodles or dumplings	do	1.00	15	8	1.20	2.00	12½	50
Chicken potpie	do	1.00	14	8	1.12	2.00	12½	50
Chicken stew	do	1.00	12	8	.96	2.00	12½	50
Chicken tamales	do	1.00	6	8	.48	2.00	12½	50
Creamed chicken	do	1.00	20	8	1.60	2.00	12½	50
Creamed turkey	do	1.00	20	8	1.60	2.00	12½	50
Minced chicken barbecue	do	1.00	40	3	1.20	5.33	4¾	19
Noodles or dumplings with chicken	do	1.00	6	8	.48	2.00	12½	50
Sliced chicken with gravy	do	1.00	35	6	2.10	2.67	9½	37½
Sliced turkey with gravy	do	1.00	35	6	2.10	2.67	9½	37½
Turkey a la king	do	1.00	20	8	1.60	2.00	12½	50
Turkey fricassee	do	1.00	20	8	1.60	2.00	12½	50
Turkey potpie	do	1.00	14	8	1.12	2.00	12½	50

[1] There is no standardization of can or carton sizes for canned and frozen poultry products. Information given for a pound may be related to the weight of the contents of the can or carton.

TABLE 5.—FISH AND SHELLFISH

Fish and shellfish as purchased	Unit of purchase	Weight per unit	Yield, as served	Portion as served	Portions per purchase unit	Approximate purchase units for— 25 portions	100 portions
FISH, CANNED		*Pounds*	*Percent*		*Number*	*Number*	*Number*
Gefiltefish	16-ounce can (9¼ ounces drained).	1.00	58	3 ounces drained	3.08	8¼	32½
				2 ounces drained	4.62	5½	21¾
	32-ounce can (20½ ounces drained).	2.00	64	3 ounces drained	6.83	3¾	14¾
				2 ounces drained	10.25	2½	10
	51-ounce can (39 ounces drained).	3.19	76	3 ounces drained	13.00	2	7¾
				2 ounces drained	19.50	1⅓	5¼
Mackerel	15-ounce can (12½ ounces drained).	.94	83	3 ounces drained	4.17	6	24
				2 ounces drained	6.25	4	16
Salmon	3¾-ounce can (2¼ ounces drained).	.23	60	2¼ ounces drained	1.00	25	100
	16-ounce can (13 ounces drained).	1.00	81	3 ounces drained	4.33	6	23¼
				2 ounces drained	6.50	4	15½
	64-ounce can (50 ounces drained).	4.00	78	3 ounces drained	16.67	1½	6
				2 ounces drained	25.00	1	4
Sardines:							
Maine	3¾- to 4-ounce can (3¾ ounces drained).	.23 to .25	100	3 ounces drained	1.25	20	80
				2 ounces drained	1.87	13½	53½
	12-ounce can (10¾ ounces drained).	.75	90	3 ounces drained	3.58	7	28
				2 ounces drained	5.38	4¾	18¾
Pacific:							
In brine	15-ounce can (11½ ounces drained).	.94	77	3 ounces drained	3.83	6¾	26¼
				2 ounces drained	5.75	4½	17½
In mustard or tomato sauce	15-ounce can	.94	100	3 ounces	5.00	5	20
				2 ounces	7.50	3½	13⅓
Tuna	3½- to 4-ounce can (3¼ ounces drained).	.22 to .25	93	3¼ ounces drained	1.00	25	100
	6- to 7-ounce can (6 ounces drained).	.38 to .44	100	3 ounces drained	2.00	12½	50
				2 ounces drained	3.00	8½	33⅓
	60- to 66½-ounce can (58 ounces drained).	3.75 to 4.16	97	3 ounces drained	19.33	1½	5¼
				2 ounces drained	29.00	(1)	3½
FISH, DRIED							
Salt cod	Pound	1.00	72	3 ounces	3.84	6¾	26¼
				2 ounces	5.76	4½	17½
FISH, FRESH OR FROZEN							
Fillets	do	1.00	64	3 ounces	3.41	7½	29½
				2 ounces	5.12	5	19¾
Steaks (backbone in)	do	1.00	[2] 58	3 ounces	3.09	8¼	32½
				2 ounces	4.64	5½	21¾
Dressed (scaled and eviscerated, usually head, tail, and fins removed).	do	1.00	[2] 45	3 ounces	2.40	10½	41¾
				2 ounces	3.60	7	28
Drawn (entrails removed)	do	1.00	[2] 32	3 ounces	1.71	14¾	58½
				2 ounces	2.56	10	39¼
Whole, or round (as caught)	do	1.00	[2] 27	3 ounces	1.44	17½	69½
				2 ounces	2.16	11¾	46½

See footnotes at end of table.

TABLE 5.—FISH AND SHELLFISH—Continued

Fish and shellfish as purchased	Unit of purchase	Weight per unit	Yield, as served	Portion as served	Portions per purchase unit	Approximate purchase units for— 25 portions	100 portions
FISH, FROZEN							
Portions:							
Breaded, fried or raw:		*Pounds*	*Percent*		*Number*	*Number*	*Number*
5⅓-ounce	Pound	1.00	95	1 portion	3.00	8⅓	33⅓
4-ounce	do	1.00	95	do	4.00	6¼	25
3-ounce	do	1.00	95	do	5.33	4¾	18¾
2-ounce	do	1.00	95	do	8.00	3¼	12½
Unbreaded:							
4-ounce	do	1.00	69	do	4.00	6¼	25
3-ounce	do	1.00	69	do	5.33	4¾	18¾
2-ounce	do	1.00	68	do	8.00	3¼	12½
Sticks, breaded, fried or raw, 1-ounce	do	1.00	85	4 sticks	4.00	6¼	25
				3 sticks	5.33	4¾	18¾
				2 sticks	8.00	3¼	12½
SHELLFISH, CANNED							
Clam chowder	8-ounce can, ready-to-serve.	.50	100	8 ounces	1.00	25	100
	10½-ounce can, condensed.	.66	200	do	2.62	9¾	38¼
	15-ounce can, condensed	.94	200	do	3.75	6¾	26¾
	50- to 51-ounce can, condensed.	3.12 to 3.19	200	do	12.50	2	8
Clam juice	8-fluid-ounce can		100	3 fluid ounces	2.67	9½	37½
	12-fluid-ounce can		100	do	4.00	6¼	25
Clams, minced	7½-ounce can	.47	100	3 ounces	2.50	10	40
				2 ounces	3.75	6¾	26¾
	51-ounce can	3.19	100	3 ounces	17.00	1½	6
				2 ounces	25.50	1	4
Crabmeat	6½-ounce can (5½ ounces drained).	.41	85	3 ounces drained	1.83	13¾	54¾
				2 ounces drained	2.75	9¼	36½
Oysters, whole	5-ounce can (5 ounces drained).	.31	100	3 ounces drained	1.67	15	60
				2 ounces drained	2.50	10	40
Oyster stew	10½-ounce can, ready-to-serve.	.66	100	8 ounces	1.31	19¼	76½
Shrimp	4½-ounce can (4½ ounces drained).	.28	100	3 ounces drained	1.50	16¾	66¾
				2 ounces drained	2.25	11¼	44½
SHELLFISH, FRESH, LIVE IN SHELL							
Clams:							
Hard	Dozen		[2] 14	6 clams on half shell	2.00	12½	50
Soft	do		[2] 29	12 clams in the shell	1.00	25	100
Crabs:							
Blue	Pound	1.00	14	3 ounces cooked	.75	33½	133⅓
				2 ounces cooked	1.12	22½	89⅓
Dungeness	do	1.00	24	3 ounces cooked	1.28	19¾	78¼
				2 ounces cooked	1.92	13¼	52¼

FOOD PURCHASING GUIDE

Food	Purchase unit	Weight	Percent yield, edible portion	Size of serving	Servings per purchase unit	Purchase units for 25 servings	Purchase units for 100 servings
Oysters	Dozen	----	[2]12	6 oysters on half shell	2.00	12½	50
SHELLFISH, FRESH OR FROZEN							
Clams, shucked	Pound	1.00	48	{3 ounces meat	2.56	10	39½
				{2 ounces meat	3.82	6½	26
Crabs, cooked in shell:							
Blue	do	1.00	14	{3 ounces meat	.75	33⅓	133⅓
				{2 ounces meat	1.12	22¼	89¼
Dungeness	do	1.00	24	{3 ounces meat	1.28	19¾	78½
				{2 ounces meat	1.92	13¼	52¼
Crabmeat	do	1.00	97	{3 ounces	5.17	5	19½
				{2 ounces	7.76	3½	13
Lobster, cooked in shell	do	1.00	[2]25	{1 lobster	1.00	25	100
				{½ lobster	2.00	12½	50
Lobster meat	do	1.00	91	{3 ounces	4.85	5¼	20½
				{2 ounces	7.28	3½	13¾
Oysters, shucked	do	1.00	40	{3 ounces	2.13	11¾	47
				{2 ounces	3.20	8	31¼
Scallops, shucked	do	1.00	63	{3 ounces	3.36	7½	30
				{2 ounces	5.04	5	20
Shrimp:							
Cooked, peeled, cleaned	do	1.00	100	{3 ounces	5.33	4¾	19
				{2 ounces	8.00	3½	12½
Raw, in shell	do	1.00	50	{3 ounces meat	2.67	9½	37½
				{2 ounces meat	4.00	6¼	25
Raw, peeled	do	1.00	62	{3 ounces meat	3.30	7¾	30¼
				{2 ounces meat	4.96	5¼	20¾
SHELLFISH, FROZEN							
Clams, breaded:							
Fried	do	1.00	85	{3 ounces	4.53	5½	22½
				{2 ounces	6.80	3¾	14¾
Raw	do	1.00	83	{3 ounces	4.43	5¾	22½
				{2 ounces	6.64	4	15¾
Crabcakes, fried	do	1.00	95	{3 ounces	5.07	5	19¾
				{2 ounces	7.60	3½	13¾
Lobster, spiny tails:							
8 ounce	do	1.00	[2]51	1 tail	2.00	12½	50
6 ounce	do	1.00	[2]51	do	2.67	9½	37½
4 ounce	do	1.00	[2]51	do	4.00	6¼	25
Oysters, breaded, raw	do	1.00	88	{3 ounces	4.69	5¼	21¼
				{2 ounces	7.04	3¾	14¼
Scallops, breaded:							
Fried	do	1.00	93	{3 ounces	4.96	5¼	20¾
				{2 ounces	7.44	3½	13¾
Raw	do	1.00	81	{3 ounces	4.32	6	23¾
				{2 ounces	6.48	4	15¾
Shrimp, breaded:							
Fried	do	1.00	88	{3 ounces	4.69	5¼	21½
				{2 ounces	7.04	3¾	14¼
Raw	do	1.00	85	{3 ounces	4.53	5¼	22¼
				{2 ounces	6.80	3¾	14¼

[1] Number of purchase units needed is less than one.
[2] Yield, edible portion.

TABLE 6.—EGGS

Eggs, in shell, frozen, and dried, as purchased	Unit of purchase	Weight per unit	Portion as served or used	Portions per purchase unit	Approximate purchase units for— 25 portions	Approximate purchase units for— 100 portions
		Pounds		*Number*	*Number*	*Number*
In shell:						
Large	Dozen	1.50	1 egg	12.00	2¼	8½
	Case	45.00	do	360.00	(1)	(1)
Medium	Dozen	1.31	do	12.00	2¼	8⅓
	Case	39.50	do	360.00	(1)	(1)
Small	Dozen	1.12	do	12.00	2¼	8½
	Case	34.00	do	360.00	(1)	(1)
Frozen:						
Whole eggs	Pound	1.00	1 egg (3 tablespoons thawed)	10.00	(2)	(2)
			12 eggs (2¼ cups thawed)	.83	(2)	(2)
	Can	10.00	1 egg	100.00	(2)	(2)
	do	30.00	do	300.00	(2)	(2)
Egg yolks	Pound	1.00	1 yolk (1⅔ tablespoons thawed)	26.00	(2)	(2)
			12 yolks (1 cup thawed)	2.16	(2)	(2)
Egg whites	do	1.00	1 white (2 tablespoons thawed)	16.00	(2)	(2)
			12 whites (1½ cups thawed)	1.33	(2)	(2)
Dried:						
Whole eggs	do	1.00	1 large egg (½ ounce or 2½ tablespoons dried + 2½ tablespoons water).	32.00	(2)	(2)
			12 large eggs (6 ounces or 2 cups dried + 2 cups water).	2.67	(2)	(2)
	13-ounce package	.81	1 large egg	26.00	(2)	(2)
	No. 10 can	3.00	do	96.00	(2)	(2)
	Package	25.00	do	800.00	(2)	(2)
	do	50.00	do	1,600.00	(2)	(2)
Egg yolks	Pound	1.00	1 large yolk (2 tablespoons dried + 2 teaspoons water).	54.00	(2)	(2)
			12 large yolks (1½ cups dried + ½ cup water)	4.50	(2)	(2)
	Package	3.00	1 large yolk	162.00	(2)	(2)
Egg white, spray-dried	Pound	1.00	1 large white (2 teaspoons dried + 2 tablespoons water).	100.00	(2)	(2)
			12 large whites (½ cup dried + 1½ cups water)	8.33	(2)	(2)
	Package	3.00	1 large white	300.00	(2)	(2)

[1] Number of purchase units needed is less than one.

[2] Number of purchase units needed is determined by use.

TABLE 7.—NUTS

Nuts in shell and peanut butter as purchased	Unit of purchase	Weight per unit	Yield, as served	Portion as used	Portions per purchase unit	Approximate purchase units for—	
						25 portions	100 portions
		Pounds	*Percent*		*Number*	*Number*	*Number*
Almonds:							
Nonpareil (softshell)	Pound	1.00	60	1 cup (0.31 pound)	1.94	(¹)	(¹)
Peerless (hardshell)	do	1.00	35	do	1.13	(¹)	(¹)
Brazil nuts	do	1.00	48	do	1.55	(¹)	(¹)
Cashew nuts	do	1.00	22	1 cup (0.30 pound)	.73	(¹)	(¹)
Chestnuts	do	1.00	84	8 large nuts (0.11 pound)	7.64	(¹)	(¹)
Coconut:							
Dried	do	1.00	100	1 cup (0.14 pound)	7.14	(¹)	(¹)
Fresh, in shell	do	1.00	52	1 cup (0.21 pound)	2.48	(¹)	(¹)
Filberts	do	1.00	39	1 cup (0.30 pound)	1.50	(¹)	(¹)
Peanuts, roasted	do	1.00	68	1 cup (0.32 pound)	2.12	(¹)	(¹)
Peanut butter	No. 10 can	6.75	100	2 tablespoons (0.07 pound)	14.29	1¾	7
Pecans	Pound	1.00	52	do	96.43	(¹)	1¼
Walnuts:					2.17	(¹)	(¹)
Black	do	1.00	22	1 cup halves (0.24 pound)	.79	(¹)	(¹)
English	do	1.00	45	1 cup (0.28 pound)	2.05	(¹)	(¹)
				1 cup (0.22 pound)			

¹ Number of purchase units needed is determined by use.

² Number of purchase units needed is less than one.

TABLE 8.—DAIRY PRODUCTS

Dairy products as purchased	Unit of purchase	Weight per unit	Yield, as served	Portion as served or used	Portions per purchase unit	Approximate purchase units for— 25 portions	100 portions
		Pounds	*Percent*		*Number*	*Number*	*Number*
Cheese:							
Cheddar	Pound	1.00	100	4 ounces, grated, 1 cup	4.00	6¼	25
	do	1.00	100	2 ounces	8.00	3¼	12½
	do	1.00	100	1 ounce	16.00	1¾	6¼
	Longhorn	11 to 13	100	2 ounces	88–104	(1)	1¼
	Daisies	20 to 25	100	do	160–200	(1)	(1)
	Flats	32 to 37	100	do	256–296	(1)	(1)
	Cheddars	70 to 78	100	do	560–624	(1)	(1)
	Block	20	100	do	160.00	(1)	(1)
	do	40	100	do	320.00	(1)	(1)
Cottage, small or large curd, with pineapple or chive.	Pound	1.00	100	4 ounces	4.00	6¼	25
				2 ounces	8.00	3¼	12½
	32-ounce carton	2.00	100	4 ounces	8.00	3¼	12½
	Tin	30.00	100	do	120.00	(1)	(1)
Cream	8-ounce package	.50	100	1 ounce	8.00	3¼	12½
	12-ounce package	.75	100	do	12.00	2¼	8½
	16-ounce package	1.00	100	do	16.00	1¾	6¼
Processed, cheese food	Pound	1.00	100	2 ounces	8.00	3¼	12½
				1 ounce, 1 slice	16.00	1¾	6¼
	Package	2.00	100	2 ounces	16.00	1¾	6¼
	do	5.00	100	do	40.00	(1)	2½
Cream:							
Half and half	Pint	1.07	100	1½ tablespoons	21.33	1¼	4¾
	Quart	2.14	100	do	42.67	(1)	2½
Light	Pint	1.06	100	do	21.33	1¼	4¾
	Quart	2.13	100	do	42.67	(1)	2½
Sour	½ pint	.53	100	1 tablespoon	16.00	1¾	6¼
	¾ pint	.80	100	do	24.00	1¼	4¼
Whipping (volume doubles when whipped).	Pint	1.05	100	1¼ tablespoons	25.60	1	4
	Quart	2.10	100	do	51.20	(1)	2

FOOD PURCHASING GUIDE

Food	Purchase unit		Weight	Serving	Servings per purchase unit		Purchase units for 100 servings
Ice cream:							
Brick	Quart	100	1.25	1 slice (½ cup)	8.00	3¾	12½
Bulk	Gallon	100	4.50	No. 12 scoop (sundae)	22–26	1	4
				No. 16 scoop (a la mode)	31–35	(³)	3
				No. 20 scoop	38–42	(³)	2¾
				No. 24 scoop	47–51		2
Cups	3-ounce	100	.19	1 cup	1.00	25	100
	5-ounce	100	.31	do	1.00	25	100
Sherbet	Gallon	100	6.00	No. 12 scoop	25.00	1	4
				No. 16 scoop	35.00	(³)	3
				No. 20 scoop	42.00	(³)	2¾
				No. 24 scoop	50.00	(³)	2
Milk:							
Fluid²	Quart	100	2.15	1 cup	4.00	6¼	25
	Gallon	100	8.60	do	16.00	1¼	6¼
	5-gallon	100	43.00	do	80.00	(¹)	1¼
Condensed	14-ounce can	100	.88	do	1.24	(³)	(³)
	15-ounce can	100	.94	do	1.33	(³)	(³)
Evaporated	14½-ounce can	100	.91	1 cup as is	1.67	(³)	(³)
		200	.91	1 cup reconstituted	3.33	(³)	(³)
	No. 10 can	100	8.00	1 cup as is	14.00	(³)	(³)
		200	8.00	1 cup reconstituted	28.00	(³)	(³)
Dry:							
Nonfat: Instant	Pound (about 6½ cups)	100	1.00	1 cup as is	6.50	(³)	(³)
	(measure)	267	1.00	1 cup reconstituted	17.08	(³)	(³)
Regular (USDA)	Pound (about 3¾ cups)	100	1.00	1 cup as is	3.25	(³)	(³)
	(measure)	533	1.00	1 cup reconstituted	17.06	(³)	(³)
Whole	Pound (about 3¾ cups)	100	1.00	1 cup as is	3.50	(³)	(³)
	(measure)	400	1.00	1 cup reconstituted	14.22	(³)	(³)

¹ Number of purchase units needed is less than one.
² Skim milk and buttermilk weigh slightly more than whole fluid milk.
³ Number of purchase units needed is determined by use.

154

TABLE 9.—VEGETABLES—FRESH

Fresh vegetables as purchased	Unit of purchase	Weight per unit [1]	Yield, as served	Portion as served	Portions per purchase unit	Approximate purchase units for—	
						25 portions	100 portions
		Pounds	Percent		Number	Number	Number
Asparagus	Pound	1.00	---	4 medium spears, cooked	3.38	7½	29¾
	do	1.00	49	3 ounces cut spears, cooked	2.61	9¾	38½
	Crate	28.00	49	do	73.17	[2]	1½
Beans, lima, green:							
In pod	Pound	1.00	40	3 ounces cooked	2.13	11¾	47
Shelled	Bushel	32.00	40	do	68.27	[2]	1½
	Pound	1.00	102	do	5.44	4¾	18½
Beans, snap, green or wax	do	1.00	84	do	4.48	5¾	22½
	Bushel	30.00	84	do	134.40	[2]	[2]
Beet greens, untrimmed	Pound	1.00	44	do	2.35	10¾	42¾
	Bushel	20.00	44	do	46.93	[2]	2¼
Beets:							
With tops	Pound	1.00	43	3 ounces sliced or diced, cooked	2.29	11	43¾
Without tops	do	1.00	76	do	4.05	6¼	24¾
	Burlap bag	50.00	76	do	202.67	[2]	[2]
Blackeye peas, shelled	Pound	1.00	93	3 ounces cooked	4.96	5¼	20¼
Broccoli	do	1.00	62	2 medium spears, cooked	4.57	5½	22
	do	1.00	62	3 ounces cut spears, cooked	3.31	7¾	30¼
	Crate	40.00	62	do	132.27	[2]	[2]
Brussels sprouts	Pound	1.00	77	3 ounces cooked	4.11	6¼	24½
Cabbage	Bulk	1.00	79	2 ounces coleslaw	6.32	4	16
	do	1.00	75	3 ounces sliced, cooked	4.00	6¼	25
	do	1.00	80	3-ounce wedge, cooked	4.27	6	23½
	Crate or sack	50.00	80	do	213.33	[2]	[2]
Cabbage, Chinese	Pound	1.00	88	2 ounces raw	7.04	3¾	14¼
Carrots, without tops	do	1.00	82	2 ounces shredded or grated, strips or diced, raw	6.56	4	15¼
	do	1.00	75	3 ounces sliced or diced, cooked	4.00	6¼	25
	Crate	50.00	75	do	200.00	[2]	[2]
Cauliflower	do	1.00	45	2 ounces sliced, raw	3.60	7	28
	do	1.00	44	3 ounces cooked	2.35	10¾	42¾
	Crate	37.00	44	do	86.83	[2]	1¼
	Crate, large	50.00	44	do	117.33	[2]	[2]
Celery	Pound	1.00	70	3 ounces chopped, cooked	3.73	6¾	27
	do	1.00	75	3 ounces sliced, raw	4.00	6¼	25
	do	1.00	75	3 ounces strips, raw	6.00	4¼	16¾
	Crate	60.00	75	2 ounces chopped, raw	240.00	[2]	[2]
Celery hearts (24 pack)	Crate or box	30.00	95	2 ounces strips, raw	228.00	[2]	[2]
Chard, untrimmed	Pound	1.00	56	3 ounces cooked	2.99	8½	33½
Collards	do	1.00	81	3 ounces cooked	4.32	6	23¼
	Bushel	20.00	81	do	86.40	[2]	1¼
Corn, in husks	Dozen	8.00	37	3 ounces cooked kernels	15.79	1¾	6½
	do	8.00	37	1 ear, cooked	12.00	2¼	8½
	5-dozen crate or bag	40.00	37	do	60.00	[2]	1¾

Cucumber	Pound	1.00	73	3 ounces sliced, peeled, raw	3.89	6½	25¾
	do	1.00	95	3 ounces sliced, unpeeled, raw	5.07	5	19¾
	Bushel	48.00	95	do	243.20	(²)	(²)
Eggplant	Pound	1.00	75	4 ounces cooked	3.00	8⅓	33⅓
	Bushel	33.00	75	do	100.00	(²)	1
Endive, escarole, chicory	Pound	1.00	75	1 ounce raw	12.00	2¼	8⅓
	Bushel	25.00	75	do	300.00	(²)	(²)
Kale, untrimmed	Pound	1.00	81	3 ounces cooked	4.32	6	23¼
	Bushel	18.00	81	do	77.76	(²)	1½
Kohlrabi	Pound	1.00	50	do	2.67	9½	37½
Lettuce:							
Head	do	1.00	74	2 ounces raw	5.92	4¼	17
Iceberg	Carton	2 doz. heads		¼ head, raw	144.00	4¼ heads	17 heads
Romaine	Pound	1.00	64	1 ounce raw	10.24	2½	10
Mushrooms	do	1.00	67	1 ounce sliced, cooked	10.72	2½	9½
	Basket	3.00	67	3 ounces sliced, cooked	10.72	2½	9½
	do	9.00	67	do	32.16	(²)	3¼
Mustard greens	Pound	1.00	59	3 ounces cooked	3.15	8	31¾
	Bushel	20.00	59	do	62.93	(²)	1¾
Okra	Pound	1.00	96	do	5.12	5	19¾
	Bushel	30.00	96	do	153.60	(²)	(²)
Onions:							
Green, partly topped	Pound	1.00	60	3 ounces raw	3.20	8	31¼
	Wirebound crate	50.00	60	do	160.00	(²)	(²)
Mature	Pound	1.00	89	1 ounce chopped or grated, raw	14.24	2	7¼
	do	1.00	76	3 ounces small whole or pieces, cooked.	4.05	6¼	24¾
	Sack	50.00	76	do	202.67	(²)	(²)
Parsley	Pound	1.00		½ cup	16.00	(²)	(²)
	Crate	19.00		do	304.00	(²)	(²)
Parsnips	Pound	1.00	84	3 ounces cooked	4.48	5¾	22½
	Bushel	50.00	84	do	224.00	(²)	(²)
Peas, green:							
In pod	Pound	1.00	36	do	1.92	13¼	52¼
	Basket	15.00	36	do	28.80	(²)	3½
	Bushel	28.00	36	do	53.76	(²)	2
Shelled	Pound	1.00	96	do	5.12	5	19¾
Peppers, green	do	1.00	82	1 ounce diced or strips, raw	13.12	2	7¾
	Bushel	25.00	82	do	328.00	(²)	(²)
	Carton	30.00	82	do	393.60	(²)	(²)
	Pound	1.00	75	2 ounces strips, cooked	6.00	4¼	16¾
Potatoes:							
To be pared by hand	do	1.00		1 medium, boiled	3.00	8½	33⅓
	do	1.00	54	2 ounces french fried	4.32	6	23¼
	do	1.00	80	3 ounces cubed and diced, cooked	4.27	6	23½
	do	1.00	95	4 ounces mashed	3.80	6¾	26½
To be pared by machine	do	1.00		1 medium, boiled	3.00	8½	33⅓
	do	1.00	52	2 ounces french fried	4.16	6¼	24¼
	do	1.00	76	3 ounces cubed and diced, cooked	4.05	6¼	24¾
	do	1.00	90	4 ounces mashed	3.60	7	28
Ready-to-cook	do	1.00		1 medium, boiled	3.00	8½	33⅓
	do	1.00	68	2 ounces french fried	5.44	4¾	18½
	do	1.00	119	4 ounces mashed	4.76	5¼	21¼
To be cooked in jacket	do	1.00		1 medium, baked in jacket	3.00	8½	33⅓
	do	1.00		1 medium, boiled	3.00	8½	33⅓
	do	1.00	87	3 ounces cubed and diced	4.64	5½	21¾
	do	1.00	104	4 ounces mashed	4.16	6¼	24¼

See footnotes at end of table.

TABLE 9.—VEGETABLES—FRESH—Continued

Fresh vegetables as purchased	Unit of purchase	Weight per unit [1]	Yield, as served	Portion as served	Portions per purchase unit	Approximate purchase units for— 25 portions	100 portions
		Pounds	*Percent*		*Number*	*Number*	*Number*
Pumpkin	Pound	1.00	63	4 ounces mashed, cooked	2.52	10	39¾
Radishes:							
With tops	do	1.00	63	1 ounce sliced, raw	10.08	2½	10
	do	1.00		4 small	11.34	2¼	9
Without tops	do	1.00	90	1 ounce sliced, raw	14.40	1¾	7
Rutabagas	do	1.00	79	3 ounces cubed, cooked	4.21	6	24
	do	1.00	77	4 ounces mashed	3.08	8¼	32½
	Bushel	56.00	77	do	172.48	(2)	(2)
Spinach:							
Partly trimmed	Pound	1.00	92	1 ounce raw for salad	14.72	1¾	7
Untrimmed	do	1.00	72	do	11.52	2¼	8¾
	do	1.00	67	3 ounces cooked	3.57	7¼	28¼
	Bushel	20.00	67	do	71.47	(2)	1½
Squash, summer	Pound	1.00	83	3 ounces diced or sliced, cooked	4.43	5¾	22¾
	Bushel	35.00	83	do	154.93	(2)	(2)
	Pound	1.00	83	4 ounces mashed	3.32	7¾	30¼
Squash, winter:							
Acorn	do	1.00		½ medium, baked	2.00	12½	50
Hubbard	do	1.00	58	4 ounces cubed, cooked	2.32	11	43¼
	do	1.00	57	4 ounces mashed	2.28	11	44
Sweetpotatoes	do	1.00		1 medium, cooked in jacket	2.00	12½	50
	do	1.00	83	3 ounces sliced	4.43	5¾	22¾
	do	1.00	81	4 ounces mashed	3.24	7¾	31
	Bushel	50.00		1 medium, cooked in jacket	100.00	(2)	1
Tomatoes (medium)	Pound	1.00	91	2 slices	7.50	3½	13½
	do	1.00		1 wedge	12.00	2¼	8½
	Lug	32.00		do	384.00	(2)	(2)
	Bushel	53.00		do	636.00	(2)	(2)
Turnip greens, untrimmed	Pound	1.00	48	3 ounces cooked	2.56	10	39¼
	Bushel	20.00	48	do	51.20	(2)	(2)
Turnips, without tops	Pound	1.00	74	3 ounces cubed, cooked	3.95	6½	25½
	do	1.00	73	4 ounces mashed	2.92	8¾	34¼
	Bushel	50.00	73	do	146.00	(2)	(2)
Watercress	Bunch	1.00	92	½ cup	27.77	(3)	(3)

[1] Legal weights for contents of bushels, lugs, crates, and boxes vary among States.

[2] Number of purchase units needed is less than one.

[3] Number of purchase units needed is determined by use.

TABLE 10.—VEGETABLES—CANNED

Canned vegetables as purchased	Unit of purchase	Weight per unit	Yield, as served	Portion as served	Portions per purchase unit	Approximate purchase units for— 25 portions	Approximate purchase units for— 100 portions
		Pounds	*Percent*		*Number*	*Number*	*Number*
Asparagus:							
Cuts and tips	No. 300 can	0.88	61	3 ounces	2.80	8¾	35
	No. 10 can	6.31	60	do	20.10	1¼	5
Spears	No. 300 can	.91		6 medium	2.57	9¾	39
	No. 10 can	6.44		do	18.53	1½	5½
Beans, lima, green	No. 303 can	1.00	69	3 ounces	3.08	7	27¼
	No. 10 can	6.56	69	do	24.14	1¼	4¼
Beans, snap, green or wax	No. 303 can	.97	59	do	3.05	8¼	33
	No. 2½ can	1.75	59	do	5.51	4¾	18¼
	No. 10 can	6.31	62	do	20.87	1¼	5
Beans, dry—kidney, lima, or navy	No. 303 can	1.00	80	6 ounces	2.13	11¾	47
	No. 10 can	6.75	80	do	14.40	1¾	6¾
Bean sprouts	do	6.62	52	3 ounces	18.37	1½	5½
Beets:							
Diced	No. 303 can	1.00	66	do	3.52	7¼	28½
	No. 10 can	6.50	69	do	23.92	1¼	4¼
Sliced	No. 303 can	1.00	61	do	3.25	7¾	31
	No. 10 can	6.50	65	do	22.53	1¼	4½
Whole baby beets	No. 303 can	1.00	62	do	3.31	7¾	30¼
	No. 10 can	6.50	66	do	22.88	1¼	4½
Carrots:							
Diced	No. 303 can	1.00	62	do	3.31	7¾	30¼
	No. 10 can	6.50	69	do	23.92	1¼	4¼
Sliced	No. 303 can	1.00	62	do	3.31	7¾	30¼
	No. 10 can	6.50	66	do	22.88	1¼	4½
Chop suey vegetables	do	6.38	100	do	34.00	(1)	3
Collards	No. 303 can	.94	72	4 ounces	2.71	9¼	37
	No. 2½ can	1.69	70	do	4.73	5½	21¼
	No. 10 can	6.12	61	do	14.93	1¾	6¾
Corn:							
Cream style	No. 303 can	1.00	100	do	4.00	6¼	25
	No. 10 can	6.62	100	do	26.48	1	4
Whole kernel	No. 303 can	1.00	66	3 ounces	3.52	7¼	28½
	No. 10 can	6.62	66	do	23.30	1¼	4½
Kale	No. 303 can	.94	72	4 ounces	2.71	9¼	37
	No. 2½ can	1.69	70	do	4.73	5½	21¼
	No. 10 can	6.12	61	do	14.93	1¾	6¾
Mushrooms	No. 8 Z	.78	64	3 ounces	2.66	9½	37¾
	No. 10 can	6.44	66	do	22.67	1¼	4½
Mustard greens	No. 303 can	.94	72	4 ounces	2.71	9¼	37
	No. 2½ can	1.69	70	do	4.73	5½	21¼
	No. 10 can	6.12	61	do	14.93	1¾	6¾
Okra	No. 303 can	.97	68	3 ounces	3.51	7¼	28½
	No. 10 can	6.19	61	do	20.14	1¼	5
Okra and tomatoes	No. 303 can	.94	100	do	5.01	5	20
	No. 10 can	6.31	100	do	33.05	(1)	3

See footnotes at end of table.

TABLE 10.—VEGETABLES—CANNED—Continued

Canned vegetables as purchased	Unit of purchase	Weight per unit	Yield, as served	Portion as served	Portions per purchase unit	Approximate purchase units for— 25 portions	100 portions
		Pounds	*Percent*		*Number*	*Number*	*Number*
Olives, large:							
Ripe:							
Pitted	No. 1 tall	[2] 0.47		2 olives	21.33	1¼	4¾
Whole	do	[2] .56		do	25.60	1	4
	No. 10	[2] 4.12		do	187.69	(1)	(1)
Green, whole	Gallon	[2] 5.50		do	250.25	(1)	(1)
Onions, small, whole	No. 303 can	1.00	56	3 ounces	2.99	8½	33½
	No. 10 can	6.31	59	do	19.86	1½	5¼
Peas, green	No. 303 can	1.00	64	do	3.41	7½	29½
	No. 10 can	6.56	64	do	22.39	1¼	4½
Peas and carrots	No. 303 can	1.00	69	do	3.68	7	27¼
	No. 10 can	6.56	69	do	24.14	1¼	4¼
Pickles:							
Dill or sour:							
Sliced or cut	Quart jar	[2] 1.38	100	1 ounce	22.00	1¼	4¾
	No. 10 jar	[2] 4.50	100	do	72.00	(1)	1½
	Gallon jar	[2] 5.62	100	do	90.00	(1)	1¼
Whole	No. 2½ jar	[2] 1.19	100	do	19.00	1½	5½
	Quart jar	[2] 1.31	100	do	21.00	1¼	5
Sweet:							
Sliced or cut	do	[2] 1.50	100	do	24.00	1¼	4¼
	No. 10 jar	[2] 4.88	100	do	78.00	(1)	1½
	Gallon jar	[2] 5.94	100	do	95.00	(1)	1¼
Whole	No. 2½ jar	[2] 1.28	100	do	20.50	1¼	5
	Quart jar	[2] 1.38	100	do	22.00	1¼	4¾
Pickle relish:							
Sour	Quart	[2] 1.61	100	do	25.75	1	4
	No. 10 jar	[2] 5.73	100	do	91.75	(1)	1¼
	Gallon jar	[2] 7.16	100	do	114.50	(1)	(1)
Sweet	Quart	[2] 1.75	100	do	28.00	1	3¾
	No. 10 jar	[2] 6.25	100	do	100.00	(1)	1
	Gallon jar	[2] 7.81	100	do	125.00	(1)	(1)
Pimientos, chopped	No. 2½ can	1.75	73	½ cup	4.80	(3)	(3)
	No. 10 can	6.81	68	do	17.39	(3)	(3)
Potatoes, small whole	No. 2 can	1.25		2–3	4.00	6¼	25
	No. 10 can	6.38		2–3	25.00	1	4
Pumpkin, mashed	No. 300 can	.91	100	4 ounces	3.64	7	27½
	No. 2½ can	1.81	100	do	7.24	3½	14
	No. 10 can	6.62	100	do	26.50	1	4
Sauerkraut	No. 303 can	1.00	82	3 ounces	4.37	5¾	23
	No. 2½ can	1.69	85	do	7.66	3½	13¼
	No. 10 can	6.19	81	do	26.74	1	3¾

Food	Purchase unit	Weight per unit (lb.)	Percent	Size of serving	Servings per purchase unit	Purchase units for 25 servings	Purchase units for 100 servings
Soups:							
Condensed	No. 1 picnic	.66 to .75	200	1 cup diluted	2.50	10	40
	No. 3 cylinder	3.12	200	---do---	11.50	2¼	8¾
Ready-to-serve	12-fluid-ounce can		100	1 cup	1.50	16¼	66¼
	25-fluid-ounce can (No. 2½)		100	---do---	3.12	8¾	32¼
Spinach	No. 303 can	.94	72	4 ounces	2.71	9¼	37
	No. 2½ can	1.69	70	---do---	4.73	5¼	21¼
	No. 10 can	6.12	61	---do---	14.93	1¼	6¾
Squash, summer	No. 303 can	1.00	69	---do---	2.75	9¼	36¼
	No. 10 can	6.62	69	---do---	17.50	1¼	5¾
Squash, winter	No. 300 can	.91	100	---do---	3.04	7	27½
	No. 2½ can	1.81	100	---do---	7.24	3½	14
	No. 10 can	6.62	100	---do---	26.48	1	4
Succotash	No. 303 can	.62	65	3 ounces	3.47	7¼	29
	No. 10 can	6.75	65	---do---	23.40	1¼	4½
Sweetpotatoes	No. 3 vacuum or squat	1.44	66	4 ounces	3.74	6¾	26¾
	No. 2½ can, with sirup	1.81	71	---do---	4.78	5¼	21
	No. 10 can, with sirup	6.38	100	---do---	18.00	1¼	5¾
Tomatoes	No. 303 can	1.00	100	---do---	4.00	6¾	25
	No. 2½ can	1.75	100	---do---	7.00	3¾	14½
	No. 10 can	6.38	100	---do---	25.52	1	4
Tomato products:							
Catsup	14-ounce bottle	.88	100	1 ounce	14.00	2	7¾
	No. 10 can	6.94	100	---do---	111.00	(¹)	1
Chili sauce	12-ounce jar	.75	100	1 tablespoon	20.27	1¼	5
	No. 10 can	6.56	100	---do---	177.30	(¹)	(¹)
Juice, concentrate [4]	6-fluid-ounce can	.43	400	4 fluid ounces	6.00	4¼	16¾
Turnip greens	No. 303 can	.94	72	4 ounces	2.71	9¼	37
	No. 2½ can	1.69	70	---do---	4.73	5¼	21¼
	No. 10 can	6.12	61	---do---	14.93	1¼	6¾
Vegetable juices	23-fluid-ounce can	1.54	100	4 fluid ounces	5.75	4¼	17½
	46-fluid-ounce can	3.07	100	---do---	11.50	2¼	8¾
	96-fluid-ounce can	6.41	100	---do---	24.00	1¼	4½
Vegetables, mixed	No. 303 can	1.00	68	3 ounces	3.63	7	27½
	No. 10 can	6.50	68	---do---	23.57	1¼	4¼

[1] Number of purchase units needed is less than one.
[2] Drained weight.
[3] Number of purchase units needed is determined by use.
[4] See vegetable juices for canned tomato juice.

TABLE 11.—VEGETABLES—FROZEN

Frozen vegetables as purchased	Unit of purchase	Weight per unit	Yield, as served	Portion as served	Portions per purchase unit	Approximate purchase units for— 25 portions	100 portions
		Pounds	*Percent*		*Number*	*Number*	*Number*
Asparagus:							
Spears	Pound	1.00		4 medium, cooked	3.38	7½	29¾
	Package	2.50		do	8.44	3	12
Cuts and tips	Pound	1.00	80	3 ounces cooked	4.27	6	23½
	Package	2.50	80	do	10.67	2½	9½
Beans, butter (lima)	Pound	1.00	100	do	5.33	4¾	19
	Package	2.50	100	do	13.33	2	7½
	do	3.00	100	do	16.00	1¾	6¼
Beans, lima, green	Pound	1.00	100	do	5.33	4¾	19
	Package	2.50	100	do	13.33	2	7½
Beans, snap, green or wax	Pound	1.00	91	do	4.85	5¼	20¾
	Package	2.50	91	do	12.13	2¼	8¼
Blackeye peas	Pound	1.00	111	do	5.92	4¼	17
	Package	2.50	111	do	14.80	1¾	7
	do	3.00	111	do	17.76	1½	5¾
Broccoli:							
Spears	Pound	1.00		2 medium	4.57	5½	22
	Package	2.50		do	11.43	2¼	8¾
Cut or chopped	Pound	1.00	85	3 ounces cooked	4.53	5¾	22¼
	Package	2.50	85	do	11.33	2¼	9
Brussel sprouts	Pound	1.00	96	do	5.12	5	19¾
	Package	2.50	96	do	12.80	2	8
Carrots, sliced or diced	Pound	1.00	96	do	5.12	5	19¾
	Package	2.50	96	do	12.80	2	8
Cauliflower	Pound	1.00	90	do	4.80	5¼	21
	Package	2.50	90	do	12.00	2¼	8½
Collards	Pound	1.00	89	do	4.75	5½	21¼
	Package	2.50	89	do	11.87	2¼	8½
Corn:							
On cob	Pound (about three 5-inch ears).	1.00		1 ear, cooked	3.00	8½	33⅓
Whole kernel	Pound	1.00	97	3 ounces cooked	5.17	5	19½
	Package	2.50	97	do	12.93	2	7¾
Kale	Pound	1.00	77	do	4.11	6¼	24½
	Package	2.50	77	do	10.27	2½	9¾
	do	3.00	77	do	12.32	2¼	8¼

Mustard greens, leaf or chopped	Pound	1.00	80	do	4.27	6	23½
	Package	2.50	80	do	10.67	2½	9½
	do	3.00	80	do	12.80	2	8
Okra, whole	Pound	1.00	82	do	4.37	5¾	23
	Package	2.50	82	do	10.93	2½	9¼
	do	3.00	82	do	13.12	2	7¾
Peas, green	Pound	1.00	96	do	5.12	5	19¾
	Package	2.50	96	do	12.80	2	8
	do	3.00	96	do	15.36	1¾	6¾
Peas and carrots	Pound	1.00	98	do	5.23	5	19¼
	Package	2.50	98	do	13.07	2	7¾
Peppers, green:							
Whole	do	1.00		½ pepper, cooked	12.00	2¼	8½
	do	2.50		do	30.00	(1)	3½
Diced or sliced	Pound	1.00	97	1 ounce cooked	15.52	1¾	6½
	Package	2.50	97	do	38.80	(1)	2¾
Potatoes:							
French fried	do	1.00		10 pieces	8.00	3¼	12½
	do	5.00		do	40.00	(1)	2½
Small whole	Container	5.00		3 cooked	16.67	1½	6
Spinach	Pound	1.00	80	3 ounces cooked	4.27	6	23½
	Package	2.50	80	do	10.67	2½	9½
	do	3.00	80	do	12.80	2	8
Squash, summer, sliced	Pound	1.00	87	do	4.64	5½	21¾
	Package	2.50	87	do	11.60	2¼	8¾
	do	3.00	87	do	13.92	2	7¼
Squash, winter, mashed	Pound	1.00	92	4 ounces cooked	3.68	7	27¼
	Package	2.50	92	do	9.20	2¾	11
Sweetpotatoes:							
Whole	Pound	1.00		1 whole, cooked	2.63	9¾	38¼
	do	1.00	98	4 ounces cooked	3.92	6½	25¾
Sliced	Package	2.50	98	do	9.80	2¾	10¼
	do	3.00	98	do	11.76	2¼	8¾
Succotash	Pound	1.00	106	3 ounces cooked	5.65	4½	17¾
	Package	2.50	106	do	14.13	2	7¼
Turnip greens, leaf or chopped	Pound	1.00	80	do	4.27	6	23½
	Package	2.50	80	do	10.67	2½	9½
	do	3.00	80	do	12.80	2	8
Turnip greens with turnips	Pound	1.00	89	do	4.75	5½	21¼
	Package	3.00	89	do	14.24	2	7¼
Vegetables, mixed	Pound	1.00	95	do	5.07	5	19¾
	Package	2.50	95	do	12.67	2	8

[1] Number of purchase units needed is less than one.

TABLE 12.—VEGETABLES—DRIED

Vegetables, dried, regular and low-moisture, as purchased	Unit of purchase	Weight per unit	Yield, as served	Portion as served	Portions per purchase unit	Approximate purchase units for—	
						25 portions	100 portions
REGULAR		*Pounds*	*Percent*		*Number*	*Number*	*Number*
Beans (includes white beans, lima beans, kidney beans, blackeye beans or peas).	Pound	1.00	232	3 ounces cooked	12.37	2¼	8¼
Peas (includes any type, whole peas, split peas, or lentils).	do	1.00	223	do	11.89	2¾	8½
	Bushel	60.00	223	do	713.60	(¹)	(¹)
LOW-MOISTURE							
Onions, sliced	Pound	1.00	417	do	22.24	1¼	4¼
Potatoes, white:							
Flakes	do	1.00	521	4 ounces cooked	20.84	1¼	5
	Package	2.50	521	do	52.10	(¹)	2
Granules	Pound	1.00	506	do	20.24	1¼	5
	Package	2.50	506	do	50.60	(¹)	2
Sweetpotatoes, flakes	Pound	1.00	294	do	11.76	2¼	8¾

¹ Number of purchase units needed is less than one.

TABLE 13.—FRUITS—FRESH

Fresh fruits as purchased	Unit of purchase	Weight per unit [1]	Yield, as served	Portion as served	Portions per purchase unit	Approximate purchase units for—	
						25 portions	100 portions
		Pounds	*Percent*		*Number*	*Number*	*Number*
Apples	Pound	1. 00		1 medium, baked or raw	3. 00	8½	33½
	Bushel	40. 00		do	120. 00	(2)	(2)
	Pound	1. 00	76	2 ounces raw, chopped or diced	6. 08	4¼	16½
	do	1. 00	87	4 ounces applesauce	3. 48	7¼	28¾
	do	1. 00	63	4 ounces cooked, sliced or diced	2. 52	10	39¾
	do	1. 00		⅙ 9-inch pie (2.12 pounds of apples per pie).	2. 83	9	35½
	do	1. 00		⅛ 9-inch pie	3. 77	6¾	26¾
Apricots	do	1. 00		2 medium	6. 00	4¼	16¾
	Lug	24. 00		do	144. 00	(2)	(2)
Avocados	Pound	1. 00	75	2 ounces sliced, diced, or wedges	6. 00	4¼	16¾
	Lug	12. 00	75	do	72. 00	(2)	1½
	Box (⅝ bushel)	36. 00	75	do	216. 00	(2)	(2)
Bananas	Pound	1. 00		1 medium	3. 00	8½	33½
	Box	25. 00		do	75. 00	(2)	1½
	Pound	1. 00	68	2 ounces sliced for fruit cup	5. 44	4¾	18½
	do	1. 00	68	3 ounces sliced for dessert	3. 63	7	27¾
	do	1. 00	68	4 ounces mashed	2. 72	9¼	37
Blackberries	Quart	1. 42	95	1 ounce salad garnish	21. 53	1¼	4¾
	do	1. 42	95	3 ounces	7. 18	3½	14
	Crate (24 quarts)	34. 00	95	do	172. 22	(2)	(2)
	Quart	1. 42		⅙ 9-inch pie (0.92 quart per pie)	6. 54	4	15½
	do	1. 42		⅛ 9-inch pie	8. 70	3	11½
Blueberries	do	1. 97	92	1 ounce salad garnish	28. 98	(2)	3½
	do	1. 97	92	3 ounces	9. 66	2¾	10½
	Crate (24 quarts)	47. 25	92	do	231. 84	(2)	(2)
	Quart	1. 97		⅙ 9-inch pie (0.59 quart per pie)	10. 20	2½	10
	do	1. 97		⅛ 9-inch pie	13. 51	2	7½
Cantaloup	Pound	1. 00	50	3 ounces sliced or diced	2. 67	9½	37½
	1 (No. 36 size)	2. 50		½ medium	2. 00	12½	50
	Crate (No. 36)	80. 00		do	64. 00	(2)	1¾
Cherries	Pound	1. 00	89	3 ounces pitted, raw	4. 75	5½	21¼
	Lug	16. 00	89	do	75. 95	(2)	1½
	Pound	1. 00		⅙ 9-inch pie (1.60 pounds per pie)	3. 75	6¾	26¾
	do	1. 00		⅛ 9-inch pie	5. 00	5	20
Cranberries	do	1. 00	96	1 ounce raw, chopped, for relish	15. 36	1¾	6¾
	do	1. 00	182	2 ounces sauce, strained	14. 56	1¾	7
	do	1. 00	239	2 ounces cooked, whole	19. 12	1½	5¼
	Box	25. 00	239	do	478. 00	(2)	(2)
Figs	Pound	1. 00		3 medium	4. 00	6¼	25
	Box	6. 00		do	24. 00	1¼	4¼

See footnotes at end of table.

TABLE 13.—FRUITS—FRESH—Continued

Fresh fruits as purchased	Unit of purchase	Weight per unit [1]	Yield, as served	Portion as served	Portions per purchase unit	Approximate purchase units for— 25 portions	100 portions
		Pounds	*Percent*		*Number*	*Number*	*Number*
Grapefruit	Pound	1.00	44	4 fluid ounces juice	1.61	15¾	62¼
	Dozen (No. 64 size)	15.00	44	do	24.22	1¼	4¼
	Pound	1.00	47	4 ounces segments	1.88	13½	53¼
	Dozen	15.00	47	do	28.20	([2])	3¾
	do	15.00		½ medium	24.00	1¼	4¼
Grapefruit segments	½-gallon jar	4.22	100	4 ounces	16.88	1½	6
Grapes:							
With seeds	Pound	1.00	89	4 ounces, seeds removed	3.56	7¼	28¼
Seedless	do	1.00	94	4 ounces	3.76	6¾	26¾
	Lug	24.00	94	do	90.24	([2])	1¼
Honeydew melon	Pound	1.00	60	3 ounces sliced or diced	3.20	8	31¼
	1 melon	4.00		Wedge, ⅛ melon	8.00	3¼	12½
	do	4.00	60	3 ounces sliced or diced	12.80	2	8
Lemons	1 lemon (medium)	.23		1 slice	8.00	3¼	12½
	do	.23		1 wedge	6.00	4¼	16¾
	Pound (about 4 lemons)	1.00	43	2 fluid ounces juice	3.16	8	31¾
	Carton	36.00	43	do	113.76	([2])	([2])
Limes	1 lime (medium)	.15		Wedge, ¼ lime	4.00	6¼	25
	Pound	1.00	48	2 fluid ounces juice	3.52	7¼	28½
	Box (⅘ bushel)	40.00	48	do	140.80	([2])	([2])
Mangoes	Pound	1.00	67	3 ounces sliced or diced	3.57	7¼	28¼
	Lug	24.00	67	do	85.76	([2])	1¼
Oranges	Pound	1.00	50	4 fluid ounces juice	1.83	13¾	54¾
	do	1.00	56	4 ounces sections (no membrane)	2.24	11¼	44¾
	do	1.00	70	4 ounces sections (with membrane)	2.80	9	35¾
California	Carton	38.00	70	do	106.40	([2])	([2])
Florida	Box	85.00	50	4 fluid ounces juice	155.55	([2])	([2])
Medium No. 176	Pound	1.00		1 whole	2.00	12½	50
	Dozen	6.00	50	4 fluid ounces juice	11.01	2¼	9¼
	do	6.00	56	4 ounces sections (no membrane)	13.44	2	7½
Small No. 250	Pound	1.00		1 whole	3.00	8½	33½
	Dozen	4.00	50	4 fluid ounces juice	7.34	3½	13¾
	do	4.00	56	4 ounces sections (no membrane)	8.96	3	11¼
Orange segments	½-gallon jar	4.28	100	4 ounces	17.12	1½	6
Peaches	Pound	1.00		1 medium	4.00	6¼	25
	do	1.00	76	3 ounces sliced or diced	4.05	6¼	24¾
	Bushel	48.00	76	do	194.56	([2])	([2])
	Pound	1.00		⅙ 9-inch pie (1.88 pound per pie)	3.19	8	31½
	do	1.00		⅛ 9-inch pie	4.26	6	23½
Pears	do	1.00		1 medium	3.00	8½	33½
	do	1.00	78	3 ounces sliced or diced	4.16	6¼	24¼
	Bushel	46.00	78	do	191.36	([2])	([2])

Pineapples	Pound	1.00	52	3 ounces cubed	2.77	9¼	36¼
	½ crate	35.00	52	do	97.07	(2)	1¼
Pineapple chunks	½-gallon jar	4.36	100	4 ounces	17.44	1½	5¾
Plums	Pound	1.00		3 medium	2.67	9½	37½
	do	1.00	94	3 ounces halves pitted	5.01	5	20
	4-basket crate	28.00	94	do	140.37	(2)	(2)
Raspberries	Quart	1.47	97	1 ounce salad garnish	22.87	1¼	4½
	do	1.47	97	3 ounces	7.62	3½	13¼
	Crate (24 quarts)	35.00	97	do	181.07	(2)	(2)
	Quart	1.46		⅙ 9-inch pie (0.68 quart per pie)	8.85	3	11½
	do	1.46		⅛ 9-inch pie	11.76	2¼	8¾
Rhubarb, trimmed	Pound	1.00	103	3 ounces cooked	5.49	4¾	18¼
	do	1.00		⅙ 9-inch pie (1.44 pounds per pie)	4.17	6	24
	do	1.00		⅛ 9-inch pie	5.56	4½	18
Strawberries	Quart	1.48	87	1 ounce salad garnish	20.53	1¼	5
	do	1.48	87	3 ounces	6.84	3¾	14¾
	Crate (24 quarts)	35.00	87	do	162.40	(2)	(2)
	Quart	1.46		⅙ 9-inch pie (1 quart per pie)	6.00	4¼	16¾
	do	1.46		⅛ 9-inch pie	8.00	3¼	12½
Tangerines	Pound	1.00		1 medium	4.00	6¼	25
	Box	45.00		do	180.00	(2)	(2)
	Pound	1.00	74	3 ounces sections	3.95	6½	25½
Watermelon	do	1.00	46	3 ounces	2.45	10¼	41
	1 melon	18 to 30		1/16 melon	16.00	1¾	6¼

[1] Legal weights for contents of bushels, lugs, crates, and boxes vary among States.

[2] Number of purchase units needed is less than one.

TABLE 14.—FRUITS—CANNED

Canned fruits as purchased	Unit of purchase	Weight per unit (Pounds)	Yield, as served (Percent)	Portion as served	Portions per purchase unit (Number)	Approximate purchase units for 25 portions (Number)	Approximate purchase units for 100 portions (Number)
Apples, solid pack	No. 2 can	1.12	100	4 ounces	4.48	5¾	22½
	No. 2½ can	1.62	100	do	6.48	4	15½
	No. 10 can	6.00	100	{4 ounces	24.00	1¼	4¼
				{⅛ 9-inch pie	24.00	1¼	4¼
Apple juice	No. 23-fluid-ounce can	1.57	100	4 fluid ounces	5.75	4½	17½
	No. 46-fluid-ounce can	3.14	100	do	11.50	2¼	8¾
	No. 96-fluid-ounce can	6.56	100	do	24.00	1¼	4¼
Applesauce	No. 303 can	1.00	100	4 ounces	4.00	6¼	25
	No. 2½ can	1.81	100	do	7.24	3½	14
	No. 10 can	6.75	100	do	27.00	1	3¾
Apricots, halves	No. 303 can	1.00	------	3–5 medium	4.00	6¼	25
	No. 2½ can	1.88	------	do	7.00	3¾	14½
	No. 10 can	6.62	------	do	25.00	1	4
Blackberries	No. 303 can	1.00	100	4 ounces	4.00	6¼	25
	No. 10 can	6.62	100	do	26.48	1	4
Blueberries	No. 300 can	.91	100	do	3.64	7	27½
	No. 10 can	6.56	100	do	26.24	1	4
Boysenberries	No. 303 can	.94	100	do	3.76	6¾	26¾
	No. 10 can	6.62	100	do	26.48	1	4
Cherries:							
Red, sour, pitted	No. 303 can	1.00	100	do	4.00	6¼	25
	No. 10 can	6.56	100	{4 ounces	26.24	1	4
				{⅛ 9-inch pie	24.00	1¼	4¼
Sweet	No. 303 can	1.00	100	4 ounces	4.00	6¼	25
	No. 2½ can	1.81	100	do	7.24	3½	14
	No. 10 can	6.75	100	do	27.00	1	3¾
Cranberries, strained or whole	No. 300 can	1.00	100	2 ounces	8.00	3¼	12½
	No. 10 can	7.31	100	do	58.50	(¹)	1¾
Cranberry juice	1 pint	1.11	100	4 fluid ounces	4.00	6¼	25
	1 quart	2.23	100	do	8.00	3¼	12½
	1 gallon	8.92	100	do	32.00	(¹)	3¼
Figs	No. 303 can	1.06	------	3–4 figs	4.00	6¼	25
	No. 2½ can	1.88	------	do	7.00	3¾	14½
	No. 10 can	7.00	------	do	25.00	1	4

Fruit cocktail or salad	No. 303 can	1.06	100	4 ounces	4.24	6	23¾
	No. 2½ can	1.88	100	do	7.52	3½	13½
	No. 10 can	6.75	100	do	27.00	1	3¾
Grapefruit juice	18-fluid-ounce can	1.24	100	4 fluid ounces	4.50	5¾	22¼
	46-fluid-ounce can	3.14	100	do	11.50	2¼	8¾
	96-fluid-ounce can	6.57	100	do	24.00	1¼	4¼
Grapefruit sections	No. 303 can	1.00	100	4 ounces	4.00	6¼	25
	No. 3 cylinder	3.12	100	do	12.48	2¼	8¼
Lemon juice	32 fluid-ounce can	2.16	100	2 fluid ounces	16.00	1¾	6¼
Lime juice	do	2.17	100	do	16.00	1¾	6¼
Orange juice	18-fluid-ounce can	1.24	100	4 fluid ounces	4.50	5¾	22¼
	46-fluid-ounce can	3.16	100	do	11.50	2¼	8¾
	96-fluid-ounce can	6.59	100	do	24.00	1¼	4¼
Oranges, mandarin	No. 10 can	6.38	100	4 ounces	25.50	1	4
Peaches:							
Halves or slices	No. 303 can	1.00	----------	2 medium	3.00	8½	33½
	No. 2½ can	1.81	----------	do	7.00	3¾	14½
	No. 10 can	6.75	----------	{2 medium	25.00	1	4
				{⅙ 9-inch pie	24.00	1¼	4¼
Whole, spiced	do	6.88	----------	1 each	25.00	1	4
Pears, halves	No. 303 can	1.00	----------	2 medium	3.00	8½	33½
	No. 2½ can	1.81	----------	do	7.00	3¾	14½
	No. 10 can	6.62	----------	do	25.00	1	4
Pineapple:							
Chunks and cubes	No. 2½ can	1.88	100	4 ounces	7.52	3½	13½
	No. 10 can	6.75	100	do	27.00	1	3¾
Crushed	No. 2½ can	1.88	100	do	7.52	3½	13½
	No. 10 can	6.81	100	do	27.24	1	3¾
Sliced	No. 2½ can	1.88	----------	1 large	8.00	3¼	12½
	No. 10 can	6.81	----------	1 large or 2 small	25.00	1	4
Pineapple juice	18-fluid-ounce can	1.24	100	4 fluid ounces	4.50	5¾	22¼
	46-fluid-ounce can	3.17	100	do	11.50	2¼	8¾
	96-fluid-ounce can	6.62	100	do	24.00	1¼	4¼
Plums	No. 2½ can	1.88	----------	2–3 plums	7.00	3¾	14½
	No. 10 can	6.75	----------	do	25.00	1	4
Prunes	No. 2½ can	1.88	100	4 ounces	7.52	3½	13½
	No. 10 can	6.88	100	do	27.52	1	3¾
Raspberries	No. 303 can	1.00	100	do	4.00	6¼	25
	No. 10 can	6.75	100	do	27.00	1	3¾
Strawberries	No. 303 can	1.00	100	do	4.00	6¼	25
	No. 10 can	6.75	100	do	27.00	1	3¾

[1] Number of purchase units needed is less than one.

TABLE 15.—FRUITS—FROZEN

Frozen fruits as purchased	Unit of purchase	Weight per unit	Yield, as served	Portion as served	Portions per purchase unit	Approximate purchase units for— 25 portions	100 portions
		Pounds	*Percent*		*Number*	*Number*	*Number*
Apples, sliced	Pound	1.00	106	4 ounces	4.24	6	23¾
				⅙ 9-inch pie (1.50 pounds per pie).	4.00	6¼	25
	Package	2.50	106	4 ounces	10.60	2½	9½
	do	5.00	106	do	21.20	1¼	4¾
	Can	30.00	106	do	127.20	[1]	[1]
Apricots	Pound	1.00	95	do	3.80	6¾	26½
	Can	25.00	95	do	95.00	[1]	1¼
	do	30.00	95	do	114.00	[1]	[1]
Blackberries	Pound	1.00	103	do	4.12	6¼	24½
	Can	30.00	103	do	123.60	[1]	[1]
Blueberries	Pound	1.00	108	do	4.32	6	23¼
	Package	2.50	108	do	10.80	2½	9½
	Can	25.00	108	do	108.00	[1]	1
	do	30.00	108	do	129.60	[1]	[1]
Cherries, red, sour, pitted	Pound	1.00	100	4 ounces	4.00	6¼	25
				⅙ 9-inch pie (1.50 pounds per pie).	4.00	6¼	25
	Can	30.00	100	4 ounces	120.00	[1]	[1]
Grapefruit sections	Pound	1.00	100	do	4.00	6¼	25
	Package	3.00	100	do	12.00	2¼	8½
Grapefruit juice, concentrate	6-fluid-ounce can	.46	400	4 fluid ounces	6.00	4¼	16¾
	32-fluid-ounce can	2.46	400	do	32.00	[1]	3¼
Grape juice, concentrate	6-fluid-ounce can	.48	400	do	6.00	4¼	16¾
	32-fluid-ounce can	2.54	400	do	32.00	[1]	3¼
Lemon juice, concentrate	4-fluid-ounce can	.31	500	2 fluid ounces	10.00	2½	10
	6-fluid-ounce can	.47	500	do	15.00	1¾	6¾
Lemonade, concentrate	6-fluid-ounce can	.49	700	do	21.00	1¼	5
	18-fluid-ounce can	1.46	700	do	63.00	[1]	1¾
Melon scoops	Pound	1.00	100	3 ounces	5.33	4¾	19
	Package	6.50	100	do	34.67	[1]	3

Orange juice, concentrate	6-fluid-ounce can	.46	400	4 fluid ounces	6.00	4¼	16¾
	12-fluid-ounce can	.93	400	do	12.00	2¼	8½
	32-fluid-ounce can	2.48	400	do	32.00	(1)	3¼
Peaches, sliced	Pound	1.00	95	4 ounces	3.80	6¾	26½
				⅛ 9-inch pie (1.33 pounds per pie).	4.50	5¾	22¼
	Can	6.50	95	4 ounces	24.70	1¼	4¼
	do	10.00	95	do	38.00	(1)	2¾
	do	30.00	95	do	114.00	(1)	(1)
Pineapple:							
Chunks	Pound	1.00	100	do	4.00	6¼	25
	Can	10.00	100	do	40.00	(1)	2½
Crushed	do	30.00	100	do	120.00	(1)	(1)
Pineapple juice, concentrate	6-fluid-ounce can	.47	400	4 fluid ounces	6.00	4¼	16¾
	32-fluid-ounce can	2.53	400	do	32.00	(1)	3¼
Raspberries	Pound	1.00	100	4 ounces	4.00	6¼	25
	Can	6.50	100	do	26.00	1	4
	do	10.00	100	do	40.00	(1)	2½
	do	30.00	100	do	120.00	(1)	(1)
Rhubarb	Pound	1.00	106	4 ounces	4.24	6	23¾
				⅛ 9-inch pie (1.50 pounds per pie).	4.00	6¼	25
	Package	2.50	106	4 ounces	10.60	2½	9½
	Can	10.00	106	do	42.40	(1)	2½
	do	25.00	106	do	106.00	(1)	1
	do	30.00	106	do	127.20	(1)	(1)
Strawberries	Pound	1.00	100	do	4.00	6¼	25
	Can	6.50	100	do	26.00	1	4
	do	10.00	100	do	40.00	(1)	2½
	do	30.00	100	do	120.00	(1)	(1)
Tangerine juice, concentrate	6-fluid-ounce can	.47	400	4 fluid ounces	6.00	4¼	16¾
	32-fluid-ounce can	2.48	400	do	32.00	(1)	3¼

[1] Number of purchase units needed is less than one.

TABLE 16.—FRUITS—DRIED

Fruits, dried, regular and low-moisture, as purchased	Unit of purchase	Weight per unit	Yield, as served	Portion as served	Portions per purchase unit	Approximate purchase units for— 25 portions	Approximate purchase units for— 100 portions
		Pounds	*Percent*		*Number*	*Number*	*Number*
REGULAR							
Apple slices	Pound	1. 00	412	4 ounces	16. 48	1¾	6¼
				⅛ 9-inch pie (½ pound per pie)	18. 00	1½	5¾
	Carton	5. 00	412	4 ounces	82. 40	(1)	1¼
Apricots	11-ounce package	. 69	344	do	9. 46	2¾	10¾
	Pound	1. 00	344	do	13. 76	2	7½
	Carton	30. 00	344	do	412. 80	(1)	(1)
Dates	12-ounce package	. 75	100	3 ounces	4. 00	6¼	25
	Pound	1. 00	100	do	5. 33	4¾	19
	Carton	15. 00	100	do	80. 00	(1)	1¼
Peaches	11-ounce package	. 69	422	4 ounces	11. 60	2¼	8¾
	Pound	1. 00	422	4 ounces	16. 88	1½	6
				⅛ 9-inch pie (½ pound per pie)	18. 00	1½	5¾
	Carton	30. 00	422	4 ounces	506. 40	(1)	(1)
Prunes	Pound	1. 00	253	do	10. 12	2½	10
	2-pound package	2. 00	253	do	20. 24	1¼	5
	Carton	30. 00	253	do	303. 60	(1)	(1)
Raisins	Pound	1. 00	100	½ cup	6. 00	4¼	16¾
LOW-MOISTURE							
Apples	Pound	1. 00	584	4 ounces	23. 36	1¼	4½
				⅛ 9-inch pie (¾ pound per pie).	24. 00	1¼	4¼
	No. 10 can	1. 50	584	4 ounces	35. 04	(1)	3
Applesauce	Pound	1. 00	911	do	36. 44	(1)	2¾
	No. 10 can	2. 50	911	do	91. 10	(1)	1¼
Apricots	Pound	1. 00	505	do	20. 20	1¼	5
	No. 10 can	3. 50	505	do	70. 70	(1)	1½
Fruit cocktail	Pound	1. 00	558	do	22. 32	1¼	4½
	No. 10 can	2. 75	558	do	61. 38	(1)	1¾
Peaches	Pound	1. 00	534	4 ounces	21. 36	1¼	4¾
				⅛ 9-inch pie (¾ pound per pie).	24. 00	1¼	4¼
	No. 10 can	3. 00	534	4 ounces	64. 08	(1)	1¾
Prunes, whole, pitted	Pound	1. 00	462	do	18. 48	1½	5½
	No. 10 can	3. 00	462	do	55. 44	(1)	2

[1] Number of purchase units needed is less than one.

TABLE 17.—FLOUR, CEREALS, AND MIXES

Flour, cereals, and mixes as purchased	Unit of purchase	Weight per unit	Yield, as served	Portion as served or used	Portions per purchase unit	Approximate purchase units for— 25 portions	Approximate purchase units for— 100 portions
		Pounds	*Percent*		*Number*	*Number*	*Number*
Flour	5-pound bag	5.00		1 cup	20.00	(1)	(1)
	25-pound bag	25.00		do	100.00	(1)	(1)
	100-pound sack	100.00		do	400.00	(1)	(1)
Cereals, uncooked:							
Bulgur, cracked wheat (USDA)	Pound	1.00	401	¾ cup cooked	10.67	2½	9½
				1 cup uncooked	2.67	(1)	(1)
Cornmeal	1-pound box	1.00	628	¾ cup cooked	15.33	1¾	6¾
	5-pound bag	5.00	628	do	76.65	(2)	1½
	10-pound bag	10.00	628	do	153.30	(2)	(2)
	1-pound box	1.00	100	1 cup uncooked	3.00	(1)	(1)
Corn grits	do	1.00	628	¾ cup cooked	16.43	1¾	6¼
	do	1.00	100	1 cup uncooked	2.75	(1)	(1)
Farina	do	1.00	855	¾ cup cooked	21.92	1¼	4¾
	5-pound bag	5.00	855	do	109.60	(2)	1
Macaroni	1-pound box	1.00	311	do	12.00	2¼	8½
	20-pound box	20.00	311	do	240.00	(2)	(2)
	1-pound box	1.00	100	1 cup uncooked	3.75	(1)	(1)
Noodles	do	1.00	329	¾ cup cooked	10.67	2½	9½
	20-pound box	20.00	329	do	213.40	(2)	(2)
	1-pound box	1.00	100	1 cup uncooked	7.25	(1)	(1)
Rice	do	1.00	320	¾ cup cooked	11.27	2¼	9
	10-pound box	10.00	320	do	112.70	(2)	(2)
	100-pound sack	100.00	320	do	1,127.00	(2)	(2)
	1-pound box	1.00	100	1 cup uncooked	2.75	(1)	(1)
Rolled oats	do	1.00	610	¾ cup cooked	15.33	1¾	6¾
	3-pound box	3.00	610	do	46.00	(2)	2¼
	50-pound sack	50.00	610	do	766.50	(2)	(2)
	1-pound box	1.00	100	1 cup uncooked	4.50	(1)	(1)
Rolled wheat (USDA)	do	1.00	375	¾ cup cooked	8.89	3	11¼
	3-pound box	3.00	375	do	26.67	(2)	3¾
Spaghetti	1-pound box	1.00	359	do	12.12	2¼	8¼
	20-pound box	20.00	359	do	242.40	(2)	(2)
	1-pound box	1.00	100	1 cup uncooked	6.06	(1)	(1)
Whole wheat	do	1.00	608	¾ cup cooked	15.20	1¾	6¾
	4½-pound box	4.50	608	do	68.40	(2)	1½
	50-pound sack	50.00	608	do	760.00	(2)	(2)

See footnotes at end of table.

TABLE 17.—FLOUR, CEREALS, AND MIXES—Continued

Flour, cereals, and mixes as purchased	Unit of purchase	Weight per unit	Yield, as served	Portion as served or used	Portions per purchase unit	Approximate purchase units for— 25 portions	Approximate purchase units for— 100 portions
		Pounds	*Percent*		*Number*	*Number*	*Number*
Cereals, ready-to-eat:							
Bran flakes (25–40%)	Pound	1.00	100	1 ounce	16.00	1¾	6¼
	14½-ounce package	.91	100	do	14.50	1¾	7
	10-pound package	10.00	100	do	160.00	(2)	(2)
Bran flakes with raisins	Pound	1.00	100	1¼ ounces	12.80	2	8
	14-ounce package	.88	100	do	11.20	2¼	9
	200 individuals	15.62	100	do	200.00	(2)	(2)
Corn flakes	Pound	1.00	100	1 ounce	16.00	1¾	6¼
	12-ounce package	.75	100	do	12.00	2¼	8½
	10-pound package	10.00	100	do	160.00	(2)	(2)
Puffed rice	Pound	1.00	100	⅝ ounce	25.60	1	4
	8-ounce package	.50	100	do	12.80	2	8
	10-pound package	10.00	100	do	256.00	(2)	(2)
Puffed wheat	Pound	1.00	100	½ ounce	32.00	(2)	3¼
	8-ounce package	.50	100	do	16.00	1¾	6¼
	10-pound package	10.00	100	do	320.00	(2)	(2)
Puffed wheat, presweetened	Pound	1.00	100	⅞ ounce	18.29	1½	5½
	9-ounce package	.56	100	do	10.29	2½	9¾
	200 individuals	10.94	100	do	200.00	(2)	(2)
Rice flakes	Pound	1.00	100	do	18.29	1½	5½
	9½-ounce package	.59	100	do	10.86	2½	9¼
	10-pound package	10.00	100	do	182.86	(2)	(2)
Shredded wheat	Pound	1.00	100	1⅗ ounces	10.00	2½	10
	12-ounce package	.75	100	1⅗ ounces (2 small)	7.50	3½	13½
	200 individuals	20.00	100	1⅗ ounces	200.00	(2)	(2)
Wheat flakes	Pound	1.00	100	1 ounce	16.00	1¾	6¼
	10-ounce package	.62	100	do	10.00	2½	10
	10-pound package	10.00	100	do	160.00	(2)	(2)
Mixes: [3]							
Cake:							
Angel food	Pound	1.00		$\frac{1}{12}$ 10-in. cake	12.00	2¼	8½
	12-cake case	12.00		do	144.00	(2)	(2)
Other	Pound	1.00		2 in. x 3 in. cut	15–20	1¾	6¾
				Cupcake	20.00	1¼	5
	5-pound box	5.00		2 in. x 3 in. cut	75–100	(2)	1½
				Cupcake	100.00	(2)	1
Frosting	Pound	1.00		2 in. x 2 in.	38–39	(2)	2¾
				Cupcake	36–37	(2)	3
	5-pound box	5.00		2 in. x 2 in.	190–195	(2)	(2)
				Cupcake	180–185	(2)	(2)

Cookie:							
Basic sugar	Pound	1.00		2 ½-ounce cookies	17–20	1¼	6
	5-pound box	5.00		do	85–100	(2)	1¼
Brownie	Pound	1.00		2 in. x 2 in.	20–30	1¼	5
	5-pound box	5.00		do	100–150	(2)	1
Hot bread:[3]							
Biscuit	Pound	1.00		2-inch biscuit	20.00	1¼	5
	5-pound box	5.00		do	100.00	(2)	1
Muffins	Pound	1.00		1½-ounce muffin	14–16	2	7¼
	5-pound box	5.00		do	70–80	(2)	1½
Rolls:							
Sweet	Pound	1.00		1¼-ounce roll	18–19	1½	5¾
	5-pound box	5.00		do	90–95	(2)	1¼
Yeast	Pound	1.00		1-ounce roll	23–25	1¼	4½
	5-pound box	5.00		do	115–120	(2)	(2)
Piecrust	Pound	1.00		9-inch shell	3.00	8½	33½
	5-pound box	5.00		do	16.00	1¾	6¼

[1] Number of purchase units needed is determined by use.
[2] Number of purchase units needed is less than one.
[3] Yields of mixes vary widely, depending on manufacturer, size of pan, and baking time and temperature. See instructions on package or box.

Table 18.—BAKERY FOODS

Bakery foods as purchased	Unit of purchase	Weight per unit	Portion as served	Portions per purchase unit	Approximate purchase units for— 25 portions	Approximate purchase units for— 100 portions
		Pounds		*Number*	*Number*	*Number*
Bread: [1]						
Raisin	1-pound loaf	1.00	1 slice	18.00	1½	5¾
	2-pound loaf	2.00	do	36.00	(2)	3
Rye	1-pound loaf	1.00	do	23.00	1¼	4½
	1½-pound loaf	1.50	do	28.00	1	3¾
	2-pound loaf	2.00	do	33.00	(2)	3¼
White and whole wheat	1-pound loaf	1.00	⅝-inch slice	16.00	1¾	6¼
	1¼-pound loaf	1.25	do	19.00	1½	5½
	1½-pound loaf	1.50	do	24.00	1¼	4¼
	2-pound loaf	2.00	½-inch slice	28.00	1	4
			⅜-inch slice	36.00	(2)	3
	3-pound loaf	3.00	½-inch slice	44.00	(2)	2½
			⅜-inch slice	56.00	(2)	2
Cake:						
Layer	8-inch		1/12 cake	12.00	2¼	8½
	9-inch		1/16 cake	16.00	1¾	6¼
	12-inch		1/30 cake	30.00	(2)	3½
	14-inch		1/40 cake	40.00	(2)	2½
Loaf	Pound	1.00	⅛ cake	8.00	3¼	12½
			1 cup soft cubes or crumbs	18.00	1½	5¾
			1 cup toasted cubes	13.50	2	7½
			1 cup dry crumbs	6.00	4¼	16¾
Sheet	8-inch square		2 in. x 2 in. (small)	16.00	1¾	6¼
	9 in. x 13 in		3 in. x 3 in. (regular)	12.00	2¼	8½
	12 in. x 10 in		2 in. x 2 in	54.00	(2)	2
			3 in. x 3 in	24.00	1¼	4¼
	16 in. x 24 in		2 in. x 2 in	96.00	(2)	1¼
			3 in. x 3 in	40.00	(2)	2½
Cookies:						
Brownies	Pound	1.00	2 cookies	18.00	1½	5¾
Butter	do	1.00	do	46.50	(2)	2¼
Chocolate chip	do	1.00	do	21.50	1¼	4¾
Cream filled	do	1.00	do	19.50	1½	5¼
Fig bars	do	1.00	do	15.50	1¾	6½
Ginger snaps	do	1.00	do	30.00	(2)	3½
Shortbread	do	1.00	do	29.00	(2)	3½
Sugar	do	1.00	do	10.50	2½	9¾
Vanilla	do	1.00	do	46.50	(2)	2¼
Crackers:						
Graham	do	1.00	2 crackers	32.50	(2)	3¼
Saltines	do	1.00	do	65–70	(2)	1¾
Soda	do	1.00	do	30–35	(2)	3½

Rolls:						
Frankfurter	do	1.00	1 roll (1⅓ ounces)	12.03	2¼	8½
Hamburger	do	1.00	1 roll (1¾ ounces)	9.14	2¾	11
Hard, round	do	1.00	1 roll (1⅚ ounces)	8.74	3	11½
Plain, pan	do	1.00	1 roll (1⅓ ounces)	12.03	2¼	8½
Sweet, pan	do	1.00	1 roll (1½ ounces)	10.67	2½	9½
Pie	8-inch		⅙ pie	6.00	4¼	16¾
	9-inch		⅐ pie	7.00	3¾	14½
	10-inch		⅛ pie	8.00	3¼	12½

[1] End crusts of bread were excluded in determining portions per purchase unit.

[2] Number of purchase units needed is less than one.

Table 19.—FATS AND OILS

Fats and oils as purchased	Unit of purchase	Weight per unit	Portion as served or used	Portions per purchase unit	Approximate purchase units for— 25 portions	Approximate purchase units for— 100 portions
		Pounds		*Number*	*Number*	*Number*
Butter or margarine:						
Pound print	Carton	1.00	1 cup	2.00	(1)	(1)
			1 pat	72.00	(2)	1½
¼-pound print	do	1.00	1 pat	72.00	(2)	1½
Chips	Case	5.00	do	360.00	(2)	(2)
Lard	Carton	1.00	1 cup	2.00	(1)	(1)
	Can	50.00	do	100.00	(1)	(1)
Salad dressing (oil or mayonnaise type)	Pint	1.00	1 tablespoon	32.00	(2)	3¼
	Quart	2.00	do	64.00	(2)	1¾
	Gallon	8.00	do	256.00	(2)	(2)
Salad oil	Pint	.97	1 cup	2.00	(1)	(1)
	Quart	1.94	do	4.00	(1)	(1)
	Gallon	7.76	do	16.00	(1)	(1)
Shortening (Hydrogenated)	Can	1.00	do	2.50	(1)	(1)
	do	3.00	do	7.50	(1)	(1)
	do	50.00	do	125.00	(1)	(1)

[1] Number of purchase units needed is determined by use.

[2] Number of purchase units needed is less than one.

TABLE 20.—SUGAR AND SWEETS

Sugar and sweets as purchased	Unit of purchase	Weight per unit	Portion as served or used	Portions per purchase unit	Approximate purchase units for— 25 portions	100 portions
		Pounds		*Number*	*Number*	*Number*
Sugar:						
Brown, dark or light	Carton	1. 00	1 cup	2. 00	[1]	[1]
		25. 00	do	50. 00	[1]	[1]
Cubes	do	1. 00	2 cubes	40. 00	[2]	2½
	Bulk	25. 00	do	1, 000. 00	[2]	[2]
Granulated:						
Bulk	Carton	1. 00	2 level or 1 rounded teaspoon	54. 00	[2]	2
			1 cup	2. 25	[1]	[1]
	Bag	5. 00	1 cup	11. 25	[1]	[1]
	do	25. 00	do	56. 25	[1]	[1]
	Sack	100. 00	do	225. 00	[1]	[1]
Individuals	Package	1. 50	1 packet	100. 00	[2]	1
	Carton	45. 00	do	3, 000. 00	[2]	[2]
Powdered (confectioners)	do	1. 00	1 cup	3. 50	[1]	[1]
	Sack	25. 00	do	87. 50	[1]	[1]
Sirup:						
Blends	12-fluid-ounce bottle	1. 03	2 tablespoons	12. 00	2¼	8½
	Quart	2. 83	do	32. 00	[2]	3¼
	No. 10 can	8. 50	do	96. 00	[2]	1¼
	Gallon	11. 00	do	128. 00	[2]	[2]
Corn	Pint	1. 50	do	16. 00	1¾	6¼
	5-pound can	5. 00	do	53. 33	[2]	2
	No. 10 can	8. 79	2 tablespoons	93. 76	[2]	1¼
			1 cup	11. 72	[1]	[1]
Maple	Pint	1. 38	2 tablespoons	16. 00	1¾	6¼
	Gallon	11. 00	do	128 00	[2]	[2]
Molasses	Pint	1. 50	do	16. 00	1¾	6¼
	Jar	2. 00	do	21. 00	1¼	5
	No. 10 can	9. 31	do	99. 00	[2]	1
Jam, jelly, marmalade:						
Bulk	Jar	1. 00	1 tablespoon	23. 00	1¼	4½
	No. 10 can	8. 38	do	192. 00	[2]	[2]
Individuals	Carton		1 packet	200. 00	[2]	[2]
Other sweets:						
Apple butter	Jar	1. 00	do	11. 00	2¼	9¼
	No. 10 can	7. 50	do	81. 00	[2]	1¼
Honey	Jar	1. 00	do	11. 00	2½	9¼
	2-pound can	2. 00	do	22. 00	1¼	4¾
	5-pound can	5. 00	do	54. 00	[2]	2
Desserts, dry:						
Gelatin, flavored	3-ounce package	. 19	½ cup	4. 00	6¼	25
	6-ounce package	. 38	do	8. 00	3¼	12½
	Pound	1. 00	do	21. 33	1¼	4¾

Pudding, pie filling:						
Chocolate	4-ounce package	.25	do	4.00	6¼	25
	Pound	1.00	4 ounces	20.00	1¼	5
			Fill for ⅙ 9-inch pie	18.67	1⅓	5⅓
Lemon chiffon	do	1.00	Fill for ⅙ 9-inch pie	32.00	(²)	3¼
Vanilla	3-ounce package	.19	½ cup	4.00	6¼	25
	Pound	1.00	4 ounces	25.60	1	4
			Fill for ⅙ 9-inch pie	24.00	1¼	4¼
Pudding, instant:						
Chocolate	4½-ounce package	.28	½ cup	4.00	6¼	25
	Pound	1.00	do	14.29	1¾	7
Vanilla	3¾-ounce package	.23	do	4.00	6¼	25
	Pound	1.00	do	17.39	1½	5¾

[1] Number of purchase units needed is determined by use.

[2] Number of purchase units needed is less than one.

TABLE 21.—BEVERAGES

Beverages as purchased	Unit of purchase	Weight per unit	Portion as served	Portions per purchase unit	Approximate purchase units [1] for— 25 portions	Approximate purchase units [1] for— 100 portions
		Pounds		*Number*	*Number*	*Number*
Carbonated drinks:						
6-ounce bottles	Case (24)		6 fluid ounces	24.00		
12-ounce bottles	do		do	48.00		
16-ounce bottles	do		do	64.00		
Cocoa:						
Regular, unsweetened	Pound	1.00	1 measuring cup, prepared	50.00	½	2
Instant, sweetened:						
Bulk	8-ounce carton	.50	1 cup	28.00	(1½ c.)	(6 c.).
	38-ounce carton	2.38	do	133.00	(1½ c.)	(6 c.).
Individuals	Carton (50)		1 packet	50.00	½	2
Sirup, sweetened	16-ounce can	1.00	1 cup	29.00	1	3½.
Coffee:						
Ground	Pound	1.00	1 measuring cup, prepared	[2] 37.00		
Instant:						
Bulk	6-ounce jar	.38	1 level teaspoon	180.00	(½ c.+1 t.)	(2 c.+4 t.).
			1 rounded teaspoon	90.00	(½ c.+1 t.)	(2 c.+4 t.).
	10-ounce jar	.62	1 level teaspoon	300.00	(½ c.+1 t.)	(2 c.+4 t.).
Individuals	Carton (72)		1 packet	72.00		
Tea:						
Bulk	Pound	1.00	1 measuring cup, prepared	256.00		(6¼ oz.).
Bags	Package (48)	.24	1 measuring cup or more	48.00		
	Carton (100)	.50	do	100.00	¼	1
Instant	1½-ounce jar	.09	1 cup hot tea	96.00	(½ c.+1 t.)	(2 c.+4 t.).
			1 cup iced tea	64.00	(¾ c.)	(3 c.).

[1] Numbers in parentheses refer to approximate measure to serve 25 and 100 portions: c., cup; t., teaspoon; oz., ounces.

[2] Varies depending on brand of coffee used and method of preparation.

OTHER USEFUL INFORMATION FOR ESTIMATING FOOD QUANTITIES

TABLE 22.—*Conversion factors for computing the number of purchase units needed for portions of various sizes*

Portion size given in purchase tables (ounces)	Conversion factors for specified portion size, ounces									
	1	2	3	4	5	6	7	8	9	10
1	1.00	2.00	3.00	4.00	5.00	6.00	7.00	8.00	9.00	10.00
2	.50	1.00	1.50	2.00	2.50	3.00	3.50	4.00	4.50	5.00
3	.33	.67	1.00	1.33	1.67	2.00	2.33	2.67	3.00	3.33
4	.25	.50	.75	1.00	1.25	1.50	1.75	2.00	2.25	2.50
5	.20	.40	.60	.80	1.00	1.20	1.40	1.60	1.80	2.00
6	.17	.33	.50	.67	.83	1.00	1.17	1.33	1.50	1.67
7	.14	.29	.43	.57	.71	.86	1.00	1.14	1.29	1.43
8	.12	.25	.38	.50	.62	.75	.88	1.00	1.12	1.25

How To Use Table 22:

This table is to be used to help determine the number of purchase units if the size of portion is different from that specified in tables 1 to 21. For example, for 3-ounce portions of snap beans, five No. 10 cans are required (table 10); for other size portions, conversion factors in this table can be used to determine the number of No. 10 cans required.

The figures in the left-hand column of the conversion table represent the portion sizes given in tables 1 to 21. The figures across the top represent portion sizes that may be desired. If a 4-ounce instead of a 3-ounce portion of canned snap beans is to be used, for example, find the 3-ounce line in the left-hand column of the conversion table. Follow this line across to the factor in the 4-ounce column. Multiply this factor (1.33) by the number of purchase units (five No. 10 cans) given in table 10 for 100. Thus: 5 (No. 10 cans) × 1.33=6.65 No. 10 cans (round to 6¾ No. 10 cans) to serve 100 people each a 4-ounce portion.

Portion sizes in the purchase tables are sometimes given in terms of tablespoons, cups, slices, etc. Any of these measures can be substituted for ounces in this conversion table and the same computations performed.

TABLE 23.—*Cost per portion for food priced from 10 cents to $2 per purchase unit*

Price per purchase unit (cents)	Cost per portion for indicated portions per purchase unit							
	4	6	8	10	12	16	20	24
	Cents	Cents	Cents	Cents	Cents	Cents	Cents	Cents
10	2.5	1.7	1.2	1.0	0.8	0.6	0.5	0.4
15	3.8	2.5	1.9	1.5	1.2	.9	.8	.6
20	5.0	3.3	2.5	2.0	1.7	1.2	1.0	.8
25	6.2	4.2	3.1	2.5	2.1	1.6	1.2	1.0
30	7.5	5.0	3.8	3.0	2.5	1.9	1.5	1.2
35	8.8	5.8	4.4	3.5	2.9	2.2	1.8	1.5
40	10.0	6.7	5.0	4.0	3.3	2.5	2.0	1.7
45	11.2	7.5	5.6	4.5	3.7	2.8	2.2	1.9
50	12.5	8.3	6.2	5.0	4.2	3.1	2.5	2.1
60	15.0	10.0	7.5	6.0	5.0	3.8	3.0	2.5
70	17.5	11.7	8.8	7.0	5.8	4.4	3.5	2.9
80	20.0	13.3	10.0	8.0	6.7	5.0	4.0	3.3
90	22.5	15.0	11.2	9.0	7.5	5.6	4.5	3.7
100	25.0	16.7	12.5	10.0	8.3	6.2	5.0	4.2
110	27.5	18.3	13.8	11.0	9.2	6.9	5.5	4.6
120	30.0	20.0	15.0	12.0	10.0	7.5	6.0	5.0
130	32.5	21.7	16.2	13.0	10.8	8.1	6.5	5.4
140	35.0	23.3	17.5	14.0	11.7	8.8	7.0	5.8
150	37.5	25.0	18.8	15.0	12.5	9.4	7.5	6.2
160	40.0	26.7	20.0	16.0	13.3	10.0	8.0	6.7
170	42.5	28.3	21.2	17.0	14.2	10.6	8.5	7.1
180	45.0	30.0	22.5	18.0	15.0	11.2	9.0	7.5
190	47.5	31.7	23.8	19.0	15.8	11.9	9.5	7.9
200	50.0	33.3	25.0	20.0	16.7	12.5	10.0	8.3

How To Use Table 23:

Determine the number of portions per unit of purchase through use of the food item or from the column, "Portions per purchase unit," in appropriate table. Locate the column in the table above that is nearest to that number. Then locate in that column the number horizontal to the price paid for the purchase unit in the left-hand column. This number represents the approximate cost of a portion.

FOOD PURCHASING GUIDE

TABLE 24.—BEEF: *Approximate percentage of edible meat [1] from the carcass and wholesale cuts of Choice, Good, and Standard grades of beef*

[Steers ranging from 11 to 21 months in age]

Beef	Grade of carcass		
	Choice	Good	Standard
	Percent	*Percent*	*Percent*
Carcass	85	84	82
Wholesale cuts:			
Brisket	88	87	85
Chuck	86	85	83
Flank	100	100	100
Foreshank	58	58	56
Loin end	89	88	86
Round, with hindshank	85	84	82
Rump, knuckle out	87	86	84
Short loin	90	89	87
Standing rib	85	83	80
Short plate	90	89	86

[1] The remaining percentage of beef consists of bone, ligament, and tendon.

TABLE 25.—LAMB: *Approximate percentage of edible meat [1] from the carcass and wholesale cuts of Prime, Choice, and Good grades of lamb*

Lamb	Grade of carcass		
	Prime	Choice	Good
	Percent	*Percent*	*Percent*
Carcass	86	83	82
Wholesale cuts:			
Breast and flank	89	86	86
Leg	87	85	84
Loin	90	87	86
Neck	79	75	75
Rib cut (9 ribs)	86	82	80
Shoulder (3 ribs)	87	85	84

[1] The remaining percentage of lamb consists of bone and ligament.

TABLE 26.—PORK: *Approximate percentage of edible meat [1] from the carcass and wholesale trimmed cuts from hogs of 3 weight groups*

Pork	Weight of carcass [2]		
	200 pounds live, 158 pounds dressed	225 pounds live, 178 pounds dressed	250 pounds live, 197 pounds dressed
	Percent	*Percent*	*Percent*
Carcass	79	80	82
Wholesale cuts:			
Bacon	92	93	94
Ham	85	85	86
Head, full cut	47	50	53
Loin	78	79	79
Shoulder, full cut	84	85	86
Shoulder, ribs	40	42	45
Spareribs	58	61	63

[1] The remaining percentage consists of bone and skin.
[2] The average yield of lard per hog slaughtered is 14 percent per 100 pounds live weight. This percentage includes lard and rendered pork fat, and excludes bacon and salt pork.

TABLE 27.—VEGETABLES OR FRUITS: *Approximate amount of canned and frozen product obtained from specified quantities of fresh vegetables and fruits*

Vegetables or fruits	Home canning methods — Fresh	Home — Yield, canned (Quarts)	Commercial canning methods — Fresh	Commercial — Yield of #10 cans, canned (Number)	Frozen — Fresh	Frozen — Yield, frozen (Pounds)	Frozen — Fruit-to-sugar ratio
Vegetables:							
Asparagus	2½ to 4½ pounds		8 to 9 pounds	1	1 crate	15	
	1 crate	7–12	1 crate	3–4			
Beans, lima	3 to 5 pounds [1]		5 pounds [2]	1	1 bushel [2]	29	
	1 bushel [1]	6–11	1 bushel [2]	6			
Beans, snap	1½ to 2½ pounds		4 to 5 pounds	1	1 bushel	24	
	1 bushel	12–20	1 bushel	6–8			
Beets, without tops	2 to 3½ pounds		8 pounds	1			
	1 bushel	15–26	1 bushel	6–7			
Broccoli					1 crate	23	
Carrots, without tops	2 to 3 pounds		8 pounds	1	1 bushel	25	
	1 bushel	17–25	1 bushel	6–7			
Corn, sweet, in husks	3 to 6 pounds	[3] 1	17 to 18 pounds	[3] 1			
	1 bushel	[3] 6–12	1 bushel	[3] 2			
Okra	1½ pounds	1	7 pounds	1	1 bushel	[3] 8	
Peas, green	3 to 6 pounds [1]		4 to 5 pounds [2]	1	1 bushel [2]	27	
	1 bushel [1]	5–10	1 bushel [2]	6–8			
Pumpkin and winter squash	1½ to 3 pounds		17 to 18 pounds	1			
	1 bushel	17–33	1 bushel	3			
Spinach, other greens	2 to 6 pounds		8 pounds		1 bushel	32	
	1 bushel	3–10	1 bushel	2–3			
Sweetpotatoes	2 to 3 pounds		7 pounds	1	1 bushel	10–11	
		17–25	1 bushel	7			
Tomatoes	2½ to 3½ pounds		12 pounds				
	1 bushel	15–21	1 bushel	4–5			
Tomato catsup			19 pounds				
			1 bushel	2–3			
Tomato paste			40 to 41 pounds	1			
			1 bushel	1–2			
Tomato sauce			21 pounds	1			
			1 bushel	3–4			

FOOD PURCHASING GUIDE

Fruits							
Apples	2½ to 3 pounds	1	10 pounds	1			
	1 bushel	15–20	1 bushel	4–5	1 bushel	20–31	5 to 1
Berries, except strawberries	1½ to 3 pounds	1	5 pounds	1			
	1 crate	12–24	1 crate	7			
Cherries, sour	2 to 2½ pounds	1	7 pounds	1			
	1 bushel	22–28	1 bushel	8	1 crate	34	4 to 1
Peaches	2 to 3 pounds	1	7 pounds	1			
	1 bushel	15–25	1 bushel	6–7	1 bushel	53	4 to 1
Pears	2 to 3 pounds	1	8 pounds	1			
	1 bushel	15–24	1 bushel	5–6	1 bushel	41–44	3 to 1
Plums	1½ to 2½ pounds	1	5 pounds	1			
	1 bushel	19–32	1 bushel	9–10	1 bushel		
Strawberries	1½ to 3 pounds	1	6 pounds	1			
	1 crate	12–24	1 crate	6	1 crate	42	3 to 1

[1] In pods.　[2] Shelled basis.　[3] Whole kernel.

TABLE 28.—*Common can and jar sizes*

Container				Principal products
	Consumer description			
Can size (Industry term)	Average net weight or fluid measure per can [1] (check label)	Average cups per can	Cans per case	
		Number	*Number*	
8 ounces	8 ounces	1	48 and 72	Small cans—ready-to-serve soups, fruits, and vegetables.
No. 1 picnic	10½ to 12 ounces	1¼	48	Small cans—condensed soups, some fruits, vegetables, meat, and fish.
No. 300	14 to 16 ounces	1¾	24	Small cans—fruits, vegetables, some meat and poultry products, and ready-to-serve soups.
No. 303	16 to 17 ounces	2	24	Do.
No. 2	1 pound, 4 ounces (20 ounces) or 1 pint, 2 fluid ounces (18 fluid ounces).	2½	24	Family size—juices, ready-to-serve soups, and some fruits.
No. 2½	1 pound, 13 ounces (29 ounces)	3½	24	Family size—fruits and some vegetables.
No. 3 cylinder	3 pounds, 3 ounces (51 ounces) or 1 quart, 14 fluid ounces (46 fluid ounces).	5¾	12	"Economy family size"—fruit and vegetable juices. Institutional size—condensed soups, some vegetables, and meat and poultry products.
No. 10	6 pounds, 8 ounces (104 ounces) to 7 pounds, 5 ounces (117 ounces).	12 to 13	6	Institutional size—fruits, vegetables, and some other foods.

[1] The label on one product may show net weight that differs slightly from the label on another product in cans or jars of identical size. (An example would be lima beans (1 pound) and blueberries (14 ounces) in the same size can.)

Source: National Canners Association.

Ounce equivalents in decimal parts of pound

Ounces	Pound	Ounces	Pound
1	0. 06	9	. 56
2	. 12	10	. 62
3	. 19	11	. 69
4	. 25	12	. 75
5	. 31	13	. 81
6	. 38	14	. 88
7	. 44	15	. 94
8	. 50	16	1. 00

Approximate scoop equivalents

Scoop No.[1]	Level measure	Scoop No.[1]	Level measure
6	⅔ cup	20	3⅕ tablespoons
8	½ cup	24	2⅔ tablespoons
10	⅖ cup	30	2⅕ tablespoons
12	⅓ cup	40	1⅗ tablespoons
16	¼ cup		

[1] A serving spoon may be used to replace a scoop. Since serving spoons are not identified by number, it is necessary to measure or weigh the quantity of food from sizes of spoons used to obtain the approximate serving size desired.

Common food-measure equivalents

3 teaspoons	1 tablespoon	16 tablespoons	1 cup
2 tablespoons	1 fluid ounce	1 cup	8 fluid ounces
4 tablespoons	¼ cup	2 cups	1 pint
6 tablespoons	⅜ cup	2 pints	1 quart
8 tablespoons	½ cup		

INDEX OF FOODS IN TABLES 1 THROUGH 21

INDEX

INDEX

INDEX

FOOD SERVICE GLOSSARY

TABLE OF CONTENTS

FOOD SERVICE GLOSSARY

A

ABSORPTION CAPABILITY
The property of flour to absorb and hold liquid.

ACIDITY
Sourness or tartness in a food product; in yeast doughs, a condition indicating excess fermentation; a factor in generating carbon dioxide for cake leavening.

AERATION
See LEAVENING.

AEROBIC BACTERIA
Those that require the presence of free oxygen as found in the air for growth.

A LA CARTE
On the menu alone, not in combination with a total meal.

A LA KING
A dish served with a cream sauce, usually containing green peppers and pimentos, and sometimes mushrooms and onions.

A LA MODE
In a fashion or the style of; for example, desserts served with ice cream or pot roast of beef cooked with vegetables.

ALBUMEN
Egg white.

AMBROSIA
A favorite southern dessert made of oranges, bananas, pineapple, and shredded coconut.

AMEBA
A simple animal-like organism that grows in water.

ANAEROBIC BACTERIA
Those that grow in oxygen-free atmosphere, deriving oxygen from solid or liquid materials and producing toxic substances.

ANTIBIOTICS
Substances produced by microorganisms and capable of inhibiting or killing other microorganisms.

ANTIOXIDANT
A chemical solution in which fruits and vegetables are dipped to prevent darkening.

ANTIPASTI or ANTIPASTO
An appetizer, or a spicy first course, consisting of relishes, cold sliced meats rolled with or without stuffings, fish, or other hors d'oeuvres eaten with a fork.

ANTISEPTIC
An agent that may or may not kill microorganisms, but does inhibit their growth. Peroxide is an example.

APPETIZER
A small portion of food or drink before or as the first course of a meal. These include a wide assortment of items ranging from cocktails, canapes, and hors d'oeuvres to plain fruit juices. The function of an appetizer is to pep up the appetite.

AU GRATIN
A thin surface crust formed by either bread or cheese, or both. Sometimes used with a cream sauce.

AU JUS
With natural juice. Roast rib au jus, for example, is beef served with unthickened gravy.

B

BACILLI
Cylindrical or rod-shaped bacteria responsible for such diseases as botulism, typhoid fever, and tuberculosis.

BACTERIA
Microscopic, one-cell microbes found in soil, water, and most material throughout nature. Some are responsible for disease and food spoilage, others are useful in industrial fermentation.

BACTERICIDE
Any substance that kills bacteria and related forms of life.

BAKE
To cook by dry heat in an oven. When applied to meats, it is called roasting.

BARBECUE
To roast or broil in a highly seasoned sauce.

BASTE
To moisten foods while cooking, especially while roasting meat. Melted fat, meat drippings, stock, water, or water and fat may be used.

BATTER
A homogeneous mixture of ingredients with liquid to make a mass that is of a soft plastic character.

BAVARIAN
A style of cooking that originated in the Bavarian section of Germany.

BEAT
 To make a mixture smooth or to introduce air by using a lifting motion with spoon or whip.

BENCH TOLERANCE
 The property of dough to ferment at a rate slow enough to prevent overfermentation while dough is being made up into units on the bench.

BLANCH
 To rinse with boiling water, drain, and rinse in cold water. Used for rice, macaroni, and other pastas to prevent sticking. For potatoes, to cook in hot, deep fat for a short time until clear but not brown.

BLAND
 Mild flavored, not stimulating to the taste.

BLEACHED FLOUR
 Flour that has been treated by a chemical to remove its natural color and make it white.

BLEEDING
 Dough that has been cut and left unsealed at the cut, thus permitting the escape of leavening gas. This term also applies to icing that bleeds.

BLEND
 To mix thoroughly two or more ingredients.

BOIL
 To cook in a liquid that bubbles actively during the time of cooking. The boiling temperature of water at sea level is 212° F.

BOTULISM
 Acute food poisoning caused by botulin (toxin) in food.

BOUILLON
 A clear soup made from beef or chicken stock or soup and gravy base.

BRAISE
 To brown meat or vegetables in a small amount of fat, then to cook slowly, covered, at simmering temperature in a small amount of liquid. The liquid may be juices rendered from meat, or added water, milk, or meat stock.

BREAD
 To coat with crumbs of bread or other food; or to dredge in seasoned flour, dip in a mixture of milk and slightly beaten eggs, and then dredge again in crumbs.

BROIL
 To cook under or over direct heat.

BROWN
 To cook, usually at medium or high heat, until the item of food darkens.

BRUNSWICK STEW
A main dish composed of a combination of poultry, meats, and vegetables.

BUTTERFLY
A method of cutting double chops (usually pork) from boneless loin strips. One side of each double chop is hinged together with a thin layer of meat.

BUTTERHORNS
Basic sweet dough cut and shaped like horns.

C

CACCIATORE
Chicken cooked "hunter" style. Browned chicken is braised in a sauce made with tomatoes, other vegetables, stock, and herbs.

CANAPE
Any of many varieties of appetizers, usually spread on bread, toast, or crackers and eaten with the fingers.

CANDY
To cook in sugar or syrup.

CARAMELIZED SUGAR
Dry sugar heated with constant stirring until melted and dark in color, used for flavoring and coloring.

CARBOHYDRATES
Sugars and starches derived chiefly from fruits and vegetable sources and containing set amounts of carbon, hydrogen, and oxygen.

CARBON DIOXIDE
A colorless, tasteless edible gas obtained during fermentation or from a combination of soda and acid.

CARRIERS
Persons who harbor and disseminate germs without having symptoms of a disease. The individual has either had the disease at one time and temporarily continues to excrete the organism, or has never manifested symptoms because of good resistance to the disease.

CHIFFONADE DRESSING
A salad dressing containing chopped hard-cooked eggs and beets.

CHIFFON CAKE
A sponge cake containing liquid shortening.

CHILI
A special pepper or its fruits. Dried, ground chili peppers are used in chili powder.

CHILI CON CARNE
Ground beef and beans seasoned with chili powder.

CHILL
To place in a refrigerator or cool place until cold.

CHOP
To cut into pieces with a knife or chopper.

CHOP SUEY
A thick Chinese stew of thin slices of pork and various vegetables, such as bean sprouts, celery, and onions.

CLEAR FLOUR
Lower grade and higher ash content flour remaining after the patent flour has been separated. (Used in rye bread.)

COAGULATE
To thicken or form into a consistent mass.

COAT
To cover the entire surface of food with a selected mixture.

CONDIMENTS
Seasonings that in themselves furnish little nourishment, but which improve the flavor of food.

CONGEALING POINT
Temperature or time at which a liquid changes to a firm or plastic condition.

COOKING LOSSES
Loss of weight, liquid, or nutrients, and possibly a lowered palatability of a cooked food.

COOL
To let stand, usually at room temperature, until no longer warm to touch.

CREAM
To mix until smooth, sugar, shortening, and other ingredients; to incorporate air so that resultant mixture increases appreciably in volume and is thoroughly blended.

CREAM PUFFS
Baked puffs of cream-puff dough, which are hollow; usually filled with cream pudding, whipped topping, or ice cream.

CREOLE
A cooked sauce for poultry or shrimp. Usually served with rice.

CRISP
To make somewhat firm and brittle.

CROUTONS
Bread cut into small cubes and either fried or browned in the oven, according to the intended use. Used as a garnish, croutons are fried; as soup accompaniments, baked.

CRULLERS
Long, twisted doughnuts.

CRUMB
The soft part of bread or cake; a fragment of bread (see also BREAD).

CRUST
Hardened exterior of bread; pastry portion of pie.

CRUSTING
Formation of dry crust on the surface of doughs.

CUBE
To cut into approximately 1/4 to 1/2 inch squares.

CURDLE
To change into curd; to coagulate or thicken.

CURING
A form of processing meat, which improves its flavor and texture.

CURRY
A powder made from many spice ingredients and used as a seasoning for Indian and Oriental-type dishes, such as shrimp and chicken curry.

CUSTOM FOODS (RATION-DENSE)
Various types of labor- and space-saving foods, including canned, concentrated, dehydrated, frozen, and prefabricated items.

CUT IN (as for shortening)
To combine firm shortening and flour with pastry blender or knife.

D

DANISH PASTRY
A flaky yeast dough having butter or shortening rolled into it.

DASH
A scant 1/8 teaspoon.

DEVILED
A highly seasoned, chopped, ground, or whole mixture served hot or cold.

DICE
To cut into 1/4 inch or smaller cubes.

DISINFECTANT
A chemical agent that destroys bacteria and other harmful organisms.

DISPOSABLES
Disposable articles used for food preparation, eating, or drinking utensils, constructed wholly or in part from paper or synthetic materials and intended for one single service.

DISSOLVE
To mix a solid, dry substance with a liquid until the solid is in solution.

DIVIDER
A machine used to cut dough into a desired size or weight.

DOCKING
Punching a number of vertical impressions in a dough with a smooth round stick about the size of a pencil. Docking makes doughs expand uniformly without bursting during baking.

DOT
To place small pieces (usually butter) on the surface of food.

DOUGH
The thickened, uncooked mass of combined ingredients for bread, rolls, cookies, and pies, but usually applicable to bread.

DOUGH CONDITIONER
A chemical product added to flour to alter its properties to hold gas.

DOUGH TEMPERATURES
Temperature of dough at different stages of processing.

DRAIN
To remove liquid.

DREDGE
To sprinkle or coat with flour, sugar, or cornmeal.

DRIPPINGS
Fat and juice dripped from roasted meat.

DRY YEAST
A dehydrated form of yeast.

DU JOUR
Today's or of the day; for example, Specialite du jour — food specialty of the day.

DUSTING
Distributing a film of flour or starch on pans or work surfaces.

E

ECLAIR
A long, thin pastry made from cream puff batter, usually filled with cream pudding, whipped topping, or ice cream. The baked, filled shell is dusted with confectioner's sugar or covered with a thin layer of chocolate.

EDIBLE

Fit to eat, wholesome.

EMULSIFICATION

The process of blending together fat and water solutions of ingredients to produce a stable mixture that will not separate while standing.

ENCHILADAS

A dish consisting of tortillas, a sauce, a filling (cheese, meat, or beans) and garnished with a topping such as cheese, then rolled, stacked, or folded and baked.

ENRICHED BREAD

Bread made from enriched flour and containing federally prescribed amounts of thiamin, riboflavin, iron, and niacin.

ENTREE

An intermediary course of a meal, which in the United States is usually the "main" dish.

ENZYME

A substance, produced by living organisms, that has the power to bring about changes in organic materials.

EXTRACT

Essence of fruits or spices used for flavoring.

F

FAT ABSORPTION

Fat that is absorbed in food products as they are fried in deep fat.

FERMENTATION

The chemical changes of an organic compound caused by action of living organisms (yeast or bacteria), usually producing a leavening gas.

FILET

The English term is "fillet," designating a French method of dressing fish, poultry, or meat to exclude bones and include whole muscle strips.

FLIPPER

A can of food that bulges at one end, indicating food spoilage. If pressed, the bulge may "flip" to the opposite end. Can and contents should be discarded.

FOAM

Mass of beaten egg and sugar, as in sponge cake before the flour is added.

FOLD

To lap yeast dough over onto itself. With cake batter, to lift and lap the batter onto itself to lightly incorporate ingredients.

FOLD IN
To combine ingredients gently with an up-and-over motion by lifting one up through the other.

FOOD-CONTACT SURFACES
Those parts and areas of equipment and utensils with which food normally comes in contact. Also those surfaces with which food may come in contact and drain back into surfaces normally in contact with food.

FOOD INFECTION
A food-borne illness from ingesting foods carrying bacteria that later multiply within the body and produce disease.

FOOD INTOXICATION
Another term used synonymously with food poisoning, or the ingestion of a food containing a poisonous substance.

FOOD POISONING
A food-borne illness contracted through ingesting food that contains some poisonous substance.

FOOD VALUE
The quantity of a nutrient contained in a food substance.

FOO YOUNG
A popular dish made with scrambled eggs or omelets with cut Chinese vegetables, onions, and meat. Usually, the dish is served with a sauce.

FORMULA
A recipe giving ingredients, amounts to be used, and the method of preparing the finished product.

FRANCONIA POTATOES
Potatoes are parboiled, then oven-browned in butter.

FREEZE DRYING
Drying method where the product is first frozen and then placed within a vacuum chamber (freeze dehydration). Aided by small controlled inputs of thermal or microwave energy, the moisture in the product passes directly from the ice-crystalline state to moisture vapor that is evacuated.

FRENCH BREAD
A crusty bread, baked in a narrow strip and containing little or no shortening.

FRENCH FRY
To cook in deep fat.

FRICASSEE
To cook by braising; usually applied to fowl or veal cut into pieces.

FRITTERS

Fruit, meat, poultry, or vegetables that are dipped in batter and fried.

FRIZZLE

To cook in a small amount of fat until food is crisp and curled at the edges.

FRY

To cook in hot fat. When a small amount of fat is used, the process is known as pan-frying or sauteing; when food is partially covered, shallow frying; and when food is completely covered, deep-fat frying.

FUMIGANT

A gaseous or colloidal substance used to destroy insects or pests.

FUNGICIDE

An agent that destroys fungi.

G

GARNISH

To ornament or decorate food before serving.

GELATINIZE

To convert into a gelatinous or jelly-like form.

GERM

A pathogenic, or disease-producing bacteria. A small mass of living substance capable of developing into an organism or one of its parts.

GERMICIDE

A germ-destroying agent.

GIBLETS

The heart, gizzard, and liver of poultry cooked with water for use in preparing chicken or turkey stock or gravy.

GLAZE

A thick or thin sugar syrup or sugar mixture used to coat certain types of pastry and cakes.

GLUTEN

The elastic protein mass formed when the protein material of the wheat flour is mixed with water.

GOULASH

A Hungarian stew variously made in the United States of beef, veal, or frankfurters with onions and potatoes. The sauce has tomato paste and paprika as ingredients, served with sour cream if desired.

GOURMET
A connoisseur, or a critical judge, of good food and drink.

GRATE
To separate food into small pieces by rubbing it on a grater.

GREASE
To rub lightly with butter, shortening, or oil.

GRIDDLE
A flat surface or pan on which food is cooked by dry heat. Grease is removed as it accumulates. No liquid is added.

GRILL
See BROIL.

GRIND
To force food materials through a food chopper.

GUMBO
A Creole dish resembling soup, thickened somewhat with okra, its characteristic ingredient.

H

HARD SAUCE
A dessert sauce made of butter and confectioner's sugar, thoroughly creamed. The mixture is thinned or tempered with boiling water.

HASH
A baked dish made of chopped or minced meat and/or vegetables mixture in brown stock.

HEARTH
The heated baking surface of the floor of an oven.

HERMITS
A rich short-flake cookie.

HOLLANDAISE
A sauce made with egg yolks and butter and usually served over vegetables.

HONEY
A sweet syrupy substance produced by bees from flower nectar.

HORS D'OEUVRES
Light, snack-type foods eaten hot or cold at the beginning of a meal.

HORSESHOES
Danish pastry, shaped like horseshoes.

HOST
Any living animal or plant affording food for growth to a parasite.

HOT CROSS BUNS
Sweet, spicy, fruity buns with cross-cut on top, which usually is covered with a plain frosting.

HOT AIR DRYING
Products are cut in small pieces and spread on slat or wire bottom trays. Hot air is passed over and under trays to dry products.

HUMIDITY
The percent of moisture in air related to the total moisture capacity of that air at a particular temperature. Usually expressed as relative humidity.

HUNTER STYLE
Browned meat, usually chicken, braised in various combinations of tomatoes and other vegetables, stock, oil, garlic, and herbs.

HUSH PUPPIES
Deep-fried cornbread batter seasoned with onions. Used mostly in the South, usually with fish.

I

INCUBATION PERIOD
That time between entrance of disease-producing bacteria in a person and the first appearance of symptoms.

INSECTICIDE
Any chemical substance used for the destruction of insects.

ITALIENNE
Italian style of cooking.

J

JARDINIERE
A meat dish or garnish, "garden" style, made of several kinds of vegetables.

JULIENNE
A method of cutting meat, poultry, vegetables (especially potatoes), and fruits in long, thin strips.

K

KEBAB
Various Turkish-style dishes whose principal feature is skewered meat, usually lamb.

KNEAD
To work and press dough with the palms of the hands, turning and folding the dough at rapid intervals.

KOLACHES
A bread bun made from a soft dough and topped with fruit.

L

LACTIC ACID
An organic acid sometimes known as the acid of milk because it is produced when milk sours. Bacteria cause the souring.

LARDING
To cover uncooked lean meat or fish with strips of fat, or to insert strips of fat with a skewer.

LASAGNA
An Italian baked dish with broad noodles, or lasagna noodles, which has been cooked, drained, and combined in alternate layers with Italian meat sauce and cheese of two or three types (cottage, parmesan, and mozzarella).

LEAVENING
The aeration of a product (raising or lightening by air, steam, or gas (carbon dioxide)) that occurs during mixing and baking. The agent for generating gas in a dough or batter is usually yeast or baking powder.

LUKEWARM
Moderately warm or tepid.

LYONNAISE
A seasoning with onions originating in Lyons, France. Sauteed potatoes, green beans, and other vegetables are seasoned this way.

M

MAKEUP
Manual or mechanical manipulation of dough to provide a desired size and shape.

MARBLE CAKE
A cake of two or three colored batters partially mixed.

MARBLING
The intermingling of fat with lean in meat. Meat cut across the grain will show the presence or absence of marbling and may indicate its quality and palatability.

MARINADE
A preparation containing spices, herbs, condiments, vegetables, and a liquid (usually acid) in which a food is placed for a period of time to enhance its flavor, or to increase its tenderness.

MARINATE
To cover with dressing and allow to stand for a short length of time.

MARMALADE
A type of jam or preserve made with sliced fruits. Crushed fruits or whole fruits are used more commonly in jam.

MEAT SUBSTITUTE
Any food used as an entree that does not contain beef, veal, pork, or lamb. Some substitutes are protein-rich dishes such as eggs, fish, dried beans, and cheese.

MEDIA
The plural of medium.

MEDIUM
A material or combination of materials used for cultivation of microorganisms.

MELTING POINT
The temperature at which a solid becomes a liquid.

MERINGUE
A white frothy mass of beaten egg whites and sugar.

MILK FAT
The fat in milk and milk products.

MILK LIQUID
Fresh fluid milk or evaporated or powdered milk reconstituted to the equivalent of fresh fluid milk.

MINCE
To cut or chop into very small pieces, using knife or chopper.

MINESTRONE
Thickened vegetable soup containing lentils or beans.

MIXING
To unite two or more ingredients.

MOCHA
A flavor combination of coffee and chocolate, but predominately that of coffee.

MOLD
Microscopic, multicellular, thread-like fungi growing on moist surfaces of organic material.

MOLDER
Machine that shapes dough pieces for various shapes.

MULLIGATAWNY
A soup with a chicken-stock base highly seasoned, chiefly by curry powder.

MYOCIDE
   An agent that destroys molds.

N

NUTRIENT
   A food substance that humans require to support life and health.

O

O'BRIEN
   A style of preparing sauteed vegetables with diced green peppers and pimientos.

OLD DOUGHS
   Overfermented yeast dough that produces a finished baked loaf, dark in crumb color, sour in flavor, low in volume, coarse in grain, and tough in texture.

OMELET
   Eggs beaten to a froth, cooked with stirring until set, and served in a half-round form by folding one half over the other.

OVEN
   A chamber used for baking, heating, or drying.

OYSTER MUSCLE
   Tender, oval piece of dark poultry meat found in the recess on either side of the back.

P

PALATABLE
   Agreeable to the palate or taste.

PAN BROIL
   See BROIL.

PAN FRY
   See FRY.

PARASITES
   Organisms that live in or on a living host.

PARBOIL
   To boil in water until partially cooked.

PARE
   To trim and remove all superfluous matter from any article.

PARKERHOUSE ROLLS
Folded buns of fairly rich dough.

PARMESAN
A very hard, dry cheese with a sharp flavor.

PASTA (or PASTE)
Any macaroni product, including spaghetti, noodles, and the other pastas.

PATHOGENS
Disease-producing microorganisms.

PEEL
To remove skin, using a knife or peeling machine.

PEPPER POT
Any of a wide variety of styles of highly seasoned soup or stew.

PICKLE
A method of preserving food by a salt and water (or vinegar) solution.

PILAF
An oriental or Turkish dish made of rice cooked in beef or chicken stock and mildly flavored with onions.

PIQUANT
A tart, pleasantly sharp flavor. A piquant sauce or dressing contains lemon juice or vinegar.

PIT
To remove pits or seeds (as from dates or avocados).

PLASTICITY
The consistency or feel of shortening.

POACH
Method of cooking food in a hot liquid that is kept just below the boiling point.

POLONAISE
A garnish consisting of chopped egg and parsley served on cauliflower, asparagus, or other dishes. Bread crumbs are sometimes added.

PPM
Parts per million.

PORCUPINE
A preparation of ground beef and rice shaped into balls and cooked in tomato sauce.

POTABLE
Suitable for drinking.

POTENTIALLY HAZARDOUS pH
Any perishable food which consists in whole or in part of milk or milk products, eggs, meat, poultry, fish, shellfish, synthetic food, or other ingredient capable of supporting rapid and progressive growth of pathogens.

PREHEAT
To heat to the desired baking temperature before placing food in the oven.

PROOF BOX
A tightly closed box or cabinet equipped with shelves to permit the introduction of heat and steam; used for fermenting dough.

PROOFING PERIOD
The time between molding and baking during which dough rises.

PROTOZOA
Minute, one-celled animals.

PROVOLONE
A cured, hard cheese that has a smoky flavor.

PSYCHROPHILIC BACTERIA
Microorganisms that grow at temperatures near freezing.

PUREE
The pulp of a boiled food that has been rubbed through a sieve. Soup is called puree when it has been thickened with its sieved, pulpy ingredients.

Q

QUICK BREADS
Bread products baked from a lean, chemically leavened batter.

R

RABBIT OR RAREBIT
A melted-cheese dish.

RAGOUT
The French word for "stew."

RANCID
A disagreeable odor or flavor. Usually used to describe foods with high fat content, when oxidation occurs.

READY-TO-COOK POULTRY
Drawn or eviscerated poultry.

RECONSTITUTE
To restore the water taken from a food when it was dehydrated.

REHYDRATE
Combining a food with the same quantity of water that has been removed from it (see also RECONSTITUTE).

RELISH
A side dish, usually contrasting in color, shape, and texture to the meal. Usually designed to add flavor, zest, and interest to a meal.

RISSOLE
A French term meaning to obtain a crackling food by means of heat. Rissole potatoes are cooked to a golden brown crispness in fat.

ROAST
See BAKE.

ROPE
A spoiling bacterial growth in bread experienced when the dough becomes infected with bacterial spores. Poor sanitation can result in rope.

ROUNDING OR ROUNDING UP
Shaping of dough pieces into a ball to seal end and prevent bleeding and escape of gas.

ROUX
Preparation of flour and melted butter (or fat) used to thicken sauces, gravies, and soups.

ROYAL FROSTING
Decorative frosting of cooked sugar and egg whites.

S

SAFE HOLDING TEMPERATURE
A range of cold and hot temperatures considered safe for holding potentially hazardous foods, including those refrigeration temperatures 40° F, or below, or heating temperatures 140° F, or above.

SALISBURY STEAK
A ground meat dish cooked with onions and made to resemble steak in shape. Sometimes referred to as hamburg steak.

SALMONELLA INFECTION
A type of food poisoning transmitted through foods such as poultry and poultry products containing salmonella bacteria.

SANITIZE
Effective bactericidal treatment of clean surfaces of equipment and utensils by an established process that is effective in destroying microorganisms.

SAPONIFY
To convert to soap.

SATURATION
Absorption to the limit of the capacity.

SAUERBRATEN
A beef pot roast cooked in a sour sauce variously prepared with spices and vinegar, and sometimes served with sour cream.

SAUTE
See FRY.

SCALD
To heat a liquid over hot water or direct heat to a temperature just below the boiling point.

SCALE
An instrument for weighing.

SCALING
Apportioning batter or dough according to unit of weight.

SCALLOP
To bake food, usually cut in pieces, with a sauce or other liquid.

SCORE
To cut shallow slits or gashes in the surface of food with a knife.

SCORING
Judging finished goods according to points of perfection; or to cut or slash the top surface of dough pieces.

SEASON
To add, or sprinkle, with seasonings or condiments.

SHRED
To cut or tear into thin strips or pieces using a knife or a shredder attachment.

SIFTING
Passing through fine sieve for effective blending and to remove foreign or oversize particles.

SIMMER
To cook in liquid at a temperature just below the boiling point.

SKEWER
A sharp metal or wood pin used to hold parts of poultry meat or skin together while being roasted.

SKIM
To remove floating matter from the surface of a liquid with a spoon, ladle, or skimmer.

SLACK DOUGH
This is a dough that is soft and extensible but has lost its resiliency.

SLIVER
To cut or split into long, thin pieces.

SMOKING
A treatment used on most cured meat to add color and flavor.

SMORGASBORD
A Scandinavian-type luncheon or supper, served buffet style. Many different dishes are served, including hot and cold hors d'oeuvres, pickled vegetables, fish, assorted cheeses, jellied salads, cold and hot fish, and meats.

SMOTHER
To cook in a covered container, as smothered onions.

SNAPS
Small cookies that run flat during baking and become crisp on cooking.

SNICKERDOODLE
A coffeecake with a crumb topping.

SOLIDIFYING POINT
Temperature at which a fluid changes to a solid.

SPORE
Any one of various small or minute primitive reproductive bodies, capable of maintaining and reproducing itself. These are unicellular, produced by plants, molds, and bacteria.

SPRAY DRYING
Used for liquids and thick materials such as soup. Hot air coming into a drier contacts the small globules of the product and causes the water to be evaporated.

SPRINGER
A marked bulging of a food can at one or both ends. Improper exhausting of air from the can before sealing, or bacterial or chemical growth may cause swelling and spoilage.

SPRINKLE
To scatter in drops or small particles, such as chopped parsley, over a finished product.

STAPHYLOCOCCI
A family of bacteria formed in grapelike clusters, living as parasites on the outer skin and mucous membrane.

STEAM
To cook in steam with or without pressure.

STEEP
To let stand in hot liquid below boiling temperature to extract flavor, color, or other qualities from a specific food.

STERILIZE
To destroy microorganisms by chemical or mechanical means.

STEW
To simmer in liquid.

STIR
To blend or mix ingredients by using a spoon or other implement.

STREPTOCOCCI
Single-celled, globular-shaped bacteria.

STROGANOFF
Beef prepared with sour cream.

STRONG FLOUR
One that is suitable for the production of bread of good volume and quality.

SUCCOTASH
A combination of corn and lima beans.

SUGAR
To sprinkle or mix with sugar; refers to granulated unless otherwise specified in recipe.

SUKIYAKI
A popular Japanese dish consisting of thin slices of meat fried with onions and other vegetables, including bean sprouts, and soy sauce containing seasoning, herbs, and spices.

SWELLER
A can of food having both ends bulging as a result of spoilage. Swellers should be discarded, except molasses, in which this condition is normal in a warm climate.

T

TABLEWARE
A general term referring to multi use eating and drinking utensils, including knives, forks, spoons, and dishes.

TACO
An open-face sandwich, Mexican style, made of fried tortillas shaped like a shell and filled with a hot meat-vegetable mixture.

TAMALE
A highly seasoned steamed dish made of cornmeal with ground beef or chicken rolled in the center.

TARTAR
A rich sauce made with salad dressing, onions, parsley, and sometimes pickle relish, olives, and cucumbers, served with fish and shellfish.

TARTS
Small pastries with heavy fruit or cream filling.

TEMPERING
Adjusting temperature of ingredients to a certain degree.

TETRAZINNI
An Italian dish with chicken, green peppers, and onions mixed in spaghetti and served with shredded cheese.

TEXTURE
The quality of the interior structure of a baked product. Usually sensed by the touch of the cut surface as well as by sight and taste.

THERMOSTAT
A device for maintaining constant temperature.

THICKEN
To transform a thin liquid into a thick one either by the gelatinization of flour starches or the coagulation of egg protein.

TOAST
To brown the surface of a food by the application of direct heat.

TORTILLA
A Mexican bread made with white corn flour and water. Special techniques are used in handling the dough to roll it thin as a pie crust. It is baked on an ungreased griddle or in the oven.

TOSS
To lightly mix one or more ingredients. Usually refers to salad ingredients.

TOXIN
A waste product, given off by an organism causing contamination of food and subsequent illness in human beings. It is the toxin of a disease-producing germ that causes the poisoning.

TRICHINOSIS
A food-borne disease transmitted through pork containing a parasite, Trichinella spirallis, or its larvae, which infects animals.

TROUGHS
Large containers, usually on wheels, used for holding large masses of raising dough.

TRUSS
To bind or fasten together the wings and legs of poultry with the aid of string or metal skewers.

V

VACUUM DRYING
Vacuum is applied to liquids and fills the liquid with bubbles, creating a puffing effect. The puffed product is then dried, leaving a solid fragile mass. This is then crushed to reduce bulk.

VERMICELLI
A pasta, slightly yellow in color, shaped like spaghetti and very thin.

VINAIGRETTE
A mixture of oil and vinegar seasoned with salt, pepper, and herbs, used in sauces and dressings.

VIRUS
A group of organisms of ultramicroscopic size that grow in living tissue and may produce disease in animals and plants. Viruses are smaller than bacteria and, hence, pass through membranes or filters.

W

WASH
A liquid brushed on the surface of an unbaked or baked product (may be water, milk, starch solution, thin syrup, or egg).

WATER ABSORPTION
Water required to produce a bread dough of desired consistency. Flours vary in ability to absorb water, depending on the age of the flour, moisture content, wheat from which it is milled, storage conditions, and milling process.

WHEY
Liquid remaining after the removal of fat, casein, and other substances from milk.

WHIP
To beat rapidly to increase volume by incorporating air.

Y

YEAST
A group of small, single-celled plants, oval in shape and several times larger than bacteria. Yeast helps to promote fermentation and is useful in producing bread, cheese, wine, and so on.

YOUNG DOUGHS
Underfermented yeast dough producing finished yeast goods that are light in color, tight in grain, and low in volume (heavy).

Z

ZWIEBACK
A toast made of bread or plain coffeecake dried in slow oven.